COMMODORE 64
GAMES BOOK 2

COMMODORE 64 GAMES BOOK 2

GREGG BARNETT

MELBOURNE HOUSE PUBLISHERS

First Published in the United Kingdom
by Melbourne House

This Remastered Edition
Published in 2022 by
Acorn Books
acornbooks.uk

Contents

INTRODUCTION

I am very pleased to be able to present this book to you, the Commodore 64 Games Book II, a successor to our previous publication, the Commodore 64 Games Book.

The Commodore Games Book has been enjoyed by thousands of Commodore users throughout the world, and has been at the top of best-seller charts in the United Kingdom, United States and Australia, among others.

This book presents even more to you — exciting and different games, clear and legible listings, progressive explanations of the programs and a totally new learning experience.

We have taken a lot of trouble to ensure that the format is as easy to follow as possible, and the special Commodore characters are especially clear.

As well we offer a chexsum listing at the end of each program. This facility allows you to see at a glance whether the program you have typed in contains a transcription error, and pinpoints the line number for you!

I know that you will enjoy this book immensely, and let me wish you happy programming.

Alfred Milgrom
Publisher

Symbols appearing in this book

To aid clarity the graphic symbols of the VIC computer have been represented in this book by special symbols designed to look like the symbol as it appears on the VIC keyboard.

For this reason the programs will not look the same on your screen as they do in this book. To assist you in determining which symbol corresponds to which key the following tables are provided.

Symbol in the book	Keypress	Symbol in the book	Keypress
▨	C= E **	▨	C= R
▨	C= W	▨	C= Q
▨	C= D	▨	C= F
▨	C= C	▨	C= V
▨	C= B	▨	C= +
▨	C= T	▨	C= Y
▨	C= U	▨	C= I
▨	C= O	▨	C= P
▨	C= @	▨	C= -
▨	C= G	▨	C= H
▨	C= J	▨	C= K
▨	C= L	▨	C= N
▨	C= M	▨	C= £
▨	C= S	▨	C= X
▨	C= A	▨	C= Z
▨	C= *		
▨	SHIFT L	▨	SHIFT @
▨	SHIFT O	▨	SHIFT P
▨	SHIFT I	▨	SHIFT U
▨	SHIFT K	▨	SHIFT J
▨	SHIFT W	▨	SHIFT Q
▨	SHIFT +	▨	SHIFT V
▨	SHIFT M	▨	SHIFT N
◆	SHIFT Z	♥	SHIFT S
✚	SHIFT X	♠	SHIFT A
▨	SHIFT E	▨	SHIFT D
▨	SHIFT *	▨	SHIFT C
▨	SHIFT F	▨	SHIFT R
▨	SHIFT T	▨	SHIFT G
▨	SHIFT B	▨	SHIFT -
▨	SHIFT H	▨	SHIFT Y
▨	SHIFT £		
↑	UP ARROW	←	LEFT ARROW
π	PI		

** The C= symbol is the special shift key located to the left of the left hand shift key

As well as these there are a set of symbols used to represent control characters such as colour controls and cursor controls.

These are represented in the book by a symbol designed to look the same as it does on your screen.

The symbols are:

Upper case.

Symbol in the book	Keypress
	CLR
	HOME
	cursor down
	cursor up
	cursor right
	cursor left
	ctrl 1
	ctrl 2
	ctrl 3
	ctrl 4
	ctrl 5
	ctrl 6
	ctrl 7
	ctrl 8
	ctrl 9
	ctrl 0
	C= 1
	C= 2
	C= 3
	C= 4
	C= 5
	C= 6
	C= 7
	C= 8

SPECIAL CHARACTERS

In the program listings throughout this book spaces have been used ONLY as an aid to readability. When you type the programs in on your computer these spaces should be left out to conserve memory space.

As an example the line
            100 POKE 54273,I : POKE V + 23,0
would be typed as
            100POKE54273,I:POKEV+23,0
on your computer. As you can see the first verson is much more legible.

The only situation in which a space should be entered into a program listing is when the symbol
" ▲ "

appears. This special character does not appear on your computer's keyboard but has been placed in the listings to tell you, the programmer, when a space is necessary.

One other symbol appears in the program listings which may not at first be recognised. This is the symbol

" ᛃ "

        and is actually just the COLON symbol located on the key next to the L key.

The letter "I" and the number "1" can cause some confusion at times as well as the letter "O" and the number "0".

Once you are familiar with them they don't cause any problems, it's just a matter of recognising the difference.

The letter I looks like this: I
The number 1 looks like this: 1
The letter O looks like this: O
The number 0 looks like this: O

Frequently occurring (and easily overlooked) typing errors with the Commodore 64

1. Do not confuse the letter O with the digit 0 (zero).

2. Do not confuse the capital letter I with the digit 1.

3. A comma and a period are not interchangeable.

4. When a colon (:) is required, do not type a semi-colon (;). The reverse rule applies as well.

5. A double quote (") is not interchangeable with an apostrophe (').

6. When a program listing shows one or more spaces, do not forget to include them (press the space bar). The computer registers a space as a fullfledged character.

7. Brackets are important, particularly in the BASIC versions of mathematical formulae. A bracket too many, or a bracket short, usually causes a syntax error. Exclusion of two outer brackets may cause a "logic" error: which will enable the program to run but will deliver wrong results.

8. Do not forget to press the SHIFT key as well, when you have to enter the following characters:
!, ", #, $, %, &, ', (,), [,], <, >, and ?

9. The "plus" symbol (+) and the graphic symbol + have been placed, unfortunately, on the same key. They look alike, but they are definitely not interchangeable.

10. Brackets are ( ) and not [ ].

Overall Advice:
When you have typed in a program and you can't get in running properly, even after numerous debugging attempts, then put the job at rest for a day or so. It often happens that you will then find the bug at once after resuming the job.

Chexsum

The unique CHEXSUM program validation.

WHY

When a book of programs such as this book is keyed in, everybody invariably makes reading and typing mistakes and then spends ages trying to sort out where and what is causing the error (or errors).

Even experienced programmers often cannot identify an error by just listing the relevant line and need to do the tedious job of going back to the book, especially with DATA statements.

Realising that this is a major cause of frustration in keying the programs, we decided to do something about it.

There are two short routines in this book which you should key in and save BEFORE you key any other programs in.

Using these routines you will be able to find out if you have made any keying errors at all and in which lines, before you even run the program.

In effect this means that with this book you need not waste time looking for keying errors, you simply run the routines and look at the display to identify lines containing errors. It's that easy.

The principle behind the routines is a unique chexsum which is calculated on each individual line of the program as you have keyed it in. Compare this chexsum value with the value for that line in the list at the end of the program listing; if they are the same the line is correct, if not there is an error in that line.

WHEN

The simplest method is to enter the MERGE and CHEXSUM programs in now and save them to tape or disk.

You can type in the CHEXSUM program at any time, even if you have started to type in a program. You cannot, of course, load in CHEXSUM from tape or disk because it will erase all you have typed so far.

A solution to this is the MERGE program included here that will allow you to merge two programs. To use it, you will have to save all you have typed in so far onto your cassette or disk, load the MERGE program, and run it.

If you are using a Datasette it might be an idea to save CHEXSUM and MERGE on a separate cassette. This will enable you to save all your corrected programs on one cassette and allow you easy access to the CHEXSUM and MERGE routines without having to constantly run backwards and forwards through the tape.

HOW CAN YOU TELL IF CHEXSUM HAS BEEN CORRECTLY ENTERED?

After having keyed CHEXSUM (or MERGE) the logical thing would be to chexsum these programs too, to ensure that they are correct. But is it possible to do this? If you follow the instructions you will be able to check them both.

Type and save CHEXSUM.

Edit line 62020 and change the value of E from 61999 to 62200.

Type RUN and check output against the table of values at the end of the program.

If the program is incorrect, edit the incorrect lines and resave the program after having reset the values of E in line 62020.

Type and save MERGE.

You can only check the data in the MERGE routine. However this is the most important part of the routine. All you need to do is 'RUN' merge — it will check its own data and prompt you if there is an error.

Here are the routines and instructions on how to use them:

MERGE ROUTINE

```
10 POKE 55,0:POKE56,159:CLR
20 S=40705:FOR J=S TO S+78:READ V
30 C=C+V:POKE J,V:NEXT
40 IFC<>8756THENPRINT"DATA ERROR":END
120 DATA 169,0,133,10,32,212,225,165
130 DATA 43,72,165,44,72,56,165,45
```

7

```
140 DATA 233,2,133,43,165,46,233,0
150 DATA 133,44,169,0,133,185,166,43
160 DATA 164,44,169,0,32,213,255,176
170 DATA 14,134,45,132,46,32,51,165
180 DATA 104,133,44,104,133,43,96,170
190 DATA 201,4,144,244,240,10,104,133
200 DATA 44,104,133,43,24,108,0,3
210 DATA 164,186,136,240,209,208,239
300 NEW
```

CHEXSUM ROUTINE

```
62000 T=PEEK(62)*256+PEEK(61)+1
62010 INPUT"TO PRINTER (Y/N)";Q$
62011 IF Q$<>"Y"THEN62020
62015 CLOSE4:OPEN4,4:CMD4:PRINTCHR$(1);CHR$(129)
62020 LINK=PEEK(44)*256+PEEK(43):E=61999
62120 T=LINK
62130 LINK=PEEK(T+1)*256+PEEK(T)
62135 LN=PEEK(T+3)*256+PEEK(T+2)
62136 IF LN>E THEN PRINT:PRINT"TOTAL=";
      CH:PRINT#4:CLOSE4:END
62137 S$=STR$(LN):L=LEN(S$)-1:S$=MID$(S$,2,L)
62138 PRINT SPC(6-L);S$;
62140 CS=0:N=0:C=0
62150 FOR P=T+4 TO LINK-2 :PK=PEEK(P)
62160 IF PK=143 THEN P=LINK-2:GOTO 62190
62165 IF PK=34 THEN C=(C=0)
62170 IF C=0 AND PK=32 THEN 62190
62180 IF PK=137 THEN N=N+1:CS=CS+(203 OR N):
      PK=164
62185 N=N+1:CS=CS+(PK OR N)
62190 NEXT P:CH=CH+CS:PRINT"=";RIGHT$(STR$(CS)
      ,LEN(STR$(CS))-1):GOTO 62120
62999 REM
```

8

CHEXSUM OF CHEXSUM

```
62000=1848
62010=1618
62011=1281
62015=2020
62020=2501
62120=577
62130=2067
62135=2115
62136=2692
62137=2908
62138=931
62140=1142
62150=2251
62160=2373
62165=1431
62170=1554
62180=3320
62185=1862
62190=4228

TOTAL=. 38719
```

INSTRUCTIONS

1: LOAD and RUN MERGE.
2: type or LOAD your program.
3: save your program — type SYS 40705 "CHEXSUM".
   (SYS 40705, 8 for Disk.)
4: RUN 62000
5: answer the question.
       "Y" if you want listing on printer
       "N" if listing is to be displayed to the screen
6: hit "RUN/STOP" to halt output.
7: type "CONT" to continue.
8: if there are errors, then correct them and start again from 4.

Because MERGE, on being run, stores itself above BASIC memory it will reside there until you switch off the machine or change the top of BASIC RAM. From this it follows that you don't need to continually reload MERGE after running it the first time.

CHEXSUM AND GRAPHICS CHARACTERS

At times it might be difficult to recognise the difference between two graphics characters and when you run the CHEXSUM you will get a variance in the values. If, after having checked the line carefully, you come to the conclusion that the error must be in one of the graphics characters, and you are reasonably sure that you keyed what you think the character should be, then don't worry about the CHEXSUM variance. When you run the program it will be obvious from the screen display what the character should be if it is an important character. Some characters don't really matter that much and at times you probably won't even be able to find the wrong one in the screen display.

CHEXSUM can sometimes see a '.' as a ',' and a ';' as a ':' if they fall on certain positions in a program line. So if a program gives a correct CHEXSUM total yet still functions incorrectly, you should check these characters, especially within DATA statements.

NOTE if you decide to run your programs without first checking them, then make sure that you SAVE YOUR PROGRAM BEFORE YOU RUN IT! The reason for this is that some of the programs will corrupt themselves if RUN after being typed in incorrectly.

Dumper

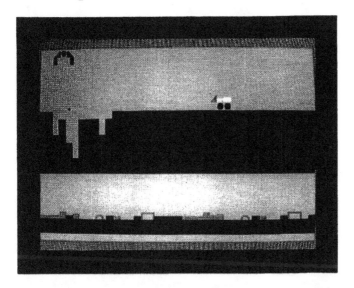

The UFO bombs are attacking the city's barricade! How can you stop the defense-wall being smashed? You must replace the bricks in the barricade as they are knocked out by the alien forces — but will you have time?

Can you fill in the holes faster than new ones are made? Points are gained by filling in the holes — the deeper the hole, the greater the number of points you score.

I moves your truck left, P moves it right and spacebar drops a brick.

You have only 3 trucks left with which to defend your city — so good luck!

VARIABLES

HS = Highest score
S = Score
B = Position of bomb
K = Inkey$
AL = Alien
P = Position of Dumper
DI = Holes
DU = Number of Dumpers

```
0     REM DUMPER
```

Print the barrier and the city, set screen up.

```
100   HS=0
110   POKE53280,5:POKE53281,3
120   PRINT"▣ ▣ ▣ ▣ ▣ ▣ ▣ ▣ ▣ ▣ ▣ ▣ ▣";
125   FORI=1TO8:PRINT"▲ ▲ ▲ ▲ ▲ ▲ ▲ ▲ ▲ ▲ ▲ ▲ ▲ ▲
      ▲ ▲ ▲ ▲ ▲ ▲ ▲ ▲ ▲ ▲ ▲ ▲ ▲ ▲ ▲ ▲ ▲ ▲
      ▲ ▲ ▲ ▲ ▲ ▲ ▲";:NEXT
130   PRINT"▬ ▣ ▣"TAB(8)"▣ ▌ ▣ ▌▌+ ▣ ▌▌ ▌ ▣ ▌▌ ▣ ▲"
140   PRINT"□ ▣ ▬ ▬ ▬ ▣ ▲ ─ ─ ▬ ▲ ▣ ╭ ╮ ■ ▬ ▣
      ▬ ▣ ╱ ╲ ▣ ▬ ▣ ┌ ┐ ▲ ■ ▬ ▬ ▬";
145   PRINT"▣ ▬ ▬ ▬ ▣ ▲ ─ ─ ▬ ▲ ▣ ╭ ╮ ■ ▬ ▣ ▬
      ▣ ╱ ╲ ▣ ▬ ▣ ┌ ┐ ▲ ■ ▬";
150   PRINT"▣ ▲ ▲ ▲ ▲ ▲ ▲ ▲ ▲ ▲ ▲ ▲ ▲ ▲ ▲ ▲ ▲
      ▲ ▲ ▲ ▲ ▲ ▲ ▲ ▲ ▲ ▲ ▲ ▲ ▲ ▲ ▲ ▲ ▲ ▲
      ▲ ▲ ▲ ▲ ▲";
155   PRINT"▣ ▲ ▲ ▲ ▲ ▲ ▲ ▲ ▲ ▲ ▲ ▲ ▲ ▲ ▲ ▲ ▲
      ▲ ▲ ▲ ▲ ▲ ▲ ▲ ▲ ▲ ▲ ▲ ▲ ▲ ▲ ▲ ▲ ▲ ▲
      ▲ ▲ ▲ ▲ ▲";
160   PRINT"□ □ □ ▣ ▣ ▣ ▣ ▬ ▣ ▬ ▣ ▣ ▣ ▣ ▣ ▣ ▣
      ▣ ▣ ▣ ▣ ▣ ▬"
170   DU=3:S=0
180   AL=1:A$="▲ ▣ ▣ ◤ ▣ ▬ ● ▣ ▣ ◥ ▬ ▲ ▣ ▌▌ ▌▌ ▌▌
      ▌▌ ▌▌ ▲ ▌ ▣ ─ ▣ ▣ ▌ ▬ ▲"
190   P=1339:CO=54272
200   B=0
210   K=64:GOTO240
```

Scan the keyboard, move the number, and alien, alien drops bricks.

```
220   K=PEEK(197):IFK=64THEN340
230   IFK=30THEN500
240   D=(K=12)-(K=20)*2+P:IFD<1303THEN340
250   IFPEEK(D)=160THEND=D-40
260   IFD>PTHEND=D-1
270   POKEP,32:POKEP-41,32:POKEP-39,32:POKEP+1,32:POKEP-40,32
280   POKEP-81,32:POKEP-80,32:POKEP-79,32:POKEP-121,32:POKEP-119
      ,32:P=D
290   POKEP+CO,0:POKEP+1+CO,0:POKEP-41+CO,4:POKEP-40+CO,1:POKEP-
      39+CO,1
300   POKEP,81:POKEP+1,81:POKEP-41,233:POKEP-40,98:POKEP-39,248
310   IFPEEK(P+40)<>32ANDPEEK(P+40)<>160THEN570
320   IFPEEK(P+40)=160THEN340
330   D=P+40:GOTO270
340   AL=AL+INT(RND(1)*3-1):IFAL<0THENAL=0
350   IFAL>18THENAL=18
360   PRINT"▣"TAB(AL)A$
370   IFB>0THEN400
```

```
380    IFRND(1)<.8THEN490
390    B=1106+AL
400    POKEB,32:B=B+40:IFPEEK(B)=32THEN480
410    IFPEEK(B)<>160THEN460
420    POKEB,32
450    B=0:GOTO490
```

> Check if this is end of game, keep game looping.

```
460    IFB>1663THEN570
470    GOTO670
480    POKEB+CO,0:POKEB,46
490    GOTO220
500    DI=P-1:IFPEEK(DI+40)<>160THENS=S+5
510    POKEP-41,95
520    POKEP-41,233:GOTO550
530    S=S+1:POKEDI+CO,2:POKEDI,160
540    FORI=1TO10:NEXT
550    IFPEEK(DI+40)=160ORDI>1623THEN340
560    POKEDI,32:DI=DI+40:GOTO530
570    GOTO660
660    GOTO760
```

> Print scores for game, check if another game, if no then stop.

```
670    POKEB+CO,7:POKEB-1+CO,7:POKEB+1+C0,7
680    POKEB-1,77:POKEB,121:POKEB+1,78
710    IFDU=1THEN760
720    POKEB,32:POKEB-1,32:POKEB+1,32
730    POKEP,32:POKEP+1,32:POKEP-41,32:POKEP-40,32:POKEP-39,32
740    PRINT" 🔲 "TAB(AL+1)" ▲ ▲ ▲ ▲ 🔲 🔲 🔲 🔲 ▲ ▲ ▲ "
750    DU=DU-1:GOTO190
760    FORI=1TO1000:NEXT:PRINT" 🔲 🔲 🔲 🔳 SCORE"S
770    IFS>HSTHENHS=S
780    PRINT" 🔲 HI ▲ ▲ ▲ "HS
790    PRINT" 🔲 ANOTHER ▲ GAME?":POKE198,0
800    GETA$:IFA$="Y"THEN120
810    IFA$<>"N"THEN800
820    PRINT:PRINT" 🔲 🔲 🔲 🔳 TOO ▲ TOUGH ▲ FOR ▲ YOU, ▲ EH ▲ ?"
830    END
```

CHECKSUM

```
        0=0                   670=2615
      100=387                 680=1832
      110=1177                710=872
      120=720                 720=1778
      125=3160                730=3465
      130=2018                740=1762
      140=5020                750=1334
      145=4551                760=2084
      150=2151                770=1179
      155=2151                780=696
      160=1716                790=1746
      170=779                 800=1306
      180=3865
      190=1198
      200=296
      210=974                 810=1120
      220=1621                820=2640
      230=836                 830=129
      240=2963
      250=1652          TOTAL=  113958
      260=1198
      270=3449
      280=4378
      290=4991
      300=3580
      310=3059
      320=1503
      330=1231
      340=2965
      350=1203
      360=721
      370=768
      380=1109
      390=781
      400=2312
      410=1395
      420=374
      450=900
      460=959
      470=532
      480=1100
      490=527
      500=2909
      510=679
      520=1348
      530=1979
      540=908
      550=2320
      560=1925
      570=531
      660=531
```

Mind Quiz

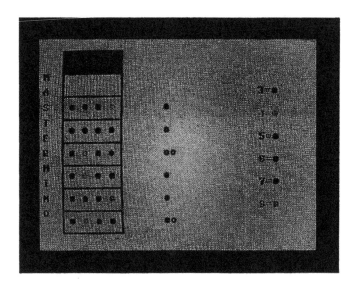

The computer will generate a sequence of four random coloured beads which you must guess. You will get eight tries. After each try, the computer will respond with a coloured bead to indicate either a right colour in the correct place or a right colour in the wrong place. By a process of elimination you should be able to guess the correct colour code combination, eventually.

VARIABLES

D$ = Message "instructions Y/N"
A$ = Response to input
Y = Flag for end of game and screen position of beads
X = General purpose variable
G$ = Response to colour bead input
D% = Array containing random numbers
B% = Array containing input numbers

16

```
Ø       REM MIND QUIZ
```

Set screen colours, draw borders, print moving title.

```
5       POKE54296,15
1Ø      POKE5328Ø,1:POKE649,1:POKE53281,1
2Ø      PRINTCHR$(8)CHR$(142):PRINT" ⬚ "
3Ø      FORX=1Ø25TO1Ø62:POKEX,64:POKEX+54272,6:NEXT
4Ø      FORX=1Ø64TO1944STEP4Ø:POKEX,93:POKEX+54272,6:NEXT
5Ø      FORX=11Ø3TO1983STEP4Ø:POKEX,93:POKEX+54272,6:NEXT
6Ø      FORX=1985TO2Ø22:POKEX,64:POKEX+54272,6:NEXT
7Ø      POKE1Ø24,85:POKE55296,6
8Ø      POKE1Ø63,73:POKE1984,74:POKE2Ø23,75:POKE55335,6
85      POKE56256,6:POKE56295,6
1Ø1     PRINT" ⬚ ⬚ ⬚ ⬚ ⬚ ▲ ▲ ▲ ▲ ▲M ▲ ▲A ▲ ▲S ▲ ▲T
        ▲ ▲ ▲E ▲ ▲R ▲ ▲M ▲ ▲I ▲ ▲N ▲ ▲D"
13Ø     DIMA%(4):DIMB%(4):DIMD%(4)
14Ø     D$=" ▲ ▲ ▲ ▲ ▲ ▲ ▲ ▲ ▲ INSTRUCTIONS ▲ Y/N ▲ ?
        ▲ ▲ ▲ ▲ ▲ ▲ ▲ ▲ "
141     PRINT" ⬚ ⬚ "
142     PRINT" ⬚ ⬚ ⬚ ⬚ ";D$:FORX=1TO79:NEXT
144     D$=D$+LEFT$(D$,1):D$=MID$(D$,2,36)
15Ø     GETA$:IFA$<>"N"ANDA$<>"Y"THEN142
17Ø     GOSUB 69Ø
18Ø     PRINT" ⬚ ⬚ "SPC(18)"M" ▲ PLAY ▲ ME"CHR$(13)SPC(18)" ⬚ S)
        ▲ PLAY ▲ SOMEONE ▲ ELSE"
```

Determine player, print board on screen, input and draw guess

```
19Ø     GETA$:IFA$<>"M"ANDA$<>"S"THEN19Ø
195     PRINT" ⬚ ⬚ "SPC(18)" ▲ ▲ ▲ ▲ ▲ ▲ ▲ ▲ ▲ "CHR$(1
        3)SPC(18)" ⬚ ▲ ▲ ▲ ▲ ▲ ▲ ▲ ▲ ▲
        ▲ ▲ ▲ ▲ "
2ØØ     IFA$="M"THENGOSUB85Ø:GOTO31Ø
23Ø     R=1
24Ø     FORX=1TO4
25Ø     GETA$:IFA$=CHR$(2Ø)ANDX>1THENX=X-1:R=R-2:POKE1Ø67+R,16Ø:
        POKE1Ø67+R+54272,14
255     IFVAL(A$)<3ORVAL(A$)>8THEN25Ø
26Ø     A%(X)=VAL(A$):POKE1Ø67+R,81:POKE1Ø67+R+54272,A%(X)-1
28Ø     R=R+2:NEXT
31Ø     GOSUB835
325     PRINT" ⬚ "SPC(32)" ⬚ ⬚ ⬚ ⬚ ⬚ ⬚3= ● ⬚ ⬚ ⬚ ⬚ ▮▮ ▮▮
        ▮▮ ◣ 4= ● ⬚ ⬚ ⬚ ⬚ ▮▮ ▮▮ ▮▮ ⬚5= ● ⬚ ⬚ ⬚ ⬚ ▮▮ ▮▮ ▮▮ ⬚6
        = ● ⬚ ⬚ ⬚ ⬚ ▮▮ ▮▮ ▮▮ ⬚7= ● ⬚ ⬚ ⬚ ⬚ ▮▮ ▮▮ ▮▮ ⬚8= ●
        ⬚.
336     Y=84Ø:R=1
34Ø     PRINT" ⬚ "SPC(25)"YOUR ▲ GUESS"
342     POKE54277,19Ø:POKE54278,248:POKE54273,17:POKE54272,37
345     POKE54276,17:FORX=1TO35Ø:NEXT:POKE54276,Ø:POKE54277,Ø:POKE
        54278,Ø
35Ø     PRINT" ⬚ "SPC(25)" ▲ ▲ ▲ ▲ ▲ ▲ ▲ ▲ ▲ ▲ ▲ ▲
        ▲ ▲ "                    "
```

```
370   FORX=1TO4:D%(X)=A%(X):NEXT
380   FORX=1TO4
390   GETA$:IFA$=CHR$(20)ANDX>1THENX=X-1:R=R-2:POKE1067+R+Y,32
400   IFVAL(A$)<3ORVAL(A$)>8THEN390
410   B%(X)=VAL(A$):POKE1067+R+Y,81:POKE1067+R+54272+Y,B%(X)-1
430   R=R+2:NEXT
```

> React to players input, generate a response, print it!

```
450   FORX=1TO4:IFB%(X)=D%(X)THENG$=G$+"  ● ":D%(X)=255:B%(X)=254
460   NEXT
470   IFD%(1)=B%(2)THENG$=G$+"  ● ":D%(1)=255:B%(2)=254
480   IFD%(1)=B%(3)THENG$=G$+"  ● ":D%(1)=255:B%(3)=254
490   IFD%(1)=B%(4)THENG$=G$+"  ● ":D%(1)=255:B%(4)=254
500   IFD%(2)=B%(1)THENG$=G$+"  ● ":D%(2)=255:B%(1)=254
510   IFD%(2)=B%(3)THENG$=G$+"  ● ":D%(2)=255:B%(3)=254
520   IFD%(2)=B%(4)THENG$=G$+"  ● ":D%(2)=255:B%(4)=254
530   IFD%(3)=B%(1)THENG$=G$+"  ● ":D%(3)=255:B%(1)=254
540   IFD%(3)=B%(2)THENG$=G$+"  ● ":D%(3)=255:B%(2)=254
550   IFD%(3)=B%(4)THENG$=G$+"  ● ":D%(3)=255:B%(4)=254
560   IFD%(4)=B%(1)THENG$=G$+"  ● ":D%(4)=255:B%(1)=254
570   IFD%(4)=B%(2)THENG$=G$+"  ● ":D%(4)=255:B%(2)=254
580   IFD%(4)=B%(3)THENG$=G$+"  ● ":D%(4)=255:B%(3)=254
600   PRINT" ▨ ":FORX=1TO((Y-40)/40):PRINT" ▨ ";:NEXT:PRINTSPC(1
      8)" ▨ "G$
620   IFG$=" ● ● ● ● "THEND$="YES":GOTO880
630   IFY=120THEND$="NO":GOTO880
640   Y=Y-120:G$="":R=1
670   GOTO340
```

> Print instructions, congratulations and prompt to play again.

```
690   IFA$="N"THEN780
692   PRINT" ▨ ▨ ▨ ▨ ▨ ▲ ▲ ▲ ▲ ▲ ▲ ▲ ▲ ▲ ▲ ▲ ▲
      ▲ INSTRUCTIONS ▲ ▲ ▲ ▲ ▲ ▲ ▲ ▲ ▲
      ▲ "
695   PRINT" ▨ ▨ IN ▲ THIS ▲ GAME ▲ YOU ▲ CAN ▲ PLAY ▲ THE ▲ CO
      MPUTER ▲ ▲ ▲ ▲ ▲ ▲ ▲ ▲ OR ▲ A ▲ HUMAN ▲ OPPON
      ENT
700   PRINT" ▨ ▲ YOU ▲ HAVE ▲ ▨ 7 ▨ ▲ CHANCES ▲ TO ▲ CRACK ▲
      THE ▲ CODE"
710   PRINT" ▨ TO ▲ ENTER ▲ COLOURS ▲ USE ▲ KEYS ▲ ▲ ▨ 3 ▲ ▶
      4 ▲ ▨ 5 ▲ ▨ 6 ▲ ▨ 7 ▲ ▨ 8 ▨ "
720   PRINT" ▨ ▲ PRESS ▲ DEL ▲ IF ▲ YOU ▲ MAKE ▲ A ▲ M
      ISTAKE"
730   PRINT" ▲ ▲ ▨ ▨ ▲ ● ▨ ▲ ▲ MEANS ▲ RIGHT ▲ COLOUR ▲
      RIGHT ▲ SPOT"
740   PRINT" ▲ ▲ ▨ ▨ ▲ ● ▨ ▲ ▲ MEANS ▲ RIGHT ▲ COLOUR ▲
      WRONG ▲ SPOT
750   PRINT" ▨ ▨ ▨ ▨ ▲ ▲ ▲ ▲ ▲ ▲ ▲ ▲ PRESS ▲ RETUR
      N ▲ TO ▲ START ▲ ▲ ▲ ▲ ▲ ▲ ▲ ▲ "
760   GETA$:IFA$<>CHR$(13)THEN760
780   PRINT" ▨ ";
790   FORX=1TO8
```

```
800    PRINT" ◧ ▴ ▴ ▴ ┌ ─ ─ ─ ─ ─ ─ ┐ ▴ ▴ ▴ ▴ ▴
       ▴ ▴ ▴ ▴ ▴ ▴ ▴ ▴ ▮ ▴ ▴ ▴ ▴ ▴ ▴ ▴ ▴ ▮"
805    PRINT" ▴ ▴ ▴ ▮ ▴ ▴ ▴ ▴ ▴ ▴ ▮ "
810    NEXT
820    PRINT" ▴ ▴ ▴ ─ ─ ─ ─ ─ ─ ─ ─ ";
830    PRINT" ▧ ▨ ▨ ▨M▨ ▨ ▮▮A▨ ▨ ▮▮S▨ ▨ ▮▮T▨ ▨ ▮▮
       E▨ ▨ ▮▮R▨ ▨ ▮▮M▨ ▨ ▮▮I▨ ▨ ▮▮N▨ ▨ ▮▮D"
835    FORX=1TO9:FORY=ØTO2:POKE1026+X+Y*4Ø,16Ø:POKE55298+X+Y*4Ø,1
       4:NEXTY,X
840    RETURN
850    FORX=1TO4
860    FORY=1TO3:E=RND(1)*5+3:NEXTY
870    A%(X)=E:NEXT:RETURN
880    FORX=1TO4:POKE1Ø68+C,81:POKE1Ø68+C+54272,A%(X)-1:C=C+2:
       NEXT
890    PRINT" ▨ ";:IFD$="NO"THENPRINTSPC(16)"BAD ▴ LUCK ▴ IT ▴ WA
       S ▴ THIS"
900    IFD$="YES"THENPRINTSPC(16)"GOOD ▴ ON ▴ YOU ▴ YOU ▴ GOT ▴ I
       T"
910    PRINT" ▨ ▨ ▨ "SPC(16)"PLAY ▴ AGAIN ▴ Y/N ▴ ?"
920    GETA$:IFA$<>"N"ANDA$<>"Y"THEN92Ø
930    IFA$="N"THENPOKEØ,Ø:SYSØ
940    RUN
```

CHECKSUM

	280=770	670=525
	310=303	690=938
	325=7246	692=2938
	336=823	695=5768
Ø=Ø	340=1477	700=3494
5=595	342=2775	710=3815
10=1646	345=3562	720=3093
20=1439	350=1456	730=3447
30=2644	370=1762	740=3415
40=2939	380=670	750=3009
50=2938	390=4335	760=1710
60=2658	400=1972	780=435
70=1176	410=4205	790=678
80=2359	430=770	800=5002
85=1178	450=4424	805=992
101=2483	460=131	810=131
130=1376	470=3439	820=2104
140=2568	480=3439	830=3392
141=266	490=3441	835=5130
142=1684	500=3439	840=143
144=2231	510=3441	850=670
150=2324	520=3443	860=2107
170=306	530=3439	870=935
180=4416	540=3441	880=4297
190=2322	550=3443	890=3678
195=3002	560=3441	900=3442
200=1676	570=3443	910=1979
230=312	580=3443	920=2330
240=670	600=3301	930=1366
250=5527	620=2860	940=139
255=1967	630=1923	
260=3595	640=1542	TOTAL= 214998

Treasure Hunt

Move the little man round the maze collecting the dollars as you go along but keep moving quickly. If you stay still for too long a killer duck will eat the little man so beware. The more dollars you collect, the higher your score.

VARIABLES

L   = Difficulty level of game
A$ = Key pressed
X   = X position on screen
Y   = Y position on screen
Z   = Player screen position
SC = Score
BX = Ducks X position
BY = Ducks Y position
NN = Number of dollars collected
BZ = Ducks screen position

```
0     REM TREASURE HUNT
```

Set the screen colours, dimension arrays, set difficulty
level.

```
10    POKE53280,4:POKE53281,0:PRINT" ⛶ "
20    DIM D(50)
25    IFPEEK(53272)=21THENGOSUB9000
26    PRINT" ⛶ ▮ ◧ ◧ ◧ ▲ ▲ ▲ ▲ ▲ ▲ ▲ ▲ ▲ ▲
      ▲ !TREASURE ▲ HUNT!"
28    PRINT" ◧ ◧ ◧ ▲ WHAT ▲ LEVEL ▲ DO ▲ YOU ▲ WANT(1=EASY,3=
      HARD)"
30    GETA$:IFA$=""THEN30
32    IFA$="1"THENL=0.99
34    IFA$="2"THENL=0.97
36    IFA$="3"THENL=0.95
37    IFA$<>"1"ANDA$<>"2"ANDA$<>"3"THEN30
38    FORI=55296TO56295:POKEI,14:NEXTI
39    PRINT" ◼ ◧ ◧ ◧ ◧ ◧ ◧ ▲ ▲ ▲ ▲ ▲ ▲ ▲ ▲ ▲
      ▲ ▲ ▲ ▲ ▲ ▲ ▲ ▲ ▲ ▲ ▲ ▲ ▲ ▲ ▲ ▲ ▲
      ▲ ▲ ▲ ▲ ▲ ▲ ▲ ▲ "
40    GOSUB10000
```

Move the man around the maze and randomly fire the duck.

```
190   Y=17:X=11:Z=1024+40*Y+X:POKEZ,0
200   GETA$
210   IF A$="A"THEN1000
220   IF A$="Z"THEN1100
230   IF A$="."THEN1200
240   IF A$=","THEN1300
250   IF RND(0)>LTHENGOSUB2000
300   GOTO 200
1000  POKEZ,32:Y=Y-1:Z=1024+40*Y+X
1010  IF PEEK(Z)=160THENY=Y+1:Z=1024+40*Y+X:GOTO1030
1020  IF PEEK(Z)<>32THENGOSUB 1500
1030  POKEZ,0:GOTO250
1100  POKEZ,32:Y=Y+1:Z=1024+40*Y+X
1110  IF PEEK(Z)=160THENY=Y-1:Z=1024+40*Y+X:GOTO1130
1120  IF PEEK(Z)<>32THENGOSUB 1500
1130  POKEZ,0:GOTO250
1200  POKEZ,32:X=X+1:Z=1024+40*Y+X
1210  IF PEEK(Z)=160THENX=X-1:Z=1024+40*Y+X:GOTO1230
1220  IF PEEK(Z)<>32THENGOSUB 1500
1230  POKEZ,0:GOTO250
1300  POKEZ,32:X=X-1:Z=1024+40*Y+X
1310  IF PEEK(Z)=160THENX=X+1:Z=1024+40*Y+X:GOTO1330
1320  IF PEEK(Z)<>32THENGOSUB 1500
1330  POKEZ,0:GOTO250
1500  NN=1:FORN=49TO57
1510  IF PEEK(Z)=NTHENSC=SC+NN
```

```
1520    NN=NN+1:NEXTN
1530    IF SC=83THEN1600
1540    RETURN
```

> Print the number of dollars collected, check if end of game.

```
1600    PRINT" ▣ ▣ ▣ ▬ ▬ YOU ▬ COLLECTED";SC;"DOLLARS"
1610    PRINT" ▣ ▣ ▣ ▬ ▬ DO ▬ YOU ▬ WANT ▬ TO ▬ PLAY ▬ AGAIN(
        ▬ Y ▣ / ▣ N ▣ )"
1620    GETA$:IFA$=""THEN1620
1630    IFA$="Y"THENRUN
1640    IFA$="N"THENPRINT" ▣ ▣ BYE ▬ BYE":END
1650    GOTO 1620
1700    PRINT" ▣ ▣ ▣ ▣ ▬ THE ▬ BIRD ▬ GOT ▬ YOU!"
1710    PRINT" ▣ ▣ ▣ ▬ YOU ▬ COLLECTED";SC;"DOLLARS"
1720    GOTO 1610
```

> Fire the duck at player and check if duck has killed player.

```
2000    REM
2005    I=0:BY=Y:BX=29
2010    BZ=1024+40*BY+BX:I=I+1
2020    D(I)=PEEK(BZ)
2030    POKEBZ,28:POKEBZ+54272,3
2040    IF Z=BZORBX=XTHEN1700
2050    GETA$:IF A$=" ▬ " THEN2500
2060    BX=BX-1:GOTO2010
2500    N=I:IFBX=29THEN2540
2510    POKEBZ,D(N):POKEBZ+54272,14
2520    BX=BX+1:BZ=1024+40*BY+BX:N=N-1
2530    IF BX<29THEN2510
2540    POKE BZ,160:POKEBZ+54272,14:RETURN
```

> Set up graphics for program.

```
9000    PRINT" ▣ ▣ ▣ ▣ ▣ ▣ ▣ ▣ ▣ ▣ ▬ ▬ ▬ PLEASE ▬ W
        AIT ▬ - ▬ SETTING ▬ UP ▬ GRAPHICS":SS=12288
9010    POKE56334,PEEK(56334)AND254
9020    POKE1,PEEK(1)AND251
9030    FORI=SSTOSS+2047
9040    POKEI,PEEK(53248+I-SS)
9050    NEXTI
9060    POKE1,PEEK(1)OR4
9070    POKE56334,PEEK(56334)OR1
9080    POKE53272,(PEEK(53272)AND240)+12
9100    FORI=SSTOSS+7:READA:POKEI,A:NEXTI
9110    FORI=SS+224TOSS+231:READA:POKEI,A:NEXTI
9190    PRINT" ▣ ":RETURN
9200    DATA60,60,24,60,90,153,36,66
```

```
9210    DATA192,97,99,127,124,60,16,16
10000   RESTORE:FORI=1TO16:READA:NEXTI:Y=6
10010   READX
10020   IFX=-1THENY=Y+1:GOTO10010
10030   IFX=-2THEN10200
10040   Z=1024+40*Y+X:POKEZ,160:GOTO10010
10050   DATA15,17,18,25,-1
10060   DATA12,14,15,20,21,23,24,27,28,-1
10070   DATA11,12,16,18,21,22,24,26,27,-1
10080   DATA14,16,18,19,24,-1
10090   DATA12,14,15,19,21,23,24,26,27,28,-1
10100   DATA12,15,17,19,21,23,26,-1
10110   DATA12,13,17,19,21,22,23,25,26,28,-1
10120   DATA14,15,17,18,19,21,23,26,-1
10130   DATA12,14,17,23,24,26,28,-1
10140   DATA11,12,14,15,16,19,20,21,22,24,26,-1
10150   DATA16,17,19,24,26,27,-1
10160   DATA12,14,15,17,19,21,23,24,-1
10170   DATA12,17,21,26,27,-2
10200   FORX=1234TO1253:POKEX,160:NEXTX
10210   FORX=1794TO1813:POKEX,160:NEXTX
10220   FORX=1234TO1794STEP40:POKEX,160:NEXTX
10230   FORX=1253TO1813STEP40:POKEX,160:NEXTX
10240   CC=49
10250   READXX,YY
10260   IFYY=-1THENCC=CC+1:GOTO10250
10270   IFYY=-2THENRETURN
10280   ZZ=1024+40*YY+XX:POKEZZ,CC:GOTO10250
10300   DATA11,14,15,16,17,15,-1,-1
10310   DATA16,6,-1,-1
10320   DATA15,9,18,12,15,14,16,17,23,15,-,-1
10330   DATA22,7,22,13,-1,-1
10340   DATA11,7,22,11,23,8,-1,-1
10350   DATA24,6,-1,-1
10360   DATA28,8,28,18,-1,-1
10370   DATA28,13,-1,-1
10380   DATA28,11,-2,-2
```

CHEXSUM

0=0	200=267	1200=2474
10=1646	210=985	1210=3720
20=401	220=1009	1220=1564
25=1526	230=960	1230=954
26=2513	240=961	1300=2475
28=3520	250=1282	1310=3720
30=1152	300=525	1320=1564
32=1227	1000=2475	1330=954
34=1226	1010=3719	1500=1271
36=1227	1020=1564	1510=1825
37=2749	1030=954	1520=997
38=1929	1100=2474	1530=991
39=2181	1110=3721	1540=143
40=402	1120=1564	1600=2503
190=2692	1130=954	1610=3164

```
1620=1277          10230=2153
1630=914           10240=426
1640=2095          10250=548
1650=583           10260=2354
1700=1797          10270=1041
1710=2456          10280=2987
1720=581           10300=1410
2000=0             10310=637
2005=1342          10320=1945
2010=2195          10330=962
2020=867           10340=1278
2030=1436          10350=636
2040=1615          10360=974
2050=1308          10370=695
2060=1406          10380=698
2500=1429
2510=1599          TOTAL= 179384
2520=3097
2530=1001
2540=1748
9000=4532
9010=1428
9020=950
9030=1312
9040=1473
9050=206
9060=839
9070=1301
9080=1836
9100=2170
9110=2671
9190=577
9200=1467
9210=1585
10000=1874
10010=225
10020=2107
10030=1092
10040=2595
10050=871
10060=1758
10070=1762
10080=1057
10090=1920
10100=1404
10110=1923
10120=1588
10130=1414
10140=2075
10150=1228
10160=1582
10170=1055
10200=1867
10210=1871
10220=2155
```

Stepping Stones

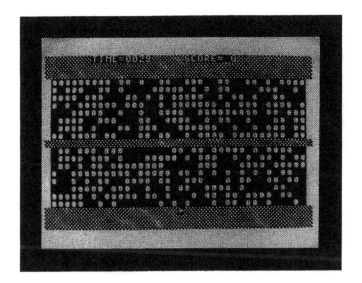

Move to and fro on the magic floating stepping stones. Step off the stone and you will sink like a rock. You can take respite on each bank or the island in the centre of the river, but the longer you wait, the less score you make. You can move up and down or sideways from one stepping stone to another but not diagonally.

VARIABLES

MM$ = Stepping stones and river space

C   = Colour offset to screen address

BG$ = River bank and island

RR$ = Empty river

TI$ = Time

R   = On/off river switch

P   = Your location on screen

Q   = Crossed river switch

SC   = Score

PH   = Previous high score

K   = Key pressed

X   = Movement increment/decrement

```
10     REM STEPPING STONES
```

Define variables

```
20     MM$(0)=" ▣ ▤ ● ":MM$(1)=" ▣ ▤ ▲ ":MM$(2)=" ▣ ▤ ● ":M
       M$(3)=" ▣ ▤ ▲ ":MM$(4)=" ▣ ▤ ● "
30     C=54272:POKE54296,15:POKE54276,0
40     BG$=" ▦ ※ ※ ※ ※ ※ ※ ※ ※ ※ ※ ※ ※ ※ ※ ※ ※
        ※ ※ ※ ※ ※ ※ ※ ※ ※ ※ ※ ※ ※ ※ ※ ※ ※ ※
        ※ ※ ※ ※ ※ "
50     RR$=" ▣ ▣ ▲ ▤ ▲ ▲ ▲ ▲ ▲ ▲ ▲ ▲ ▲ ▲ ▲ ▲ ▲
        ▲ ▲ ▲ ▲ ▲ ▲ ▲ ▲ ▲ ▲ ▲ ▲ ▲ ▲ ▲ ▲ ▲ ▲
        ▲ ▲ ▲ ▲ ▲ ▲ "
60     GOTO1000
```

Place a new set of stepping stones at right of river, clear left side.

```
100    PRINT" ▣ ▣ ▣ ▣ ▣ ▣ ▣ ▣ ▣ ▣ ▣ ▣ ▣ ▣ ▣ ▣ ▣ ▣
        ▣ ▣ ▣ ▣ ▣ ▣ ▣ ▣ ▣ ▣ ▣ ▣ ▣ ▣ ▣ ▣ ▣ ▣
        ▣ ▣ ▣ ▣ ▣ ▣ ▣ ";
101    FORI=1TO8:PRINT" ▣ ■■ ";MM$(RND(.)*5);:NEXT
102    PRINT" ▣ ";
103    FORI=1TO8:PRINT" ▣ ■■ ";MM$(RND(.)*5);:NEXT
104    RETURN
110    FORI=1TO8:PRINT" ▣ ▣ "CHR$(20):NEXT:RETURN
```

Move river, print time, score, check if key was pressed and move player.

```
130    GOSUB100
135    PRINT" ▣ ▣ ▣ ▣ ▣ ▣ ▣ ▣ ▣ TIME="RIGHT$(TI$,4)" ▣
        ▣ ▣ ▣ ▣ SCORE="SC
140    PRINT" ▣ ▣ ▣ ▣ ▣ ";:GOSUB110:PRINT" ▣ ▣ ▣ ▣ ▣ ▣
        ▣ ▣ ▣ ▣ ▣ ▣ ▣ ▣ ";:GOSUB110
145    IFINT(ABS(R)/9)=0ANDR<>0THENP=P-1
150    K=PEEK(197)
160    IFK=64THENX=0:GOTO197
170    IFK=10THENX=-1:GOTO195
175    IFK=9THENX=-40:R=R-1:GOTO195
180    IFK=18THENX=1:GOTO195
185    IFK=12THENX=40:R=R+1
195    IFP+X>1903THENX=0
196    IFP+X<1144THENX=0
```

Stepped in river, generate sound of player movement, check if river crossed.

```
197    IFPEEK(P+X)=32ORPEEK(P+X)=160THEN600
200    IFP<1184THENPOKEP,102:GOTO205
201    IFP<1504THENPOKEP,209:GOTO205
```

```
202  IFP<1544THENPOKEP,102:GOTO205
203  IFP<1864THENPOKEP,209:GOTO205
204  IFP<1904THENPOKEP,102
205  IFX<>0THENPOKE54273,20:POKE54272,10:POKE54277,22:POKE54276
     ,0:POKE54276,129
206  POKE54276,0:P=P+X:POKEP,170
207  IFP<1184ANDQ=0THENQ=1:SC=SC+INT(1000000/TI):TI$="000000":
     GOSUB300
208  IFP>1863ANDQ=1THENQ=0:SC=SC+INT(1000000/TI):TI$="000000":
     GOSUB300
210  GOTO130
```

> Sound routine for crossing river, print message, check if another game.

```
300  POKE54276,0:POKE54278,240
310  POKE54276,33:POKE54273,6:POKE54272,206
320  FORT=1TO200:NEXT:POKE54273,0:POKE54272,0
330  POKE54278,0:RETURN
600  PRINT" ▨ ▨ ▨ ▨ ▨ ▨ ▨ ▨ ▨ ▨ ▨ ▨ ▨ ▨ ▨ ▨ ▨
     ▨ ▨ ▨ ▨ ▨ ▨ ▨ ▨ ▨ ▨ ▨ ▨ ▨ ▨ ▨ ▨ ▨ "
610  PRINT" ▲  ▲ DROWNED ▲ LIKE ▲ A ▲ RAT!":PRINT" ▨ ▨ ▲  ▲
     ▲  ▲  ▲  ▲  ▲ SCORE ▲ ="SC
620  PRINT" ▨ ▨ ▲  ▲ PREVIOUS ▲ HIGH ▲ ="PH
630  IFSC>PHTHENPH=SC
640  PRINT" ▨ ▨ ▨ ▲  ▲ ANOTHER ▲ GAME ▲ (Y/N) ▨ ▨ ▨ ▨ ▨
     "
650  GETG$:IFG$="Y"THEN1100
660  IFG$="N"THENPOKE54276,0:PRINT" ▨ ":END
670  GOTO650
```

> Print instruction and print the game screen.

```
1000 POKE53280,1:POKE53281,1:PRINT" ▨ ▨ ▨ ▨ ▨ ▲  ▲  ▲  ▲
     ▲  ▲  ▲  ▲  ▲ STEPPING ▲ STONES"
1020 FORX=1TO1000:NEXT
1050 PRINT" ▨ ▨ ▨ YOUR ▲ MISSION ▲ IS ▲ TO ▲ MOVE ▲ BACK ▲ &
     ▲ FORTH ▲ "
1060 PRINT" ▨ ▲ ACROSS ▲ THE ▲ SWOLLEN ▲ RAGING ▲ RIVER."
1070 PRINT" ▨ ▨ ▲ TIPPY-TOE ▲ ON ▲ THE ▲ MAGIC ▲ STEPPING ▲ S
     TONES"
1075 PRINT" ▨ ▲ USING ▲ THE ▲ KEYBOARD ▲ CHARACTERS:-"
1076 PRINT" ▨ ▨ ▲  ▲  ▲  ▲  ▲  ▲  ▲  ▲  ▲  ▲  ▲
     ▲ W ▨ ▨ ▮▮ ▮▮ ▮▮A ▲  ● ▲ D ▨ ▨ ▮▮ ▮▮ ▮▮Z"
1080 PRINT" ▨ ▨ ▲  ▲  ▲  ▲  ▲  ▲  ▲ HIT ▲ KEY ▲ TO ▲ BE
     GIN."
1090 WAIT198,1
1100 PRINT" ▨ "
1110 PRINTBG$BG$BG$;:FORI=1TO8:PRINTRR$:NEXT
1120 PRINTBG$;:FORI=1TO8:PRINTRR$:NEXT:PRINTBG$BG$BG$" ▨ "
1130 P=1864+INT(RND(1)*35):POKEP,170:R=9:Q=0:SC=0:TI$="000000"
1140 GOTO130
```

28

CHECKSUM

```
  10=0              1070=3727
  20=5017           1075=2840
  30=1799           1076=2910
  40=7696           1080=2041
  50=2362           1090=417
  60=579            1100=372
 100=2017           1110=2183
 101=2427           1120=2898
 102=307            1130=4342
 103=2427           1140=528
 104=143
 110=1877      TOTAL= 128238
 130=295
 135=2641
 140=1883
 145=2710
 150=704
 160=1625
 170=1795
 175=2480
 180=1632
 185=1730
 195=1415
 196=1415
 197=2618
 200=1895
 201=1889
 202=1887
 203=1897
 204=1278
 205=4165
 206=1740
 207=4896
 208=4896
 210=528
 300=1273
 310=1957
 320=2222
 330=736
 600=1374
 610=3439
 620=1736
 630=1317
 640=1923
 650=1359
 660=2013
 670=530
1000=4031
1020=1036
1050=3377
1060=2992
```

Plane Chase

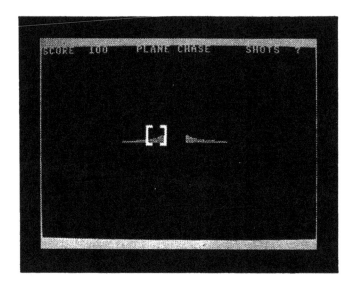

You are the pilot of a jet fighter. Immediately in front of you is a sequence of planes moving across your missile sight. The missile sight can only be moved up and down by pressing the Q and Z keys. Hitting the spacebar will fire one of these lethal projectiles. Beware, it takes time for the missile to get to its target. Each hit on the plane will result in a score of a hundred points. It is quite difficult to hit a plane so be exacting with shots. In each game a player will be given fifteen planes to shoot down with one missile per plane. The more planes you shoot down with fewer missiles the better your points per shot ratio.

VARIABLES

K	= Keyboard scan
A	= Sprite register
B	= Pointer to sprite
C	= Sprite colour register
D	= Colour of sprite
E	= Number of bytes in sprite
S	= Byte of machine language program
W	= Y axis increment of plane
D1	= Collision register
Z	= Position of sprite in memory
XL	= Passes X data to machine program
V	= Flag to indicate a missile used
F	= Flag missile in flight
CN	= Timer for missile
MS	= Is this missile's first pass
TG	= Top of missile sprite
TP	= Bottom of missile
M3	= X axis increment of plane
T	= Video chip register
K1	= Entry point of machine program
SC	= Player score
PL	= Player number
P1	= Start of plane movement
P2	= End of plane movement
CT	= Start of Y axis of plane
I	= General purpose variable
SH	= Number of shots
T+21	= Sprite on/off switch
O	= X position of plane for memory
S1	= Y position of plane in memory
C1	= X position gun sight register
C2	= Y position gun sight register
M1	= X position of missile register
M2	= Y position of missile register
F1	= X position of fuselarge register
F2	= Y position of fuselarge register
L1	= X position of left wing register
L2	= Y position of left wing register
R1	= X position of right wing register
R2	= Y position of right wing register
X2	= X co-ordinate of gun sight
Y2	= Y co-ordinate of gun sight

```
5      REM PLANE CHASE
```

> Clear the screen, define variables, build the plane, set colours.

```
10     CLR:PRINT" 🖥 ";CHR$(158);"SETTING ▲ UP ▲ GAME"
15     K=197:D1=53278:POKE53280,3:POKE53281,9
20     T=53248:O=17000:S1=17001:KI=18000
25     C1=T+0:C2=T+1:M1=T+2:M2=T+3
50     F1=T+4:F2=T+5:L1=T+6:L2=T+7
70     R1=T+8:R2=T+9:M=T+16
95     POKE T+21,0:X2=148:Y2=100
100    FORI=0TO62:POKE16128+I,85:POKE16064,170:NEXT
130    FORJ=1TO5
135    READA,B,C,D,E:POKEA,B:POKEC,D:Z=B*64
155    IF E=0 THEN 180
160    FOR Q1=0 TO E
165    READ H:POKEZ+Q1,H
175    NEXT
180    NEXT
182    GOSUB 593
183    FORI=18000 TO 18000+33
184    READ S:POKEI,S:NEXT
190    GOSUB24000:GOSUB25000:POKET+21,255
195    POKE 53277,24:POKE53271,4
```

> Give player's 1 and 2 each 15 goes and print the score.

```
200    FOR JP=1TO2STEP0
210    FORC9=1TO15:GOSUB600:NEXT
235    PL=1
240    GOSUB 300:SC=0:SH=0
250    FORC9=1TO15:GOSUB600:NEXT
275    PL=2
280    GOSUB300:SC=0:SH=0:NEXT
295    STOP
```

> Print number of shots, hits and the score.

```
300    PRINT" 🖥 ";:POKET+21,0
315    PRINT TAB(13);"PLAYER:";PL
320    PRINT" 🔲 🔲 🔲 "
325    PRINT TAB(13);"SCORE ▲ ▲ ▲ ▲ ▲ ▲ ▲ ▲ : ▲ ";SC
330    PRINT TAB(13);"SHOTS ▲ ▲ ▲ ▲ ▲ ▲ ▲ ▲ : ▲ ";SH
331    IFSH=0THENSH=.01
332    PRINT TAB(13);"HITS ▲ ▲ ▲ ▲ ▲ ▲ ▲ ▲ ▲ ▲ : ▲ ";
       SC/100
335    PRINT TAB(13);"POINT ▲ PER ▲ SHOT ▲ : ▲ ";
340    PRINT INT(SC/SH)
```

```
345    PRINT" ◧ ◧ ◧ ◧ ◧ ◧ ◧ ◧ ◧ ◧ ◧ ◧ ";
350    PRINT TAB(13);"PRESS ▲ ANY ▲ KEY ▲ TO ▲ RUN"
353    FORK1=1TO100:GETA$:NEXT
355    GETA$:IFA$=""THEN355
360    POKET+21,31:PRINT" ◨ ";
365    RETURN
```

> Launch the missile on its way and keep it going.

```
500    AS=PEEK(D1):V=1
505    IFMSTHEN520
510    MS=1:SH=SH+1:POKET+21,30
515    CN=10:TG=14*64+1:TP=14*64+61
520    X1=X2:Y1=Y2:POKEM1,X1:POKEM2,Y1
530    POKETG,0:POKETP,0:TG=TG+3:TP=TP-3
535    CN=CN-1
537    POKEM1,X1:POKEM2,Y1
540    IFCN=1THENGOSUB550:E=0:MS=0:F=0:POKET+21,31:RETURN
545    RETURN
550    IFPEEK(D1)AND6=6THENGOSUB1000:E=1
590    POKEM1,0:POKEM2,0:RETURN
593    FORI=0TO62STEP3:POKEI+896,0:POKEI+1+896,255:POKEI+896+2,0:
       NEXT:RETURN
```

> Launch a plane at random and let player shoot it down.

```
600    POKET+21,1:MS=0:CN=0
607    FORJ=1TO100:GETA$:NEXT
610    RN=INT(RND(1)*5):IFRN>40RRN=0THEN610
620    IFRN=1THENP1=0:P2=184:M3=7:W=RND(1)*3:CT=60:REM RIGHT DOWN
630    IFRN=2THENP1=184:P2=0:M3=-7:W=RND(1)*3:CT=60:REM LEFT DOWN
640    IFRN=3THENP1=184:P2=0:W=-3*RND(1):M3=-7:CT=150:REM LEFT UP
650    IFRN=4THENP1=0:P2=184:W=3*RND(1):M3=7:CT=150:REM RIGHT UP
660    POKEL2,Y4:POKEF2,Y3:POKER2,Y5
720    E=0:F=0:POKEC1,X2:POKEC2,Y2:GOSUB593:POKET+21,31:V=0:POKEM
       1,0:POKEM2,0
725    PRINT" ◨ SCORE ▲ ▲ ▲ ▲ ▲ ▲ ▲ ▲ ▲ PLANE ▲ CHASE ▲
       ▲ ▲ ▲ ▲ SHOTS";
730    FORXL=P1TOP2STEPM3:POKEO,XL:POKES1,CT:SYSKI:CT=CT+W:IFV
       THEN790
750    A=PEEK(K):IFA=0THEN890
760    IFA=62THENGOSUB955:GOTO890
770    IFA=12THENGOSUB970:GOTO890
780    IFA=60THENF=1
790    IFFTHENGOSUB500:IFETHENRETURN
795    PRINT" ◨ ";TAB(6);SC;TAB(36);SH;
890    NEXTXL
895    POKET+21,3
900    RETURN
```

33

```
955    IFY2=30THENRETURN
960    Y2=Y2-5:POKEC2,Y2:RETURN
970    IFY2=190THENRETURN
975    Y2=Y2+5:POKEC2,Y2:RETURN
1000   FORI=1TO10:POKE2041,252
1030   FORJ=1TO30:NEXT:POKE2041,251
1045   FORJ=1TO30:NEXT
1050   NEXT
1060   SC=SC+100:POKE2041,14:RETURN
```

```
11000  DATA 2040,13,53287,1,62
11010  DATA 255,0,255,255,0,255,255,0,255
11020  DATA 224,0,7,224,0,7,224,0,7
11030  DATA 224,0,7,224,0,7,224,0,7
3616   DATA 224,0,7,224,0,7,224,0,7
11050  DATA 224,0,7,224,0,7,224,0,7
11060  DATA 224,0,7,224,0,7,224,0,7
11070  DATA255,0,255,255,0,255,255,0,255
11090  REM
12000  DATA 2041,14,53288,1,0
13000  DATA 2042,15,53289,0,62
13010  DATA0,24,0,0,24,0,0,24,0,0,24,0,0,24,0,0,24,0,0,24,0,0,24,
       0,0,24,0,0,24,0
13020  DATA0,24,0,0,60,0,0,60,0,0,126,0,0,126,0,255,255,255,255,2
       55,255
13030  DATA 146,66,73,146,66,73,255,255,255,255,255,255
14000  DATA 2043,253,53290,5,62
14010  DATA0,0,0,0,0,0,0,0,0,0,0,0,0,0,0,0,0,0,0,0,0,0,0,0,0,0,0,
       0,0,0,0,0
14020  DATA0,0,0,0,0,0,0,0,0,3,0,0,7,0,0,15,0,0,63,0,7,255,0,255,
       255,255,255,255
14030  DATA 255,255,255
15000  DATA 2044,254,53291,5,62
15010  DATA 0,0,0,0,0,0,0,0,0,0,0,0,0,0,0,0,0,0,0,0,0,0,0,0,0,0,0
       ,0,0,0,0,0,0,0
15020  DATA 0,0,0,0,0,192,0,0,224,0,0,240,0,0,254,0,0,255,224,0,2
       55,255,128
15030  DATA 255,255,255,255,255,255
24000  PRINT" ";:PRINT:PRINT:PRINT:PRINT"
24010  PRINT"
24020  PRINT"
24030  PRINT"
```

```
24040 PRINT"  ▲  ▲  ▲  ▲  ✺  ▲  ▲  ▲  ▲  ▲  ✺  ▲  ▲  ▲  ▲
      ✺  ▲  ▲  ✺  ▲  ▲  ✺  ▲  ▲  ▲  ▲  ✺  ✺  ▲  ▲  ✺  ▲  ▲  ▲  ▲ "
24050 PRINT"  ▲  ▲  ✺  ▲  ▲  ✺  ▲  ▲  ▲  ▲  ▲  ✺  ✺  ✺  ✺  ▲  ▲
      ✺  ▲  ▲  ▲  ✺  ▲  ▲  ✺  ▲  ▲  ▲  ▲  ▲  ✺  ▲  ▲  ✺  ✺  ✺ "
24070 PRINT:PRINT
24100 PRINT"  ▲  ▲  ▲  ▲  ✺  ✺  ✺  ✺  ▲  ▲  ✺  ▲  ▲  ✺  ▲  ▲
      ▲  ▲  ✺  ▲  ▲  ▲  ✺  ✺  ✺  ✺  ▲  ▲  ✺  ✺  ✺  ✺ "
24110 PRINT"  ▲  ▲  ▲  ▲  ✺  ▲  ▲  ▲  ▲  ▲  ✺  ▲  ▲  ✺  ▲  ▲
      ▲  ✺  ▲  ✺  ▲  ▲  ✺  ▲  ▲  ▲  ▲  ✺  ▲  ▲  ▲  ▲ "
24120 PRINT"  ▲  ▲  ▲  ▲  ✺  ▲  ▲  ▲  ▲  ▲  ✺  ▲  ▲  ✺  ▲  ▲
      ✺  ▲  ▲  ✺  ▲  ▲  ✺  ▲  ▲  ▲  ▲  ✺  ▲  ▲  ▲  ▲ "
24130 PRINT"  ▲  ▲  ▲  ▲  ✺  ▲  ▲  ▲  ▲  ▲  ✺  ▲  ▲  ✺  ✺  ✺
      ✺  ▲  ▲  ✺  ▲  ✺  ✺  ✺  ✺  ▲  ✺  ✺  ✺  ✺ "
24140 PRINT"  ▲  ▲  ▲  ▲  ✺  ▲  ▲  ▲  ▲  ▲  ✺  ▲  ▲  ✺  ▲  ▲  ✺  ▲  ▲
      ✺  ▲  ▲  ✺  ▲  ▲  ▲  ▲  ✺  ▲  ▲  ▲  ▲ "
24150 PRINT"  ▲  ▲  ▲  ▲  ✺  ✺  ✺  ✺  ▲  ▲  ✺  ▲  ▲  ✺  ▲  ▲
      ✺  ▲  ▲  ▲  ✺  ▲  ▲  ✺  ✺  ✺  ✺  ▲  ▲  ✺  ✺  ✺ "
24160 FORI=1TO1000:GETA$:NEXT
24200 RETURN
25000 REM PRINT THE INSTRUCTIONS
25010 PRINT" ⬛ ";
25020 PRINT
25030 PRINT TAB(13);"PLANE ▲ CHASE"
25040 PRINT
25050 PRINT "THE ▲ OBJECT ▲ OF ▲ THIS ▲ GAME ▲ IS ▲ ▲ TO ▲ SHOO
      T":PRINT
25060 PRINT "DOWN ▲ THE ▲ PLANE ▲ WANDERING ▲ ACROSS ▲ YOUR":
      PRINT
25070 PRINT "GUN ▲ SIGHT. ▲ A ▲ TOTAL ▲ OF ▲ 15 ▲ PLANES ▲ PER":
      PRINT
25080 PRINT "GAME ▲ WILL ▲ FLY ▲ ACROSS ▲ YOUR ▲ SCREEN.":PRINT
25090 PRINT "YOU ▲ CAN ▲ MOVE ▲ YOUR ▲ GUN ▲ UP ▲ AND ▲ DOWN ▲ W
      ITH":PRINT
25100 PRINT "THE ▲ Q ▲ AND ▲ Z ▲ KEYS. ▲ A ▲ MISSILE ▲ CAN ▲ BE"
      :PRINT
25110 PRINT "FIRED ▲ BY ▲ PRESSING ▲ THE ▲ SPACEBAR":PRINT:PRINT
25115 PRINT TAB(10);"PRESS ▲ KEY ▲ ANY ▲ TO ▲ START";
25120 GETA$:IFA$=""THEN25120
25130 PRINT" ⬛ ";
25999 RETURN
28500 REM --------------------------
29000 REM DATA FOR MACHINE SUBROUTINE
29500 REM --------------------------
30000 DATA 173,104,66,141,6,208,24,105,48,141,4,208,24,105,25,14
      1,8,208
30010 DATA 173,105,66,141,7,208,141,9,208,56,233,21,141,5,208,96
```

35

CHECKSUM

5=0	537=1031	14020=4390
10=2595	540=3281	14030=731
15=2350	545=143	15000=1205
20=2535	550=1958	15010=4088
25=2756	590=1037	15020=3685
50=2766	593=4358	15030=1404
70=2057	600=1537	24000=4493
95=1729	607=1320	24010=3033
100=2650	610=2779	24020=3565
130=655	620=3702	24030=3551
135=2285	630=3880	24040=2905
155=782	640=4102	24050=3433
160=735	650=3747	24070=366
165=951	660=1593	24100=3787
175=131	720=4418	24110=2737
180=131	725=2884	24120=2743
182=310	730=4478	24130=3787
183=1413	750=1490	24140=2739
184=835	760=1597	24150=3923
190=1729	770=1593	24160=1380
195=1217	780=973	24200=143
200=968	790=1272	25000=0
210=1363	795=1512	25010=435
235=391	890=300	25020=153
240=1237	895=616	25030=1470
250=1363	900=143	25040=153
275=392	955=881	25050=3398
280=1446	960=1467	25060=3542
295=145	970=952	25070=3241
300=1133	975=1466	25080=3120
315=1415	1000=1379	25090=3660
320=286	1030=1589	25100=3122
325=1900	1045=907	25110=3195
330=1917	1050=131	25115=2500
331=1211	1060=1674	25120=1325
332=2224	11000=1112	25130=435
335=1976	11010=1763	25999=143
340=912	11020=1379	28500=0
345=627	11030=1379	29000=0
350=2258	3616=1379	29500=0
353=1380	11050=1379	30000=3496
355=1215	11060=1379	30010=3106
360=1199	11070=1763	
365=143	11090=0	TOTAL= 259173
500=1137	12000=1057	
505=630	13000=1115	
510=1980	13010=4357	
515=2629	13020=3449	
520=2146	13030=2528	
530=2580	14000=1205	
535=704	14010=3638	

Minotaur

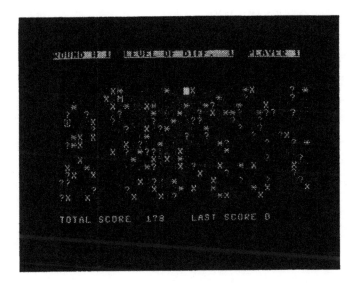

Move the cursor to the exit (white), using smallest possible numbers. If numbers used are too large, the mintaur ('M') moves one step closer.

Our object is to determine an integer between 0 and 1000; 'X' squares provide clues; '?' squares have random values and '*' may improve your total score. The smallest total scores are the better ones. Hit 'T' if trapped.

VARIABLES

LD%	= Level of difficulty
R%	= Round
SN%	= Secret number
D1%,D2%,D3%	= Digits of SN%
PP%	= Player's position
M%	= Minotaur's position
LS%	= Last score
TS%	= Total score
CU	= Character under minotaur
NC%	= Number of clues
T%(I)	= Truth array for clues
61%,62%,63%	= Digits of guess
MR%,MC%	= Minotaur's row, colour
PR%,PC%	= Player's row, colour

```
0       REM MINOTAUR
```

> Print the board, position player and minotaur, set difficulty level.

```
1       PRINT" 💾 ";:POKE53280,14:POKE53281,13:PRINTTAB(10);" ▪ MIN
        OTAUR ▲ MASTER-MIND":
2       PRINT:PRINTTAB(30);"BY ▲ A.LACEY":PRINT
4       PRINT:PRINT"LEVEL ▲ OF ▲ DIFFICULTY?(1-9)";
5       GETX$:IFX$=""THEN5
6       IFVAL(X$)<1ORVAL(X$)>9THEN5
7       LD%=VAL(X$):PRINTLD%
8       FORT=1TO1000:NEXT
10      GOTO68
20      FORI=1225TO1785STEP40
22      FORJ=0TO37
24      K1=INT(RND(0)*13)
26      IFK1>9THEN30
27      POKEI+J,K1+48:POKEI+J+54272,2
28      GOTO40
30      IFK1<>10THEN33
31      POKEI+J,24:POKEI+J+54272,3
32      GOTO40
33      IFK1<>11THEN35
34      POKEI+J,63:POKEI+J+54272,5:GOTO40
35      POKEI+J,42:POKEI+J+54272,7
40      NEXT:NEXT
42      POKE1244,160:POKE55516,1
45      RETURN
68      R%=1:SN%=INT(RND(0)*999+1)
69      D1%=INT(SN%/100):D2%=INT((SN%-D1%*100)/10):D3%=SN%-D1%*100
        -D2%*10
70      PRINT" 💾 ";:POKE53280,0:POKE53281,0:GOSUB20
72      PP%=1804:M%=1524:IFPEEK(1804)>48THENLS%=PEEK(1804)-48
73      IFPEEK(1804)=63ORPEEK(1804)=42ORPEEK(1804)=24THENLS%=0:
        POKE1804,48
74      TS%=TS%+LS%:CU=PEEK(1524):POKE1524,13:POKE55796,7:POKE1244
        ,160:POKE55516,1
75      PRINT" ◣ 🄻 ROUND ▲ #";R%;" ▬ ▲ 🄻 LEVEL ▲ OF ▲ DIFF. ▲ "
        ;LD%;" ▬ ";TAB(30);" 🄻 PLAYER ▲ 1 ▬ "
76      FORI=1TO21:PRINT:NEXT:PRINT" ◣ ▲ TOTAL ▲ SCORE ▲ ";TS%;
        TAB(21);"LAST ▲ SCORE";LS%;
```

> Move the player round the board and calculate new player position.

```
80      C=0:Q=1
81      GETX$:C=C+1
82      IFC=7THENQ=1-Q:C=0
83      IFQ<>0THEN86
84      IFPEEK(PP%)>63THENPOKEPP%,PEEK(PP%)-128:Q=1:GOTO86
85      POKEPP%,PEEK(PP%)+128:Q=1
86      IFX$=""THEN81
87      GOSUB480:IFPEEK(PP%)>64THENPOKEPP%,PEEK(PP%)-128
```

39

```
89      IFX$="P"THEN100
90      IFX$="O"THEN110
92      IFX$="@"THEN120
93      IFX$=":"THEN130
94      IFX$="+"THEN140
95      IFX$="0"THEN150
96      IFX$="L"THEN160
97      IFX$=";"THEN170
98      IFX$="T"THEN178
99      GOTO81
100     IFPEEK(PP%-40)=32THEN81
102     LS%=PEEK(PP%)-48
104     POKEPP%,32:PP%=PP%-40
105     GOTO180
110     IFPEEK(PP%-1)=32THEN81
112     LS%=PEEK(PP%)-48
114     POKEPP%,32:PP%=PP%-1
115     GOTO180
120     IFPEEK(PP%+1)=32THEN81
122     LS%=PEEK(PP%)-48
124     POKEPP%,32:PP%=PP%+1
125     GOTO180
130     IFPEEK(PP%+40)=32THEN81
132     LS%=PEEK(PP%)-48
134     POKEPP%,32:PP%=PP%+40
135     GOTO180
140     IFPEEK(PP%-39)=32THEN81
142     LS%=PEEK(PP%)-48
144     POKEPP%,32:PP%=PP%-39
145     GOTO180
150     IFPEEK(PP%-41)=32THEN81
152     LS%=PEEK(PP%)-48
154     POKEPP%,32:PP%=PP%-41
155     GOTO180
160     IFPEEK(PP%+39)=32THEN81
162     LS%=PEEK(PP%)-48
164     POKEPP%,32:PP%=PP%+39
165     GOTO180
170     IFPEEK(PP%+41)=32THEN81
172     LS%=PEEK(PP%)-48
174     POKEPP%,32:PP%=PP%+41
175     GOTO180
178     PR%=INT((PP%-1024)/40) :PC%=PP%-PR%*40-1024:GOSUB360:IFPP%
        <>M%THEN178
179     GOTO400
```

Check if the move was valid and decide if to move minotaur.

```
180     PR%=INT((PP%-1024)/40) :PC%=PP%-PR%*40-1024
181     K1=PEEK(PP%):IFK1=63THENGOSUB200
182     IFPP%=M%THEN400
183     IFK1=24THENGOSUB210
184     IFK1=42THENGOSUB300
186     IFK1=160THEN320
190     K1=PEEK(PP%)-48:IFLS%+K1>=10-LD%THENGOSUB360
```

40

```
192    TS%=TS%+K1:GOSUB450
194    IFPP%=M%THEN400
196    GOTO80
```

```
┌─────────────────────────────────────────────┐
│                                             │
│   Give player hints about the number.       │
│                                             │
└─────────────────────────────────────────────┘
```

```
200    I=INT(RND(1)*10):POKEPP%,I+48:POKEPP%+54272,2
202    RETURN
210    POKEPP%,48
211    IFNC%>=9THENGOTO295
213    K2=INT(RND(0)*9+1):IFT%(K2)=1THEN213
214    T%(K2)=1:NC%=NC%+1
216    ONK2GOTO220,225,230,235,240,245,250,255,260
220    GOSUB460:PRINT"SUM ▲ OF ▲ DIGITS ▲ OF ▲ SECRET":PRINTTAB(9
       );"NUMBER ▲ EQUALS ▲ ";
222    PRINTD1%+D2%+D3%
224    GOSUB470:RETURN
225    GOSUB460:PRINT"SECRET ▲ NUMBER ▲ IS ▲ ";
226    IFSN%/2=INT(SN%/2)THENPRINT"EVEN":GOTO228
227    PRINT"ODD"
228    PRINT:GOSUB470:RETURN
230    K=INT(RND(1)*200)+SN%:J=K-200:IFJ<0THENJ=0
232    IFK>1000THENK=1000
233    GOSUB460:PRINT"NUMBER ▲ IS ▲ BETWEEN";J:PRINTTAB(9);"AND";
       K
234    GOSUB470:RETURN
235    GOSUB460:PRINT"NUMBER ▲ IS ▲ ";
236    IFSN%/5=INT(SN%/5)THENPRINT"DIVISIBLE":GOTO238
237    PRINT"NOT ▲ DIVISIBLE"
238    PRINTTAB(9);"BY ▲ 5":GOSUB470:RETURN
240    L=D1%:IFD2%>LTHENL=D2%
241    IFD3%>LTHENL=D3%
242    GOSUB460:PRINT"LARGEST ▲ DIGIT ▲ IN ▲ THE":PRINTTAB(9);"SE
       CRET ▲ NUMBER ▲ IS";L
243    GOSUB470:RETURN
245    GOSUB460:PRINT"FIRST ▲ DIGIT ▲ IN ▲ THE ▲ SECRET":PRINT
       TAB(9);"NUMBER ▲ IS ▲ ";
246    IFD1%>5THENPRINT"LARGER ▲ THAN ▲ 5":GOTO249
247    IFD1%<5THENPRINT"LESS ▲ THAN ▲ 5":GOTO249
248    PRINT"EQUAL ▲ TO ▲ 5"
249    GOSUB470:RETURN
250    GOSUB460:PRINT"SUM ▲ OF ▲ FIRST ▲ AND ▲ THIRD":PRINTTAB(9)
       ;"DIGITS ▲ IS ▲ ";
252    PRINTD1%+D3%
253    GOSUB470:RETURN
255    GOSUB460:PRINT"ONE ▲ OF ▲ THE ▲ DIGITS ▲ IN ▲ THE":PRINT
       TAB(9);"SECRET ▲ NUMBER ▲ IS ▲ ";
256    K=INT(RND(1)*3):IFK=0ANDSN%>99THENPRINTD1%:GOTO259
257    IFK=1ANDSN%>9THENPRINTD2%:GOTO259
258    PRINTD3%
259    GOSUB470:RETURN
260    GOSUB460:PRINT"PRODUCT ▲ OF ▲ THE ▲ NON-ZERO":PRINTTAB(9);
       "DIGITS ▲ IS";
261    IFD1%=0ANDD2%=0THENPRINTD3%:GOTO268
262    IFD1%=0ANDD3%=0THENPRINTD2%:GOTO268
```

41

```
263     IFD1%=ØTHENPRINTD2%*D3%:GOTO268
264     IFD2%=ØANDD3%=ØTHENPRINTD1%:GOTO268
265     IFD2%=ØTHENPRINTD1%*D3%:GOTO268
266     IFD3%=ØTHENPRINTD1%*D2%:GOTO268
267     PRINTD1%*D2%*D3%
268     GOSUB47Ø:RETURN
295     GOTO23Ø
```

Tell player how close he is getting to secret number.

```
3ØØ     POKEPP%,48
3Ø2     IFTS%<11THENRETURN
3Ø4     I=INT(RND(Ø)*1ØØ):IFI>5ØTHENTS%=TS%-1Ø:RETURN
3Ø6     IFI<1ØTHENTS%=TS%+5Ø:RETURN
31Ø     TS%=TS%+1Ø:RETURN
32Ø     GOSUB46Ø:PRINT"GUESS ▲ AT ▲ THE ▲ SECRET ▲ NUMBER":PRINT
        TAB(9);
322     INPUT"AND ▲ HIT ▲ ◧ RETURN ▬ ";K$
324     I=VAL(K$):IFI=SN%THEN4ØØ
325     G1%=INT(I/1ØØ):G2%=INT((I-G1%*1ØØ)/1Ø):G3%=I-G1%*1ØØ-G2%*1
        Ø
326     PRINT" ◫ ":PRINT:IFD1%=G1%THENPRINT"FIRST ▲ DIGIT ▲ CORREC
        T":PRINT
328     IFD2%=G2%THENPRINT"SECOND ▲ DIGIT ▲ CORRECT":PRINT
33Ø     IFD3%=G3%THENPRINT"THIRD ▲ DIGIT ▲ CORRECT"
332     IFD1%<>G1%ANDD2%<>G2%ANDD3%<>G3%THENPRINT"NO ▲ DIGITS ▲ CO
        RRECT"
334     FORT=1TO2ØØØ:NEXT
336     R%=R%+1:GOTO7Ø
36Ø     MR%=INT((M%-1Ø24)/4Ø):MC%=M%-MR%*4Ø-1Ø24
362     IFMC%<>PC%THEN37Ø
364     IFMR%>PR%THENMR%=MR%-1:GOTO39Ø
366     MR%=MR%+1:GOTO39Ø
37Ø     IFMR%<>PR%THEN376
372     IFMC%>PC%THENMC%=MC%-1:GOTO39Ø
374     MC%=MC%+1:GOTO39Ø
376     IFM%>PP%THEN382
378     IFMC%<PC%THENMC%=MC%+1:GOTO39Ø
38Ø     MC%=MC%-1:GOTO39Ø
382     MR%=MR%-1
39Ø     K=1Ø24+4Ø*MR%+MC%:IFPEEK(K)=16ØTHENRETURN
391     POKEM%,CU:IFCU=63THENPOKEM%+54272,5:GOTO395
392     IFCU>=48THENPOKEM%+54272,2:GOTO395
393     IFCU=24THENPOKEM%+54272,3:GOTO395
394     POKEM%+54272,7
395     M%=K:CU=PEEK(M%)
396     POKEM%,13:POKEM%+54272,7
397     K=54272:FORL=KTOK+24:POKEL,Ø:NEXT:POKEK+5,96:POKEK+24,15:
        POKEK+4,33
398     POKEK,2Ø9:POKEK+1,18:FORT=1TO3Ø:NEXT:POKEK,Ø:POKEK+1,Ø
399     RETURN
```

> Game is finished, print congratulations or consolations and score.

```
400    PRINT" ▓ ";:IFM%=PP%THEN420
405    FORI=1TO18:PRINT" ▲ ▲ ▲ CONGRATULATIONS! ▲ ▲ ▲ CONGRAT
       ULATIONS!":NEXT:PRINT
410    PRINT"YOU ▲ HAVE ▲ DEFEATED ▲ THE ▲ MINOTAUR!!":PRINT"YOUR
       ▲ SCORE ▲ IS ▲ ";TS%;
415    PRINT"IN ▲ ";R%;" ▲ ROUNDS":GOTO440
420    FORI=1TO18:PRINT" ▲ ▲ ▲ MINOTAUR ▲ WINS! ▲ ▲ ▲ ▲ M
       INOTAUR ▲ WINS!":NEXT:PRINT
425    PRINT"THE ▲ SECRET ▲ NUMBER ▲ WAS ▲ ";SN%
440    PRINT:PRINT"HIT ▲ ANY ▲ KEY ▲ FOR ▲ ANOTHER ▲ GAME"
445    GETX$:IFX$=""THEN445
446    RUN
450    PRINTCHR$(13);CHR$(145);" ▲ TOTAL ▲ SCORE ▲ ▲ ▲ ▲ ▲
       ▲ ▲ ▲ ";TAB(21);"LAST ▲ SCORE ▲ ▲ ▲ ▲ ▲ ";
452    PRINTCHR$(13);CHR$(145);" ▲ TOTAL ▲ SCORE ▲ ";TS%;TAB(21);
       "LAST ▲ SCORE";LS%;
455    RETURN
460    PRINTCHR$(13);:FORI=1TO21:PRINTCHR$(145);:NEXT:PRINT" ▓ ";
462    PRINTTAB(9);:RETURN
470    FORI=1TO18:PRINTCHR$(17);:NEXT
472    PRINTTAB(35);" ◣ ";
474    RETURN
480    FORI=1112TO1138:POKEI,32:NEXT
482    FORI=1152TO1178:POKEI,32:NEXT
485    RETURN
2000   K1=INT(RND(0)*14):PRINTK1,:GOTO2000
```

CHECKSUM

0=0	40=320	92=947
1=4975	42=1209	93=940
2=1820	45=143	94=928
4=2389	68=2063	95=936
5=1135	69=5528	96=959
6=1902	70=1983	97=945
7=1204	72=3731	98=968
8=1032	73=4337	99=481
10=484	74=4575	100=1519
20=1310	75=5042	102=1181
22=709	76=5040	104=1506
24=1207	80=680	105=533
26=785	81=903	110=1464
27=2062	82=1587	112=1181
28=476	83=927	114=1452
30=1032	84=3465	115=533
31=1744	85=1638	120=1464
32=476	86=807	122=1181
33=1036	87=2902	124=1451
34=2328	89=963	125=533
35=1744	90=957	130=1519

132=1181	242=4801	394=836
134=1505	243=507	395=1195
135=533	245=4455	396=1351
140=1518	246=2606	397=4509
142=1181	247=2461	398=3243
144=1513	248=941	399=143
145=533	249=507	400=1513
150=1519	250=4120	405=4920
152=1181	252=656	410=4976
154=1507	253=507	415=1980
155=533	255=5060	420=4541
160=1518	256=3537	425=2254
162=1181	257=2218	440=2713
164=1512	258=311	445=1258
165=533	259=507	446=139
170=1519	260=4231	450=4669
172=1181	261=2284	452=4697
174=1506	262=2283	455=143
175=533	263=2020	460=2969
178=5364	264=2282	462=688
179=529	265=2021	470=1619
180=3530	266=2020	472=828
181=1946	267=1009	474=143
182=995	268=507	480=1677
183=1041	295=528	482=1681
184=1038	300=515	485=143
186=960	302=956	2000=2312
190=3279	304=3178	
192=1291	306=1812	
194=995	310=1086	TOTAL= 363149
196=480	320=3389	
200=3098	322=1679	
202=143	324=1664	
210=515	325=5020	
211=1480	326=3812	
213=2621	328=3022	
214=1484	330=2710	
216=2580	332=4953	
220=4728	334=1031	
222=1009	336=1211	
224=507	360=3341	
225=2034	362=1253	
226=2917	364=2420	
227=441	366=1431	
228=720	370=1286	
230=3495	372=2356	
232=1286	374=1401	
233=3259	376=999	
234=507	378=2358	
235=1426	380=1402	
236=3379	382=810	
237=1236	390=2898	
238=1421	391=2868	
240=1700	392=2453	
241=1168	393=2256	

Spy Training

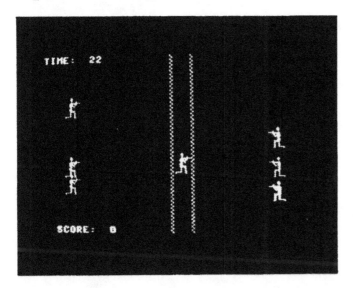

You are at the centre of the screen and the aim is to shoot as many spies as you can in the allotted time. Your colour changes randomly and if you hit a spy of the same colour, you lose 150 points and you won't get an extra round.

Otherwide scoring is 50 points per spy hit.

CONTROLS

    'Q', 'Z': up, down
    'I', 'P': fire left, right

VARIABLES

PC = Player's colour

HT = Spy hit

NK = No. (own) men shot

ER = Extra round flag

TL = Time limit

CO = Collision flags

SC = Score

```
1     REM SPY TRAINING
```

Generate the spy sprites, set screen up, push sound routine into memory.

```
10    POKE53281,0:POKE53280,0:PRINT" ◰ ▣ ▲ ▲ ▲ ▲ ▲ ▲ ▲
      ▲ ▲ ▲ ▲ ▲ ▲ SPY ▲ TRAINING"
15    PRINT" ▩ ▩ ▩ ▩ ▩ ▩ ▩ ▩ ▩ "
20    V=53248:POKEV,180:POKEV+1,200:POKE2040,192:POKEV+39,6:POKE
      V+47,1
25    POKE2041,192:POKE2042,192:POKE2043,192:POKE2044,193:POKE20
      45,193:POKE2046,193
30    FORI=12288TO12350:READQ:POKEI,Q:NEXT
40    FORI=12352TO12414:READQ:POKEI,Q:NEXT
50    POKE2047,194:FORI=12417TO12478:POKEI,0:NEXT
55    POKE12416,240:POKE12419,240
60    FORI=49152TO49369:READQ:POKEI,Q:NEXT
70    TL=60:PRINT" ▲ ▲ ▲ ▲ ▲ ▲ ▲ ▲ ▲ YOUR ▲ TIME ▲ LI
      MIT ▲ IS ▲ ";TL;" ▩ ▩ ▩ ▩ "
90    PRINT" ▲ ▲ ▲ ▲ ▲ ▲ ▲ ▲ ▲ ▲ HIT ▲ ANY ▲ KEY ▲ T
      O ▲ START"
95    GETX$:IFX$=""THEN95
100   PRINT" ◰ ";:FORI=1TO23:PRINTTAB(19);" ◙ ≷ ▲ ▲ ≷ ":NEXT
      :PRINT" ▥ ▧ ";:GOSUB1000
110   PC=6
120   FORI=1TO3:POKEV+2*I,50:NEXT:FORI=4TO6:POKEV+2*I,30:NEXT:
      POKEV+16,112
130   POKEV,180:POKEV+1,150:POKEV+39,6:POKEV+21,1
150   TI$="000000"
160   POKEV+15,150:GOSUB305
```

Driver logic, call up spies randomly and move spy master.

```
200   SYS(49152)
210   SYS(49182)
220   OS=PEEK(V+21):IF(OSAND128)<>0THENGOSUB500:POKEV+30,0
230   GOSUB300:IF(PEEK(V+30)AND126)<>0THENGOSUB305
250   GOSUB1100:IFTI/60>TLTHEN900
260   GOTO200
```

Place spies on screen, move them up and down randomly.

```
300   IFRND(1)<.95THENRETURN
305   Y=PEEK(V+15)-30+INT(RND(1)*60):IFY>230ORY<35THENRETURN
310   I=RND(1):IFI<.2THENPC=2:GOTO330
312   IFI<.6THEN335
315   IFI<.8THENPC=6:GOTO330
320   PC=8
330   POKEV+39,PC:IFRND(1)<.5THEN360
```

47

```
335    IFRND(1)<.5THEN345
340    POKEV+3,Y:POKEV+40,2:POKEV+21,PEEK(V+21)OR2:RETURN
345    POKEV+3,Y:POKEV+5,Y-35:POKEV+7,Y+25
350    FORI=1TO3:K=RND(1):IFK<.3THENPOKEV+39+I,2:GOTO358
352    IFK<.6THENPOKEV+39+I,8:GOTO358
354    POKEV+39+I,6
358    NEXT:POKEV+21,PEEK(V+21)OR14:RETURN
360    IFRND(1)<.5THEN385
365    POKEV+9,Y:POKEV+43,2:POKEV+21,PEEK(V+21)OR16:RETURN
385    POKEV+9,Y:POKEV+11,Y-30:POKEV+13,Y+25
390    FORI=4TO6:K=RND(1):IFK<.3THENPOKEV+39+I,2:GOTO396
392    IFK<.6THENPOKEV+39+I,8:GOTO396
394    POKEV+39+I,6
396    NEXT:POKEV+21,PEEK(V+21)OR112:RETURN
```

```
┌─────────────────────────────────────────────────────────────┐
│ A spy has been shot, increment score, was he one of yours.    │
└─────────────────────────────────────────────────────────────┘
```

```
500    CO=PEEK(V+30):X=PEEK(V+14)+2*(PEEK(V+16)AND128)
505    IFX>200THEN550
510    POKEV+13,PEEK(V+13)+1:HT=0:FORI=1TO3:IF(COAND2^I)=2^ITHENH
       T=I
515    NEXT
517    IFHT=0THENPOKEV+21,PEEK(V+21)AND127:RETURN
520    IFPC=(PEEK(V+39+HT)AND15)THENSC=SC-200:NK=NK+1:GOSUB1200
525    SC=SC+50:GOSUB1000:POKEV+21,PEEK(V+21)AND(127-2^HT)
530    RETURN
550    POKEV+13,PEEK(V+13)-1:HT=0:FORI=4TO6:IF(COAND2^I)=2^ITHENH
       T=I
555    NEXT
560    GOTO517
```

```
┌─────────────────────────────────────────────────────────────┐
│ Terminate the game, print score and number of men killed.     │
└─────────────────────────────────────────────────────────────┘
```

```
900    POKEV+21,0:PRINT" ▧ ▨ ▲ ▲ ▲ ▲ ▲ ▲ ▲ ▲ ▲ ▲
       ▲ ▲ ▲ ▲ GAME ▲ OVER":PRINT" ▨ ▨ ▨ ▨ ▨ ▨ ▨ ▨ ▨
       ▨ ▨ "
910    PRINT" ▲ ▲ ▲ ▲ ▲ ▲ ▲ ▲ ▲ ▲ ▲ YOUR ▲ SCORE ▲ W
       AS";SC;" ▨ ▨ ▨ ▨ "
920    IFNK<>0THENPRINT"BUT ▲ YOU ▲ KILLED ▲ ";NK;" ▲ OF ▲ YOUR
       ▲ OWN ▲ MEN!!":ER=1:GOTO935
930    PRINT"WELL ▲ DONE!! ▲ - ▲ YOU ▲ DIDN'T ▲ KILL ▲ ANY ▲ OF
       ▲ ▲ ▲ ▲ ▲ ▲ ▲ ▲ ▲ ▲ ▲ ▲ ▲ ▲ YOUR
       ▲ OWN ▲ MEN"
935    IFER=0THENPRINT" ▨ ▲ ▲ ▲ ▲ ▲ ▲ ▲ ▲ ▲ ▲ EXT
       RA ▲ ROUND!!!":FORT=1TO4000:NEXT:ER=1:GOTO100
950    GETX$:IFX$=""THENEND
960    GOTO950
```

48

```
1000    FORI=1913TO1917:POKEI,32:NEXT
1005    PRINT" 🔲 🔲 🔲 🔲 🔲 🔲 🔲 🔲 🔲 🔲 🔲 🔲 🔲 🔲 🔲 🔲 🔲 🔲 🔲
        🔲 🔲 🔲 🔲 🔲 🔲 🔲 🔲 SCORE: ▲ ";SC;" 🔲 ";
1010    RETURN
1100    PRINT"TIME: ▲ ";INT(TI/60);" 🔲 ";
1110    RETURN
1200    PRINT" 🔲 YOU ▲ HAVE ▲ JUST ▲ SHOT ▲ ONE ▲ OF ▲ YOUR ▲ OWN
        ▲ MEN!! 🔲 ";
1210    FORT=1TO3000:NEXT
1220    PRINT" ▲ ▲ ▲ ▲ ▲ ▲ ▲ ▲ ▲ ▲ ▲ ▲ ▲ ▲ ▲ ▲
        ▲ ▲ ▲ ▲ ▲ ▲ ▲ ▲ ▲ ▲ ▲ ▲ ▲ ▲ ▲ ▲
        ▲ ▲ ▲ ▲ 🔲 ";
1230    RETURN
10000   DATA0,96,0,0,240,0,0,240,0,0,97,0,0,65,128,0,255,248,1,255
        ,128,1,243,0
10010   DATA1,254,0,0,236,0,0,228,0,1,224,0,1,224,0,1,254,0,0,254,
        0,0,198,0
10020   DATA0,198,0,0,198,0,0,198,0,63,199,0,48,7,0
10030   DATA0,12,0,0,30,0,0,30,0,1,12,0,3,4,0,63,254,0,3,255,0,1,1
        43,0
10040   DATA0,255,0,0,111,0,0,14,0,0,15,0,0,15,0,0,255,0,0,254,0,0
        ,198,0
10050   DATA0,198,0,0,198,0,0,198,0,0,199,248,1,192,24
10100   DATA165,197,201,62,208,10,56,173,1,208,233,6,141,1,208,96,
        201,12,208
10110   DATA251,24,173,1,208,105,6,141,1,208,96
10200   DATA165,197,201,33,208,67,169,193,141,248,7,169,160,141,14
        ,208,173,16
10210   DATA208,41,127,141,16,208,173,1,208,141,15,208,173,21,208,
        9,128,141
10220   DATA21,208,32,196,192,56,173,14,208,233,2,141,14,208,173,3
        0,208,41,128
10230   DATA208,15,173,14,208,201,2,176,230,173,21,208,41,127,141,
        21,208,96
10240   DATA201,41,208,251,169,192,141,248,7,169,210,141,14,208,17
        3,16,208,41
10250   DATA127,141,16,208,173,1,208,141,15,208,173,21,208,9,128,1
        41,21,208,32
10260   DATA196,192,24,173,14,208,105,2,141,14,208,173,30,208,41,1
        28,208,200
10270   DATA173,14,208,201,2,176,8,173,16,208,9,128,141,16,208,173
        ,14,208,201
10280   DATA70,144,215,173,16,208,41,128,240,208,173,21,208,41,127
        ,141,21,208
10290   DATA96,162,0,232,208,253,173,24,212,208,6,169,15,141,24,21
        2,96,169
10300   DATA0,141,24,212,96
```

49

CHECKSUM

1=0	335=1116	1000=1688
10=3868	340=3196	1005=2085
15=444	345=2588	1010=143
20=4082	350=3646	1100=1701
25=3984	352=2179	1110=143
30=2103	354=884	1200=3691
40=2095	358=1937	1210=1032
50=2432	360=1112	1220=2183
55=1364	365=3265	1230=143
60=2109	385=2682	10000=4048
70=3546	390=3644	10010=3705
90=2367	392=2181	10020=2291
95=1196	394=884	10030=3319
100=3984	396=1989	10040=3452
110=381	500=3641	10050=2483
120=4733	505=916	10100=3887
130=2690	510=5002	10110=2068
150=805	515=131	10200=3992
160=1121	517=2544	10210=3764
200=521	520=4335	10220=4061
210=528	525=3695	10230=3703
220=3472	530=143	10240=3967
230=2553	550=5011	10250=4097
250=1719	555=131	10260=3864
260=525	560=532	10270=3993
300=1133	900=3833	10280=3993
305=3958	910=2532	10290=3606
310=2352	920=5617	10300=947
312=836	930=5145	
315=1691	935=5086	TOTAL= 224289
320=387	950=1214	
330=1916	960=534	

50

Dragster 64

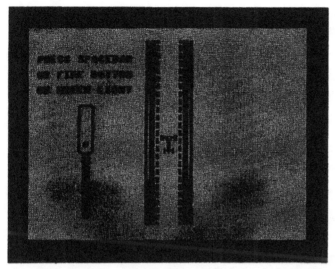

Drive the dragster down a narrow winding road. Do not crash into the armco railing and beware of spin outs off the oil slicks. Steer with the keyboard or a joystick in Port 2. Try to go as far as you can before crashing.

VARIABLES

V   = Sprite control Register

BG = Background Screen Register

MS = Sound Register

R$ &RR$ Roadway

R   = Roadway Number (1-7)

OL = Spaces to oil spill

P   = Keyboard or Joystick Value

C   = Crashed Flag

SP = Spaces to start of roadway

DS = Distance

HD = Best Distance

ES = Time lag from green light to Go

```
10      REM DRAGSTER
```

Build variables, switch repeating key on, print traffic light.

```
100     POKE650,128:V=53248:BG=53280:MS=54272:GOTO2000
130     R$=R$(R)
140     C=PEEK(V+31)AND2^0:IFC=1THEN290
150     IFTI<1000THEN160
154     TI$="000000":R=R+1:IFR>7THENR=7
155     R$=R$(R):DS=DS+1000:GOTO210
160     IFINT(RND(TI)*100)<40THENR$=RR$
180     SP=ABS(SP+(INT(RND(TI)*3)-1))
190     SP=SP-(1*(SP<(40-LEN(R$)))+1)
```

Print car track and player, move the car and scroll screen.

```
200     SP=SP*((SP<0)+1)
207     PRINT" �

210     PRINT:PRINTSPC(SP)R$
220     IFRND(.)<.2THENOL=INT(RND(.)*(LEN(R$))):PRINT" ▯ "SPC(SP+O
        L)" ▮  ● "
230     P=PEEK(203):IFP=39THEN280
240     IFP=36THEN270
250     P=PEEK(56320)AND12:IFP=8THEN280
260     IFP<>4THEN290
270     POKEV,PEEK(V)+3:POKEV,PEEK(V)+4:GOTO130
280     POKEV,PEEK(V)-3:POKEV,PEEK(V)-4:GOTO130
290     C=PEEK(V+31)AND2^0:IFC=0THEN150
```

Generate an explosion, print distance travelled, print best distance.

```
300     REM CRASHED ROUTINE
305     POKEMS+4,0:POKEMS+6,0
307     POKEMS+4,0:POKEMS+1,72:POKEMS,179:POKEMS+5,140:POKEMS+4,12
        9
310     PRINT" ▣ ▤ ":PRINT" ▣ ▥ CRASHED ▬  ▲  ▲  ▲  ▲  ▲
         ▲  ▲  ▲  ▲  ▲ "
320     FORI=0TO150STEP2:POKE2040,I:POKE2040,192:NEXT:POKEMS+4,0
330     XS=TI:DS=(XS-ES+(R+1)*1000)/100
340     PRINT" ▦ ▧ DISTANCE:"DS"KILOMETRES ▲  ▲  ▲  ▲  ▲
         ▲  ▲  ▲ "
350     IFDS>HDTHENHD=DS
355     PRINT" ▨ BEST ▲ DISTANCE:"HD"KILOMETRES ▲  ▲  ▲  ▲
         ▲  ▲  ▲  ▲ "
356     PRINT" ▩ PRESS ▲ KEY ▲ OR ▲ FIRE ▲ BUTTON ▲ TO ▲ RESTART"
358     POKE198,0
359     IF(PEEK(56320)AND16)=0THEN370
360     GETA$:IFA$=""THEN359
370     PRINT" ▪ "
```

```
410    POKE2040,192
```

> Print the title screen, instructions and move car up and
> down.

```
500    REM   TITLE SCREEN
502    PRINT" ▩ ";:POKEBG,1:POKEBG+1,1
505    POKEV+39,6
510    POKEV,0:POKEV+1,0
515    POKEV+16,PEEK(V+16)AND(255-(2^0))
520    POKE2040,192
525    POKEV+21,PEEK(V+21)OR(2^0)
530    POKEV+27,0
535    POKEV,168
540    PRINT" ▩ YOU ▲ ARE ▲ THE"
542    PRINT" ▩ YOU ▲ ARE ▲ THE"
544    PRINT" ▩ DRIVER ▲ OF ▲ A"
546    PRINT" ▩ NEW ▲ DRAGSTER."
550    PRINT" ▩ ▩ YOU ▲ MUST ▲ DRIVE"
554    PRINT" ▩ TO ▲ THE ▲ LIMIT."
560    PRINT" ▩ ▩ YOU ▲ CAN ▲ STEER"
564    PRINT" ▩ WITH ▲ M ▲ & ▲ N ▲ KEYS"
570    PRINT" ▩ OR ▲ USE ▲ THE"
574    PRINT" ▩ JOYSTICK-PORT ▲ 2"
580    PRINT" ▩ ▩ ▩ "SPC(24)"DO ▲ NOT ▲ HIT ▲ THE"
584    PRINT" ▩ ▩ ▩ ▩ ▩ "SPC(24)"ARMCO ▲ SIDING"
590    PRINT" ▩ ▩ ▩ ▩ ▩ ▩ ▩ "SPC(24)"& ▲ WATCH ▲ OUT ▲ FOR"
594    PRINT" ▩ ▩ ▩ ▩ ▩ ▩ ▩ ▩ ▩ "SPC(24)"OIL ▲ SLICKS."
600    PRINT" ▩ ▩ ▩ ▩ ▩ ▩ ▩ ▩ ▩ ▩
       ▩ ▩ ▩ ▩ HOLD ▲ SPACEBAR ▲ OR":PRINT"FIRE ▲ TO ▲ STAR
     T ▩ ";
630    FORI=1TO24
635    PRINTSPC(16);" ▩ ▨ ▮ ⊢ ▬ ▲ ▲ ▲ ▨ ◀ ▨ ▮ ▬ "
640    NEXT
645    PRINT" ▩ "SPC(19)"D ▨ ▨ ▮▮R ▨ ▨ ▮▮A ▨ ▨ ▮▮G ▨ ▨ ▮▮
     S ▨ ▨ ▮▮T ▨ ▨ ▮▮E ▨ ▨ ▮▮R ▨ ▨ ▮▮6 ▨ ▨ ▮▮4"
650    GOSUB2500:POKEMS+4,129:FORI=20TO250:POKEV+1,I:NEXT
655    IF(PEEK(56320)AND16)=0THEN665
660    GETA$:IFA$<>" ▲ "THENPOKEMS+4,0:FORT=1TO200:NEXT:GOTO650
665    POKEMS+24,5
670    FORI=VTOV+16:POKEI,0:NEXT
680    POKEV+27,253
690    FORI=1TO30
700    PRINTSPC(16);" ▩ ▨ ▮ ⊢ ▬ ▲ ▲ ▲ ▨ ◀ ▨ ▮ ▬ "
710    NEXT
720    POKEV,168:POKEV+1,70
730    GOSUB2400
740    TI$="000007"
750    PRINT" ▩ ▨ ▨ ▨ ▨ ▨ ▨ ▨ ▨ ▨ ▨ ▨ ▨ ▨ ▨ ▨ ▨
       ▨ ● ";
760    T1=INT(10-VAL(TI$))
770    IFT1<>2THEN760
772    PRINT" ▮▮ ▲ ▨ ▨ ▮▮ ▨ ● ";
774    T1=INT(10-VAL(TI$))
775    IFT1<>1THENPOKE198,0:GOTO774
776    PRINT" ▮▮ ▲ ▨ ▨ ▮▮ ▨ ● ";
```

53

```
777   IF(PEEK(56320)AND16)=ØTHEN78Ø
778   GETA$:IFA$<>" ▲ "THEN777
78Ø   POKE198,Ø:ES=TI:TI$="ØØØØØØ":DS=Ø:R=Ø:GOSUB25ØØ:POKEMS+4,1
      29
79Ø   FORI=7ØTO18Ø:POKEV+1,I:NEXT
8ØØ   SP=13:R$=R$(R):RR$=RR$(R)
82Ø   POKE198,Ø:GOTO13Ø
```

Define road data, road in sprite for dragster, make roar sound.

```
2ØØØ  REM ROAD DATA
2Ø1Ø  R$(7)=" ■ ■ ▲ ▲ ■ ▲ ▲ ▲ ▲ ▲ ■ ▲ ▲ ■ "
2Ø2Ø  R$(6)=" ■ ■ ▲ ▲ ■ ▲ ▲ ▲ ▲ ▲ ■ ▲ ▲ ■ "
2Ø3Ø  R$(5)=" ■ ■ ▲ ▲ ■ ▲ ▲ ▲ ▲ ▲ ▲ ■ ▲ ▲ ■ "
2Ø4Ø  R$(4)=" ■ ■ ▲ ▲ ■ ▲ ▲ ▲ ▲ ▲ ▲ ■ ▲ ▲ ■ "
2Ø5Ø  R$(3)=" ■ ■ ▲ ▲ ■ ▲ ▲ ▲ ▲ ▲ ▲ ■ ▲ ▲ ■ "
2Ø6Ø  R$(2)=" ■ ■ ▲ ▲ ■ ▲ ▲ ▲ ▲ ▲ ▲ ▲ ■ ▲ ▲ ■ "
2Ø7Ø  R$(1)=" ■ ■ ▲ ▲ ■ ▲ ▲ ▲ ▲ ▲ ▲ ▲ ■ ▲ ▲ ■ "
2Ø8Ø  R$(Ø)=" ■ ■ ▲ ▲ ■ ▲ ▲ ▲ ▲ ▲ ▲ ▲ ▲ ■ ▲ ▲ ■
      "
2Ø9Ø  RR$(7)=" ■ ■ ▲ ▲ ■ ▲ ▲ ▲ ▲ ▲ ■ ▲ ▲ ■ "
21ØØ  RR$(6)=" ■ ■ ▲ ▲ ■ ▲ ▲ ▲ ▲ ▲ ■ ▲ ▲ ■ "
211Ø  RR$(5)=" ■ ■ ▲ ▲ ■ ▲ ▲ ▲ ▲ ▲ ▲ ■ ▲ ▲ ■ "
212Ø  RR$(4)=" ■ ■ ▲ ▲ ■ ▲ ▲ ▲ ▲ ▲ ▲ ■ ▲ ▲ ■ "
213Ø  RR$(3)=" ■ ■ ▲ ▲ ■ ▲ ▲ ▲ ▲ ▲ ▲ ■ ▲ ▲ ■ "
214Ø  RR$(2)=" ■ ■ ▲ ▲ ■ ▲ ▲ ▲ ▲ ▲ ▲ ▲ ■ ▲ ▲ ■ "
215Ø  RR$(1)=" ■ ■ ▲ ▲ ■ ▲ ▲ ▲ ▲ ▲ ▲ ▲ ■ ▲ ▲ ■ "
216Ø  RR$(Ø)=" ■ ■ ▲ ▲ ■ ▲ ▲ ▲ ▲ ▲ ▲ ▲ ▲ ■ ▲ ▲
      ■ "
22ØØ  FORI=12288TO1235Ø:READN:POKEI,N:NEXT
23ØØ  REM DRAGSTER DATA
231Ø  DATAØ,Ø,Ø,6Ø,Ø,6Ø,6Ø,255,6Ø,63,195,252,63,255,252,6Ø,255,6
      Ø,6Ø,126,6Ø
232Ø  DATAØ,6Ø,Ø,Ø,6Ø,Ø,Ø,6Ø,Ø,Ø,6Ø,Ø,Ø,6Ø,Ø,Ø,6Ø,Ø,Ø,6Ø,Ø
233Ø  DATA3,6Ø,192,3,6Ø,192,3,255,192,3,255,192,3,6Ø,192,3,24,19
      2,Ø,Ø,Ø
235Ø  GOTO5ØØ
24ØØ  PRINT" ■ ■ ■ ■ ■ ■ ■ ■ ■ ■ ■ ■ ■ ■ ■ ■ ■
      ■ "
241Ø  FORI=1TO5:PRINTSPC(6)" ■ ▲ ■ ":NEXT
242Ø  PRINTSPC(6)" ■ ■ ■ "
243Ø  FORI=1TO8:PRINTSPC(7)" ■ ▲ ":NEXT
244Ø  PRINT" ■ ■ ■ PRESS ▲ SPACEBAR"
2445  PRINT" ■ OR ▲ FIRE ▲ BUTTON"
245Ø  PRINT" ■ ON ▲ GREEN ▲ LIGHT"
246Ø  RETURN
25ØØ  REM EHAUST NOISE
252Ø  POKEMS+4,Ø:POKEMS+24,15:POKEMS+5,85:POKEMS+6,195:POKEMS,15
      :POKEMS+1,1
254Ø  RETURN
```

CHECKSUM

10=0	564=1297	2150=1688
100=3259	570=1001	2160=1742
130=597	574=1406	2200=2124
140=2237	580=1817	2300=0
150=1058	584=1828	2310=3917
154=2547	590=2058	2320=2737
155=2197	594=1852	2330=3561
160=2235	600=4144	2350=529
180=2325	630=710	2400=1278
190=2625	635=1959	2410=1943
200=1544	640=131	2420=1077
207=814	645=3805	2430=1535
210=887	650=3084	2440=1457
220=4559	655=1670	2445=1367
230=1640	660=3692	2450=1300
240=852	665=704	2460=143
250=1991	670=1625	2500=0
260=970	680=738	2520=4635
270=2520	690=711	2540=143
280=2522	700=1959	
290=2227	710=131	TOTAL= 198280
300=0	720=1169	
305=1374	730=351	
307=3848	740=809	
310=2516	750=996	
320=3283	760=1380	
330=2976	770=1045	
340=2752	772=1061	
350=1296	774=1380	
355=3081	775=1915	
356=3265	776=933	
358=420	777=1674	
359=1666	778=1441	
360=1215	780=4197	
370=372	790=1715	
410=574	800=2053	
500=0	820=1037	
502=1632	2000=0	
505=625	2010=1453	
510=969	2020=1472	
515=2273	2030=1525	
520=574	2040=1525	
525=1817	2050=1521	
530=618	2060=1581	
535=454	2070=1581	
540=1085	2080=1640	
542=1085	2090=1553	
544=1065	2100=1573	
546=1275	2110=1633	
550=1413	2120=1633	
554=1205	2130=1629	
560=1285	2140=1688	

Astral Attack

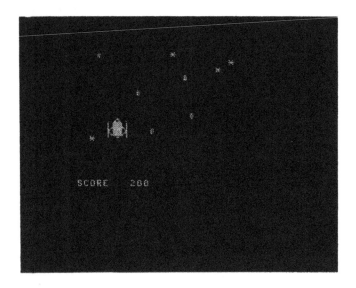

For this game you must guide your ship through space, avoiding planets (blue) and hitting asteroids (yellow to red). If a red asteroid misses your ship, then the game is over.

CONTROLS

    'I' – left
    'P' – right

VARIABLES

PC   = Player's column

VL   = Current (value of) destroyed ship

LR   = Last red asteroid

A (I,J) = Asteroid I : colour, column, row

P (I,J) = Planet I : column, row

HA   = Number of hit asteroid

SC   = Score

```
1      REM ASTRAL ATTACK
```

Clear screen, set screen colours, and prompt user to start game.

```
10     PRINT" ▨ ▨ ▬ ▬ ▬ ▬ ▬ ▬ ▬ ▬ ▬ ▬ ▬ ▬ ASTR
       AL ▬ ATTACK":POKE53280,7
15     PRINT"▨ ▨ ▨ ▨ ▨ ▨ ▨ ▨ ▨ ▨ ▨ ▬ ▬ ▬ ▬
       ▬ ▬ ▬ ▬ ▲ ▨ HIT ▬ ANY ▬ KEY ▬ TO ▬ START ▬ "
20     V=53248:POKE2040,192:POKE2041,193:POKEV+21,0:POKEV+28,2:
       POKEV+37,2:POKEV+38,8
25     POKEV+39,3:POKEV+40,1:POKEV+23,0:POKEV+29,0:POKEV+30,0:
       POKEV+31,0
30     FORI=12288TO12350:READQ:POKEI,Q:NEXT
35     FORI=12352TO12414:J=PEEK(I-64):J=J-15:IFJ<0THENJ=0
36     POKEI,J
38     NEXT
40     FORI=49152TO49271:READQ:POKEI,Q:NEXT
45     GETX$:IFX$=""THEN45
50     PRINT" ▨ ▨ ▨ ▨ ▨ ▨ ▨ ▨ ▨ ▨ ▨ ▨ ▨ ▨ ▨ ▨
       ▨ ▨ ▨ ▨ ▨ ▨ ▬ ▬ ▬ SCORE ▬ ";:POKE53280,0:POKE53281
       ,0
55     POKE53265,PEEK(53265)AND247:POKEV,170:POKEV+1,160:POKEV+21
       ,1:POKEV+16,0
57     PC=18:VL=0:LR=1:GOSUB200
```

Main logic loop, call add a planet, call add asteroid.

```
60     SYS(49152):FORI=1TO6
61     IFA(I,2)<>0THENA(I,3)=A(I,3)+1
62     IFP(I,1)<>0THENP(I,2)=P(I,2)+1
63     SYS(49225):NEXT
64     IFRND(1)<.5THEN66
65     GOSUB100
66     FORI=1TO6:IFA(I,3)>16ANDA(I,1)<>2THENA(I,3)=0:A(I,2)=0
67     SYS(49225):NEXT
68     IFRND(1)<.5THEN72
70     GOSUB150
72     FORI=1TO6:IFP(I,2)>16THENP(I,2)=0:P(I,1)=0
73     SYS(49225):NEXT
80     PC=INT((PEEK(V)+256*(PEEK(V+16)AND1)-23)/8)
81     IF(PEEK(V+31)AND1)=0THEN90
82     HA=0:FORI=1TO6:IFA(I,3)>=13AND(PC=A(I,2)ORA(I,2)=PC+1ORA(I
       ,2)=PC+2)THENHA=I
84     IFP(I,2)>=13AND(PC=P(I,1)ORP(I,1)=PC+1ORP(I,1)=PC+2)THEN27
       0
86     NEXT
88     IFHA<>0THENGOSUB250
90     FORI=1TO6:IFA(I,3)>17ANDA(I,1)=2THENM$="RED ▬ ASTEROID ▬ E
       SCAPED":GOTO300
95     SYS(49225):NEXT:GOTO60
```

Move the asteroid down the screen, move planet too.

```
100    FORI=1TO6:IFA(I,2)<>0THEN120
110    K=INT(RND(1)*33+4):POKE1025+K,42
112    IFRND(1)<.9THEN114
113    POKE55297+K,7:A(I,2)=K+1:A(I,1)=7:RETURN
114    IFA(LR,3)<6THEN113
115    LR=I:POKE55297+K,2:A(I,2)=K+1:A(I,1)=2:RETURN
120    NEXT
130    RETURN
150    FORI=1TO6:IFP(I,1)<>0THEN170
160    K=INT(RND(1)*39):POKE1025+K,81:POKE55297+K,6:P(I,1)=K+1:
       RETURN
170    NEXT
180    RETURN
200    SC=SC+VL
210    PRINTCHR$(13);CHR$(145);TAB(10);SC;
220    VL=54296:W=54276:A=54277:H=54273:L=54272
222    FORI=54272TO54296:POKEI,0:NEXT
225    POKEVL,15:POKEW,33:POKEA,190
230    FORT=1TO10:POKEH,34:POKEL,75:NEXT
235    POKEH,0:POKEL,0:POKEW,0:POKEVL,0
240    RETURN
```

Destroy the asteroid, add to score, collide with planet.

```
250    IFA(HA,1)=7THENVL=10:GOTO260
257    VL=50
260    GOSUB200:POKE1024+A(HA,2)+40*A(HA,3),32:A(HA,2)=0:A(HA,3)=
       0
265    RETURN
270    POKEV+2,PEEK(V):POKEV+3,PEEK(V+1):IFPEEK(V+16)=1THENPOKEV+
       16,3
272    POKEV+21,2
280    V=54296:W=54276:A=54277:H=54273:L=54272
282    FORI=54272TO54296:POKEI,0:NEXT
285    FORX=15TO0STEP-1:POKE53281,X+30:POKEV,X:POKEW,129:POKEA,15
       :POKEH,40
290    POKEL,200:NEXT:POKE53281,0
295    POKEW,0:POKEA,0:M$="COLLISION ▲ WITH ▲ A ▲ PLANET!"
299    FORT=1TO1000:NEXT
```

You are destroyed, print score, ask if player wants another try.

```
300    PRINT" ▨ ";:POKE53269,0:POKE53265,PEEK(53265)OR8
310    PRINTTAB(15);" ▨ ▲ GAME ▲ OVER ▬ ":PRINT" ▨ ▨ ▨ ▨ ▨
       ▨ ▨ ▨ ▨ ▨ ▨ ▲ ▲ ▲ ▲ ▲ ▲ ▲ ▲ ▲ ▲ YOUR ▲ S
       CORE ▲ WAS ▲ ";SC
315    PRINTTAB(8);" ▨ ▨ ▨ ▨ ▨ ▨ ▨ ▨ ";M$;" ▬ "
320    PRINT
```

58

```
330    GETX$:IFX$=""THENEND
340    GOTO330
10000  DATA0,24,0,0,60,0,0,102,0,64,231,2,65,255,130,195,255,195,
       195,255,195
10010  DATA195,255,195,195,255,195,199,255,227,207,255,243,219,25
       5,219
10020  DATA243,255,207,227,255,199,227,255,199,243,255,207,219,25
       5,219
10030  DATA207,255,243,199,255,227,192,85,3,192,62,3
10100  DATA169,127,133,178,169,6,133,179,160,0,177,178,160,40,145
       ,178,160,0,165
10110  DATA24,133,180,165,179,105,212,133,181,177,180,160,40,
       145,180,165
10120  DATA178,56,233,1,133,178,165,179,233,0,133,179,165,178,201
       ,255,208
10130  DATA210,165,179,201,3,208,204,169,32,162,0,157,0,4,232,224
       ,40,208,248,96
10140  DATA165,197,133,178,201,33,208,19,169,0,205,0,208,208,8,17
       3,16,208,41
10150  DATA254,141,16,208,206,0,208,96,165,178,201,41,208,13,238,
       0,208,208,8,173
10160  DATA16,208,9,1,141,16,208,96
```

CHECKSUM

1=0	86=131	280=3047
10=2909	88=1187	282=1769
15=3207	90=5768	285=4123
20=4903	95=1283	290=1279
25=4309	100=1959	295=3338
30=2103	110=2271	299=1032
35=4013	112=1107	300=2478
36=351	113=2682	310=4656
38=131	114=1163	315=1276
40=2108	115=3201	320=153
45=1195	120=131	330=1214
50=2940	130=143	340=528
55=4252	150=1974	10000=3954
57=1762	160=4215	10010=3454
60=1282	170=131	10020=3465
61=2267	180=143	10030=2409
62=2297	200=824	10100=4334
63=719	210=1780	10110=3988
64=1058	220=3125	10120=3627
65=295	222=1769	10130=4329
66=4055	225=1473	10140=3978
67=719	230=1881	10150=4455
68=1055	235=1647	10160=1467
70=299	240=143	
72=3039	250=2057	
73=719	257=450	TOTAL= 184330
80=3249	260=4159	
81=1647	265=143	
82=6537	270=4197	
84=4804	272=616	

Stuntman

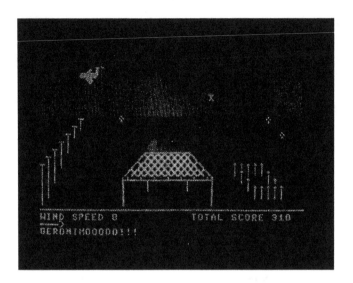

Send the stuntman from the plane, attempting to land him on red square on trampoline. Look out for the picket fence and the telephone poles! Three misses puts a stuntman out of action but you get 3 men. Use space bar to kick man out of plane.

VARIABLES

NM	= No men
SC,R	= Score, round
WS	= Wind speed
T	= Time parameter for projection equations
F	= Flying flag
NW	= No.wounds
VL,W,A,H,L	= Sound
M$	= Message
X,YI	= X,Y initial values
X,Y	= Man's X,Y co-ordinates
M	= Mass of man
XV	= Initial X velocity

```
1      REM STUNT MAN
10     V=53248:POKE2040,192:POKE2041,193:POKEV+39,7:POKEV+40,10
20     POKEV+16,0:POKEV+21,0:FORI=12288TO12350:READQ:POKEI,Q:NEXT
30     FORI=12352TO12373STEP3:READQ:POKEI,Q:POKEI+1,0:POKEI+2,0:
       NEXT
35     FORI=12376TO12414:POKEI,0:NEXT
40     POKEV+2,185:POKEV+3,170
50     FORI=49152TO49230:READQ:POKEI,Q:NEXT
60     NM=3:SC=100
```

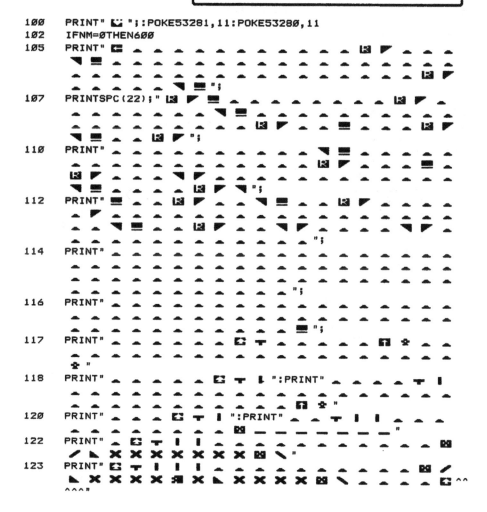

```
100    PRINT" "; :POKE53281,11:POKE53280,11
102    IFNM=0THEN600
105    PRINT"
107    PRINTSPC(22);"
110    PRINT"
112    PRINT"
114    PRINT"
116    PRINT"
117    PRINT"
118    PRINT"               ":PRINT"
120    PRINT"       ":PRINT"
122    PRINT"
123    PRINT"
```

61

```
124  PRINT"                                    
         ▓ ▓ ▓ ▓ ▓ ▓ ▓ ▓ ▓ ▓ ▓ ▓ ▓ ▓ ▓ ▓ ▓ ▓ ▓ ▓ ▓
         ▮ ▮ ^"
126  PRINT"                                    
                                    ▮
         ▮ ^"
128  PRINT"                                    
                                    
         "
130  PRINT"                                    
                                    
         ▮ ▮ ▮ ▮ "
132  PRINT"                                    
                                    
134  PRINT"                                    
                                    
                   ";
136  PRINT:PRINT"      >   ";
140  POKEV+16,1:POKEV,80:POKEV+1,80:POKEV+21,1:WS=5:GOSUB1000:F
     =0:T=0:NW=0
150  VL=54296:W=54276:A=54277:H=54273:L=54272
```

┌───┐
│ Launch and fly the plane, drop the man.   │
└───┘

```
200  SYS(49152):SYS(49152):SYS(49152)
202  IF(PEEK(V+16)AND1)<>1ORPEEK(V)<89THEN204
203  POKEV+1,INT(RND(1)*75+50):SC=SC-10:GOSUB1000
204  IFF=1THEN230
205  K=PEEK(197):IFK<>60THEN220
210  POKEV+2,PEEK(V):POKEV+3,PEEK(V+1):F=1:T=0:M$="GERONIMOOOOO
     !!!      ":GOSUB1300
212  IF(PEEK(V+16)AND1)=0THENPOKEV+16,0:GOTO217
215  POKEV+16,PEEK(V+16)OR2
217  POKEV+21,PEEK(V+21)OR2:YI=PEEK(V+1)+8:XI=PEEK(V)+256*(PEEK
     (V+16)AND1)
220  IFF=0THEN200
230  GOSUB300
240  IFX<200RX>336THEN550
250  IFY<170THEN200
260  IFX>130ANDX<220THENGOSUB350:GOTO200
270  IFX<50THEN400
280  IFX>255ANDX<300THENGOSUB450:GOTO200
290  GOSUB500:GOTO200
```

┌───┐
│ Send man hurtling to ground taking account of wind speed. │
└───┘

```
300  XV=3:M=50
310  T=T+1:POKE54278,128:POKEVL,15:POKEW,129:POKEA,15:POKEL,200
     :POKEH,80-2*T
320  X=WS*T*T/M-XV*T+XI:Y=4.9*T*T/M+YI
325  X=INT(X):Y=INT(Y)
330  IFX>255THENPOKEV+16,PEEK(V+16)OR2:POKEV+2,X-256:GOTO340
335  POKEV+16,PEEK(V+16)AND253:POKEV+2,X
```

```
340     POKEV+3,Y
345     RETURN
```

If hit target exactly then print superb else good jump.

```
350     IFX>170ANDX<185THENSC=SC+200:M$="SUPERB!!!! ▲ ▲ ▲ ▲ ▲
        ▲ ▲ ▲ ▲ ▲ ▲ ▲ ":GOTO360
355     SC=SC+100:M$="GOOD ▲ JUMP! ▲ ▲ ▲ ▲ ▲ ▲ ▲ ▲ ▲ "
360     WS=INT(RND(1)*10):GOSUB1000:GOSUB1300:F=0:T=0
370     POKEW,0:POKEA,0:RETURN
```

Increment accident count, man was electrocuted, start again.

```
400     GOSUB1200:PRINT" ▤ ▦ ▲ ▲ ▲ ▲ ▲ ▲ ▲ STUNT ▲ MAN ▲ E
        LECTROCUTED!!!":NM=NM-1:POKEV+21,0
410     FORTM=1TO3000:NEXT:SC=SC-100
440     GOTO100
```

Increment accident count, man hit fence, if too many men dead.

```
450     M$="HIT ▲ THE ▲ FENCE!!":GOSUB1300:SC=SC-50
460     WS=INT(RND(1)*10):GOSUB1000:GOSUB1300:F=0:T=0:NW=NW+1
470     POKEW,0:POKEA,0:IFNW>2THEN700
480     RETURN
```

Add to accident count, check if man out of action.

```
500     M$="OUCH!! ▲ - ▲ TRY ▲ AGAIN":GOSUB1300:SC=SC-30:NW=NW+1
510     WS=INT(RND(1)*10):GOSUB1000:GOSUB1300:F=0:T=0
540     POKEW,0:POKEA,0:IFNW>2THEN700
545     RETURN
```

Man is dead, clear screen, sprites off, print message and re-start.

```
550     GOSUB1200:PRINT" ▤ ▦ ▲ ▲ ▲ STUNT ▲ MAN ▲ DROWNED ▲ IN
        ▲ SWAMP ▲ - ▲ ":POKEV+21,0
555     PRINT" ▲ A ▲ LONG ▲ WAY ▲ FROM ▲ THE ▲ TARGET!!"
560     FORTM=1TO3000:NEXT
570     NM=NM-1
580     GOTO100
```

Print terminating message, score and stop game.

```
600     POKE53280,0:POKE53281,0
605     PRINT" ▤ ▲ ▲ ▲ ▲ ▲ ▲ ▲ ▲ ▲ ▲ ▲ ▲ ▲ ▲ ▲ ▲ ▤ G
        AME ▲ OVER ▬ ":PRINT" ▣ ▣ ▣ ▣ ▣ ▣ ▣ ▣ ▣ ▣ ▣ ▣ ▣ "
        ;
```

```
610   PRINT"  ▲  ▲  ▲  ▲  ▲  ▲  ▲  ▲  ▲  ▲ YOUR ▲ SCORE ▲ WAS
      ▲ ";SC
630   POKEV+21,0 :END
```

> Print too many accidents and restart game.

```
700   PRINT"▨ ▨ ▨  ▲  ▲  ▲  ▲  ▲  ▲ STUNT ▲ MAN ▲ OUT ▲ OF
      ▲ ACTION ▲ -":PRINT"  ▲  ▲  ▲  ▲  ▲ TOO ▲ MANY ▲ ACC
      IDENTS"
710   POKEV+21,0:NM=NM-1:FORTM=1TO3000:NEXT
720   GOTO100
```

> Print wind speed and score.

```
1000  PRINT"▨ ▨ ▨ ▨ ▨ ▨ ▨ ▨ ▨ ▨ ▨ ▨ ▨ ▨ ▨ ▨ ▨
      ▨ ▨ ▨ ▨ ▨ ";
1002  FORI=1938TO1943:POKEI,32:NEXT
1005  PRINT"▨ WIND ▲ SPEED";TAB(10);WS;SPC(10);"TOTAL ▲ SCORE";
      SC;
1010  PRINT" ▨ ";:RETURN
```

> Flash screen and generate sound effects.

```
1200  FORI=15TO0STEP-1:POKE53281,I+80:POKE53280,I+80
1220  POKEVL,I:POKEW,129:POKEA,15:POKEH,2+5*I:POKEL,200:NEXT
1230  POKEW,0:POKEA,0:RETURN
```

> Print message to user.

```
1300  PRINT"▨ ▨ ▨ ▨ ▨ ▨ ▨ ▨ ▨ ▨ ▨ ▨ ▨ ▨ ▨ ▨
      ▨ ▨ ▨ ▨ ▨ ▨ ▨ ▨ ";M$;" ▨ ";
1310  RETURN
```

> Data for sprites and machine routine.

```
10000 DATA0,0,15,0,0,15,0,15,15,0,31,15,0,62,15,0,124,15,63,255,
      255,63,255,255
10010 DATA127,255,255,255,255,254,255,255,252,127,255,248,0,255,
      0,0,127,128
10020 DATA0,63,192,0,31,192,0,15,128,0,7,0,0,0,0,0,0,0,0,0,0,0
10030 DATA184,214,124,56,56,56,108,206
10100 DATA173,16,208,41,1,208,27,56,173,0,208,233,4,141,0,208,20
      1,5,176,13,173
10110 DATA16,208,9,1,141,16,208,169,100,141,0,208,96,56,173,0,20
      8,233,4,141,0
10120 DATA208,201,252,144,8,173,16,208,41,254,141,16,208,96,238,
      0,208,238,0
10130 DATA208,238,0,208,173,0,208,208,234,173,16,208,9,1,141,16,
      208,96
```

CHECKSUM

1=0	330=3953
10=3414	335=2265
20=3668	340=603
30=3708	345=143
35=1766	350=4613
40=1449	355=2590
50=2107	360=2883
60=973	370=924
100=1778	400=5251
102=866	410=2050
105=4268	440=525
107=5169	450=2827
110=5291	460=3810
112=5898	470=1686
114=3848	480=143
116=2629	500=4031
117=2540	510=2883
118=3580	540=1686
120=3878	545=143
122=3950	550=4358
123=5780	555=2428
124=6186	560=1122
126=5458	570=722
128=3921	580=525
130=3936	600=1170
132=2266	605=3071
134=8933	610=2170
136=1360	630=811
140=4888	700=5657
150=3125	710=2656
200=1762	720=525
202=2835	1000=821
203=3040	1002=1700
204=773	1005=3856
205=1817	1010=512
210=5492	1200=3033
212=2841	1220=3134
215=1485	1230=924
217=5294	1300=1308
220=772	1310=143
230=295	10000=4273
240=1520	10010=3996
250=911	10020=2828
260=2301	10030=1713
270=849	10100=4296
280=2302	10110=4174
290=909	10120=4002
300=852	10130=3455
310=4570	
320=3988	TOTAL= 264978
325=1345	

Convoy

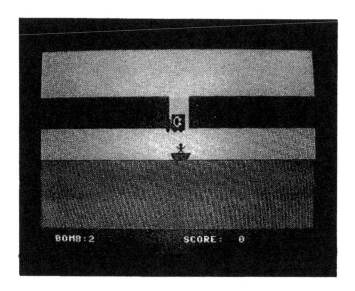

You are floating on an underground river and must blow up portions of the road above in order to drop the black trucks into the river. The red trucks must not fall into the river and the black trucks must not escape at the left side of the screen.

By pressing the space bar, you either deposit a bomb or patch up the road, depending on your position. The seconds left for the fuse are at bottom left of screen.

CONTROLS
    'I', 'P' : left, right

VARIABLES

R,SC	= Round, score
XP	= X position
PEEK (178)	= Last truck moved
C	= Column
BP	= Bomb's position
PC	= Player's column
BS	= Bomb set flag
FS	= Fuse set
TM	= Time bomb set
FL	= Fuse length
NT	= New truck (latest)
MD	= Minimum distance apart
VL,W,A,HI,LW	= Sounds
C(I)	= Truck colours

```
1       REM CONVOY
5       PRINT" ◖
        ◼ CONVOY ◙ ◙ ◙ ◙ ◙ ◙ ◙ ◙ ◙ ◙ ◙ ◙ ":POKE53281,11
        :POKE53280,11
10      V=53248:POKE2040,192:POKE2041,193:POKE2042,193:POKE2043,19
        3:POKE2044,193
15      POKEV+39,11:POKEV+40,0:POKEV+41,0:POKEV+42,0:POKEV+43,0
20      FORI=12288TO12350:READQ:POKEI,Q:NEXT
30      FORI=12352TO12414:READQ:POKEI,Q:NEXT
50      FORI=49152TO49300:READQ:POKEI,Q:NEXT
60      VL=54296:W=54276:A=54277:HI=54273:LW=54272
70      POKEV+16,0
90      PRINT" ◣ ◣ ◣ ◣ ◣ ◣ ◣ ◣ ◣ ◣ ◣ HIT ◣ ANY ◣ KEY ◣ T
        O ◣ START"
95      GETX$:IFX$=""THEN95
100     PRINT" ◖ ";
105     FORI=1024TO1263:POKEI,160:POKEI+54272,14:NEXT
110     FORI=1264TO1423:POKEI,102:POKEI+54272,9:NEXT
115     FORI=1424TO1583:POKEI,160:POKEI+54272,12:NEXT
120     FORI=1584TO1943:POKEI,160:POKEI+54272,6:NEXT
130     GOSUB1000:POKEV,178:POKEV+1,145:POKEV+21,1
140     NT=1:POKE178,1:MD=25:GOSUB400
150     POKEV+30,0:PRINT" ▨ ◙ ◙ ◙ ◙ ◙ ◙ ◙ ◙ ◙ ◙ ◙ ◙ ◙
        ◙ ◙ ◙ ◙ ◙ ◙ ◙ ◙ ◙ ◙ ◙ ◙ ◙ ◙ ◗ ◗ BOMB: ◙ ";:POKE56
        263,7
```

```
200     SYS(49152)
205     IFFS=0ANDRND(1)<.2THENFL=INT(RND(1)*9+1):FS=1:TI$="000000"
207     GOSUB1100
210     SYS(49206):IF(PEEK(V+21)AND30)=0THENJ=1:GOSUB420
212     IFPEEK(181)<>1THEN215
214     IFC(PEEK(178))=0THEN800
215     SYS(49152):K=PEEK(178):XP=PEEK(V+2*K)+2^(8-K)*(PEEK(V+16)
        AND2^K):C=INT(XP/8)
217     IFPEEK(1304+C)=160ANDPEEK(1302+C)=160ANDPEEK(1303+C)=160
        THENGOSUB550
220     K=PEEK(197):IFK<>60THEN240
225     XP=PEEK(V)+256*(PEEK(V+16)AND1):PC=INT((XP-11)/8)
230     IFPEEK(1384+PC)<>160ANDBS=0THENGOSUB500:GOTO240
235     IFPEEK(1384+PC)=160THENGOSUB350
240     SYS(49152):IFFS=1ANDBS=0ANDINT(TI/60)>FLTHEN700
245     IFBS=1ANDINT(TI/60)>FLTHENGOSUB450
250     IFRND(1)<.02+SC/10000THENGOSUB400
260     GOTO200
```

> Rebuild the road, send a new truck on its way.

```
350    IFPC<3THEN380
352    IFPC>36THEN392
355    FORJ=1264TO1384STEP40:FORK=PC-2TOPC+2
360    IFPEEK(J+K)=160THENPOKEJ+K,102:POKEJ+K+54272,9
365    NEXT:NEXT:RETURN
380    FORJ=1264TO1384STEP40:FORK=0TOPC
385    IFPEEK(J+K)=160THENPOKEJ+K,102:POKEK+J+54272,9
390    NEXT:NEXT:RETURN
392    FORJ=1264TO1384STEP40:FORK=37TO39
394    IFPEEK(J+K)=160THENPOKEJ+K,102:POKEJ+K+54272,9
396    NEXT:NEXT:RETURN
400    J=0:FORI=1TO4:IF(PEEK(V+21)AND2^I)=0THENJ=I
405    NEXT
410    IFJ=0THENRETURN
412    TE=(PEEK(V+21)AND30)
415    XP=PEEK(V+2*NT)+2^(8-NT)*(PEEK(V+16)AND2^NT):IF326-XP<MD
       ANDTE<>0THENRETURN
420    NT=J:POKEV+2*NT,70:POKEV+16,PEEK(V+16)OR2^NT:POKEV+2*NT+1,
       80
425    IFRND(1)<.6THENC(NT)=0:GOTO435
430    C(NT)=2
435    POKEV+39+NT,C(NT):POKEV+21,PEEK(V+21)OR2^NT
440    RETURN
```

> Explode the bomb, place a bomb under truck, eat away road.

```
450    GOSUB1200
460    FS=0:POKE1424+BP,160:BS=0:IFBP=39THEN480
462    IFBP=0THEN490
465    FORJ=1264TO1384STEP40:FORK=BP-1TOBP+1
470    POKEJ+K,160:POKEJ+K+54272,12:NEXT:NEXT
475    POKEVL,0:POKEA,0:POKEW,0
478    RETURN
480    FORJ=1264TO1384STEP40:FORK=37TO39
482    POKEJ+K,160:POKEJ+K+54272,12:NEXT:NEXT
485    GOTO475
490    FORJ=1264TO1384STEP40:FORK=0TO2
492    POKEJ+K,160:POKEJ+K+54272,12:NEXT:NEXT
495    GOTO475
500    BS=1:BP=PC:POKE1424+PC,209
520    RETURN
```

> Drop the truck into river, check if truck was red or black.

```
550    FORY=80TO155STEP3
555    SYS(49152):POKEV+2*K+1,Y:IF(PEEK(V+30)AND(1+2^K))<>0THEN80
       0
```

69

```
558   GOSUB1100:NEXT
560   IF(PEEK(V+39+K)AND15)=2THEN800
565   SC=SC+50:GOSUB1000:POKEV+21,PEEK(V+21)AND(255-2^K)
570   GOSUB400:RETURN
700   FORI=15TO0STEP-1:POKE12288+INT(RND(1)*62),INT(RND(1)*128)
705   POKEVL,I:POKEW,129:POKEA,15:POKEHI,40:POKELW,200:NEXT
710   POKEW,0:POKEA,0
720   FORT=1TO1000:NEXT
800   POKE53281,0:POKE53280,0:PRINT" ■  ▲  ▲  ▲  ▲  ▲  ▲
      ▲  ▲  ▲  ▲  ▲  ◤ GAME ▲ OVER"
805   POKEV+21,0
810   PRINT" ◘ ◘ ◘ ◘ ◘ ◘ ◘ ◘ ◘ ◘ ◘ ◘ ◘ ◘ ◘ ▲ ▲ ▲
      ▲  ▲  ▲  ▲  ▲  ▲ YOUR ▲ SCORE ▲ WAS: ▲ ";SC
820   GETX$:IFX$=""THENEND
830   GOTO820
```

> Update the score, generate sound and data for truck and boat man.

```
1000  PRINT" ◘ ◘ ◘ ◘ ◘ ◘ ◘ ◘ ◘ ◘ ◘ ◘ ◘ ◘ ◘ ◘ ◘ ◘
      ◘ ◘ ◘ ◘ ◘ ◘ ◘ ◙ ◙ ◙ ◙ ◙ ◙ ◙ ◙ ◙ ◙
      ◙ ◙ ◙ ◙ ◙ ◙ ◙ ◙ ◙ ▤ SCORE: ▲ ";SC;" ▨ ";
1010  RETURN
1100  I=FL-INT(TI/60):IFI<0THENI=0
1110  IFFS=0THENPOKE1991,32:RETURN
1115  POKE1991,48+I
1120  RETURN
1200  POKEVL,15:POKEW,129:POKEA,15:POKEHI,40:POKELW,200
1210  RETURN
10000 DATA0,24,0,0,60,0,0,24,0,1,24,128,0,189,0,0,90,0,0,24,0,0,
      24,0,0,36,0
10010 DATA0,66,0,255,255,255,255,255,254,127,255,252,127,255,252
      ,63,255,248
10020 DATA63,255,248,15,255,224,7,255,192,0,0,0,0,0,0,0,0,0,0
10030 DATA0,255,255,0,255,255,0,248,127,0,240,127,0,231,15,62,20
      7,15,126,207,31
10040 DATA254,207,255,254,207,31,255,207,15,255,231,15,255,240,1
      27,255,248,127
10050 DATA127,255,255,60,255,255,60,255,255,56,60,120,24,24,48,0
      ,0,0,0,0,0,0,0,0
10100 DATA165,197,201,33,208,22,56,173,0,208,233,4,141,0,208,201
      ,252,144,8,173
10110 DATA16,208,41,254,141,16,208,96,201,41,208,251,24,173,0,20
      8,105,4,141,0
10120 DATA208,201,4,176,8,173,16,208,9,1,141,16,208,96
10200 DATA169,0,133,181,230,178,165,178,201,5,208,4,169,1,133,17
      8,170,189,141
10210 DATA192,133,179,165,178,10,170,173,21,208,37,179,240,227,5
      6,189,0,208
10220 DATA233,5,157,0,208,201,251,144,11,169,255,56,229,179,45,1
      6,208,141,16
10230 DATA208,165,179,45,16,208,208,22,189,0,208,201,3,176,15,16
      9,255,56,229
10240 DATA179,45,21,208,141,21,208,169,1,133,181,96,0,2,4,8,16,3
      2,64,128
```

70

CHECKSUM

1=0	412=1389	10040=4322
5=3695	415=6400	10050=4544
10=3933	420=4911	10100=4334
15=3584	425=2132	10110=4169
20=2103	430=554	10120=2561
30=2095	435=3307	10200=4193
50=2106	440=143	10210=3991
60=3352	450=348	10220=4075
70=617	460=2923	10230=4106
90=2367	462=859	10240=3597
95=1196	465=2811	
100=435	470=2275	TOTAL= 245880
105=2738	475=1224	
110=2677	478=143	
115=2739	480=2181	
120=2687	482=2275	
130=2384	485=532	
140=1778	490=2064	
150=3015	492=2275	
200=521	495=532	
205=4437	500=1992	
207=348	520=143	
210=2955	550=1085	
212=1384	555=4409	
214=1337	558=545	
215=6283	560=2004	
217=4505	565=3580	
220=1821	570=503	
225=3844	700=3811	
230=3285	705=2859	
235=1852	710=723	
240=3398	720=1032	
245=2305	800=3569	
250=2100	805=616	
260=525	810=2916	
350=861	820=1214	
352=919	830=535	
355=2811	1000=3535	
360=3199	1010=143	
365=525	1100=2347	
380=2183	1110=1467	
385=3199	1115=778	
390=525	1120=143	
392=2181	1200=2681	
394=3199	1210=143	
396=525	10000=3925	
400=3386	10010=3995	
405=131	10020=2793	
410=753	10030=4426	

Egg Plant

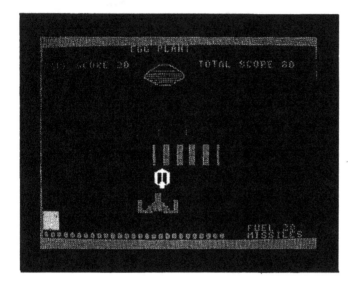

The objective of this game is to destroy the egg creature. He is protected by a moving fence with gaps in it and a shield. You must fire your missiles up at the creature through the fence and gradually eat the shield away.

When there is a complete hole in the fence you can destroy the egg creature. Beware, he can drop bombs on you which can be avoided by moving the missile launcher from side to side with the I and P keys. The missile launcher only has a limited number of missiles, thirty, and a small amount of fuel with which to move itself. Each time that you eat a chunk out of the shield you get 20 points. Hitting the Egg Plant gives 100 points.

VARIABLES

T   = Start of video driver
A$ = Missile count
L1 = Sprite collision register
O   = Keyboard scan
X1 = Horizontal position of missile launcher
Y1 = Vertical position of missile launcher
E1 = Horizontal position of Egg Plant
G1 = Vertical position of Egg Plant
LE = Driver loop variable
E   = End flag
F1 = Fences horizontal co-ordinate
F2 = Fences vertical co-ordinate
SC = Score
SL = Grand score
F   = Fuel
M   = Number of missiles
X3 = Horizontal position of launcher
Z6 = Position of shield in sprite memory

Ready.

```
Ø      REM EGG PLANT
```

Set up the sprites, egg plant, shield, missile and fence.

```
1      PRINT CHR$(147);"INTIALIZING!!!!"
999    T=53248
1010   FORI=1TO30:A$=A$+CHR$(209):NEXTI
1020   POKET+21,Ø:POKE2040,13:POKET+39,8
1070   FORI=ØTO62:READD:POKE832+I,D:NEXTI
1110   POKE2041,14:POKET+40,10:D=195
1120   FORI=ØTO62:POKE896+I,D:NEXTI
1140   POKE2042,15:POKET+41,10
1160   FORI=ØTO62:POKE960+I,D:NEXTI
1230   POKE2044,254:POKET+43,5
1240   FORI=ØTO62:READD:POKE16256+I,D:NEXTI
1255   POKE 2045,253:POKET+44,1:D=255
1265   FORI=ØTO62:POKE16192+I,D:NEXTI
1285   POKE2046,252:POKET+45,1:D=255
1290   FORI=ØTO62STEP3
1291   POKE16128+I,Ø:POKE16128+I+1,08:POKE16128+I+2,Ø:NEXTI
1310   POKE2047,251:POKET+46,Ø:D=255
1320   FORI=ØTO62:POKE16064+I,D:NEXTI
1335   X1=145:Y1=200:O=197:L1=53278
1350   E1=145:G1=70
1385   FORI=ØTO62:READD:POKE16000+I,D:NEXT
```

Print controls to use to move your missile launcher.

```
1500   PRINT" 🔲 ";:GOSUB 20000:PRINT CHR$(147);TAB(10);"EGG ▲ PLA
       NT"
1510   PRINT
1520   PRINT "PRESS ▲ THE ▲ I ▲ KEY ▲ TO ▲ MOVE ▲ LAUNCHER ▲ LEFT
       "
1530   PRINT
1540   PRINT "PRESS ▲ THE ▲ P ▲ KEY ▲ TO ▲ MOVE ▲ LAUNCHER ▲ RIGH
       T"
1550   PRINT
1560   PRINT "PRESS ▲ SPACE ▲ BAR ▲ TO ▲ FIRE ▲ ROCKET"
1570   PRINT:PRINT
1590   PRINT "PUSH ▲ ANY ▲ KEY ▲ TO ▲ START ▲ GAME"
1595   GET C$:IFC$=""THEN1595
```

Set score to nil, print fuel and missile supply and build screen.

```
2001   POKET+21,255:FOR LE=1 TO 10
2006   FORI=ØTO62:POKE16064+I,255:NEXTI
2010   PRINT " 🔲 ";TAB(13);"EGG ▲ PLANT"
2015   PRINT " 🔲 🔲 🔲 🔲 🔲 🔲 🔲 🔲 🔲 🔲 🔲 🔲 🔲 🔲 🔲
       🔲 🔲 🔲 🔲 🔲 🔲 ";
```

74

```
2020    PRINT TAB(30);"FUEL"
2030    PRINT A$;TAB(30);"MISSILES";
2040    SC=0:GOSUB7000:F=21:M=30:E=0
2080    POKE53277,223:F1=130:F2=150
2310    POKET+2,F1:POKET+3,F2
2320    POKET+4,F1+30:POKET+5,F2
2330    POKET+0,E1:POKET+1,G1
2350    POKET+8,X1:POKET+9,Y1
2360    POKET+14,145:POKET+15,120
2375    POKET+10,F:POKET+11,220
2400    SC=0:REM SET THE SCORE TO ZERO
2510    GOSUB3000:SL=SL+SC:NEXTLE:STOP
```

Main logic, move the fence, check for launched or dropped missile.

```
3000    GOSUB3200
3020    A=PEEK(O):IFA=60THENGOSUB4000:IFE=1THENRETURN
3030    IFA=33THENGOSUB4100
3040    IFA=41THENGOSUB4200
3050    IFINT(RND(1)*15)=14THENGOSUB6000:IFE=1THENRETURN
3100    F=F-.001:POKET+10,F:GOTO3000
3200    IFF1>155THENF1=130:RETURN
3220    POKET+2,F1:POKET+4,F1+30:F1=F1+1:RETURN
```

Launch a missile, check to move, launcher left or right.

```
4000    IFM=0THENRETURN
4020    M=M-1:X3=X1:Y3=Y1
4050    GOSUB9000
4052    GOSUB3200:Q2=PEEK(L1)
4058    IFQ2=70THENGOSUB7000:POKET+12,0:POKET+13,0:RETURN
4060    IFQ2=198THENGOSUB7000:GOSUB8000:POKET+12,0:POKET+13,0:
        RETURN
4062    IFQ2=71THENGOSUB7000:GOSUB7500:POKET+12,0:POKET+13,0:E=1:
        RETURN
4064    IFY3<8 THEN RETURN
4066    Y3=Y3-8:POKET+13,Y3
4070    GOTO4052
4100    IFF<1THENRETURN
4120    IFX1<110THENRETURN
4130    X1=X1-8:POKET+8,X1:F=F-.1:RETURN
4200    IFF<1THENRETURN
4220    IFX1>169THENRETURN
4230    X1=X1+8:POKET+8,X1:F=F-.1:RETURN
```

Egg Plant has launched a missile, keep moving it.

```
6000    POKE2046,250:REM POINT EGG MISSILE
6002    X3=E1:Y3=G1:POKET+12,X3:POKET+13,Y3
```

```
6030    GOSUB3200
6040    A=PEEK(L1):IFA=86THENGOSUB7000:GOSUB7600:POKET+12,0:POKET+
        13,0:E=1:RETURN
6045    IFY3>232THENPOKET+12,0:POKET+13,0:POKE2046,252:RETURN
6046    Y3=Y3+8:POKET+12,X3:POKET+13,Y3
6050    A=PEEK(O)
6060    IFA=33THENGOSUB4100:GOTO6030
6065    IFA=41THENGOSUB4200:GOTO6030
6090    GOTO6030
```

```
┌─────────────────────────────────────────────────────────┐
│ Print the scores, egg plant destroyed, missile launcher  │
│ destroyed.                                                │
└─────────────────────────────────────────────────────────┘
```

```
7000    REM PRINT THE SCORES
7010    PRINT " ▩ ";" ◪ ◪ ";"GAME ▲ SCORE";SC;TAB(23);"TOTAL ▲ SC
        ORE";SL
7020    RETURN
7500    PRINTCHR$(147);TAB(10);"EGG ▲ PLANT ▲ DESTROYED";
7501    REM EGG PLANT EXPLOSION
7502    FORI=1TO500:NEXT
7510    SC=SC+100
7540    RETURN
7600    PRINT" ▩ ";TAB(10);"NOW ▲ YOUR ▲ DESTROYED!!!!"
7620    POKE2046,252:FORI=1TO400:NEXTI:RETURN
8000    Z1=(X3+24-145)
8020    Z3=INT((Z1/16))
8025    IFZ3>2THENZ3=2
8027    IFZ3<0THENZ3=0
8030    Z5=((Y3+4)-120)
8035    Z6=(Z5*3)+Z3:SC=SC+20:GOSUB7000
8050    IFZ6>62THENZ6=62
8100    FOROL=0TO-21STEP-3:POKE16064+Z6+OL,0:NEXTOL:RETURN
```

```
┌─────────────────────────────────────────────────────────┐
│ Print fuel and missiles left, data for sprites.          │
└─────────────────────────────────────────────────────────┘
```

```
9000    PRINT " ▩ ◨ ◨ ◨ ◨ ◨ ◨ ◨ ◨ ◨ ◨ ◨ ◨ ◨ ◨ ◨ ◨ ◨ ◨
        ◨ ◨ ◨ ◨ ◨ ◨ ◨ ";
9020    J=INT(F):PRINTTAB(30);"FUEL";J;" ▲ ▲ ";:PRINTLEFT$(A$,M);
        :IF30-M=0 THEN 9025
9023    FORJ=1TO30-M:PRINT" ▲ ";:NEXTJ
9025    PRINTTAB(30);"MISSILES";
9040    POKET+12,X3:RETURN
9110    DATA0,255,0,1,129,128,3,0,192,6,0,96,12,0,48,24,0,24,63,25
        5,252
9120    DATA 48,0,6,96,0,2,255,255,255,128,0,1,255,255,255,128,0,1
        ,255,255,255
9130    DATA 96,0,6,63,255,252,24,0,24,15,255,224,6,0,96,3,0,192,0
        ,255,0
11010   DATA 0,60,0,0,60,0,0,60,0,0,60,0,0,60,0,0,60,0,0,60,0
11020   DATA 224,60,7,224,60,7,224,126,7,224,255,7,224,255,7,224,2
        55,7
11030   DATA227,255,199,227,255,199,227,255,199,231,255,231,231,25
        5,231,255,255
```

76

```
11040 DATA 255,255,129,255,255,129,255
12010 DATA0,32,0,0,112,0,0,248,0,1,252,0,3,254,0,3,38,0,3,38,0,3
      ,38,0,3,38,0
12020 DATA3,38,0,3,38,0,3,38,0,3,38,0,3,38,0,3,118,0,3,118,0,1,2
      52,0,0,248,0
12030 DATA 0,112,0,0,112,0,0,112,0
20000 PRINT:PRINT:PRINT
21000 PRINT" ▲ ▲ ▲ ▲ ▲ ▲ ▲ ✹ ✹ ✹ ✹ ✹ ▲ ▲ ✹ ✹
      ✹ ✹ ✹ ▲ ▲ ✹ ✹ ✹ ✹ ✹
22000 PRINT" ▲ ▲ ▲ ▲ ▲ ▲ ▲ ✹ ▲ ▲ ▲ ▲ ▲ ▲ ✹ ▲
      ▲ ▲ ▲ ▲ ▲ ✹
22210 PRINT" ▲ ▲ ▲ ▲ ▲ ▲ ▲ ▲ ✹ ▲ ▲ ▲ ▲ ▲ ✹ ▲
      ▲ ▲ ▲ ▲ ▲ ✹
22220 PRINT" ▲ ▲ ▲ ▲ ▲ ▲ ▲ ✹ ✹ ✹ ✹ ✹ ▲ ▲ ✹ ▲
      ✹ ✹ ✹ ▲ ▲ ✹ ▲ ✹ ✹ ✹
22230 PRINT" ▲ ▲ ▲ ▲ ▲ ▲ ▲ ✹ ▲ ▲ ▲ ▲ ▲ ▲ ✹ ▲
      ▲ ✹ ▲ ✹ ▲ ▲ ▲ ✹
22240 PRINT" ▲ ▲ ▲ ▲ ▲ ▲ ▲ ✹ ▲ ▲ ▲ ▲ ▲ ▲ ✹ ▲
      ▲ ▲ ✹ ▲ ✹ ▲ ▲ ▲ ✹
22250 PRINT" ▲ ▲ ▲ ▲ ▲ ▲ ▲ ✹ ✹ ✹ ✹ ✹ ▲ ▲ ✹ ✹
      ✹ ✹ ✹ ▲ ▲ ✹ ✹ ✹ ✹ ✹
22260 PRINT:PRINT
22270 PRINT" ▲ ▲ ▲ ▲ ▲ ✹ ✹ ✹ ✹ ✹ ▲ ▲ ✹ ▲ ▲ ▲ ▲ ▲
      ▲ ▲ ▲ ✹ ▲ ▲ ▲ ✹ ▲ ✹ ✹ ✹ ✹ ✹
22280 PRINT" ▲ ▲ ▲ ▲ ▲ ✹ ▲ ▲ ▲ ✹ ▲ ▲ ✹ ▲ ▲ ▲
      ▲ ▲ ✹ ▲ ✹ ▲ ▲ ✹ ✹ ▲ ▲ ▲ ✹ ▲ ▲ ✹
22290 PRINT" ▲ ▲ ▲ ▲ ▲ ✹ ▲ ▲ ▲ ✹ ▲ ▲ ✹ ▲ ✹ ▲
      ▲ ✹ ▲ ✹ ▲ ✹ ▲ ✹ ▲ ▲ ✹ ▲ ▲ ✹
22300 PRINT" ▲ ▲ ▲ ▲ ▲ ✹ ✹ ✹ ✹ ✹ ▲ ▲ ✹ ▲ ✹ ▲
      ▲ ✹ ▲ ▲ ✹ ▲ ✹ ▲ ▲ ▲ ✹
22310 PRINT" ▲ ▲ ▲ ▲ ▲ ✹ ▲ ▲ ▲ ▲ ▲ ▲ ✹ ▲ ▲ ✹
      ✹ ✹ ✹ ✹ ▲ ✹ ▲ ▲ ▲ ▲ ✹ ✹ ▲ ▲ ▲ ✹
22320 PRINT" ▲ ▲ ▲ ▲ ▲ ✹ ▲ ▲ ▲ ▲ ▲ ▲ ✹ ▲ ✹ ▲
      ▲ ▲ ▲ ▲ ✹ ▲ ✹ ▲ ✹ ▲ ▲ ▲ ▲ ✹ ▲ ▲ ▲ ✹
22330 PRINT" ▲ ▲ ▲ ✹ ▲ ✹ ▲ ▲ ▲ ▲ ▲ ✹ ✹ ✹ ✹ ✹
      ▲ ✹ ▲ ▲ ✹ ▲ ▲ ▲ ✹ ▲ ▲ ▲ ✹
23000 FORI=1TO5000:NEXT:RETURN
```

CHEXSUM

0=0	1290=937	1590=2290
1=1918	1291=3434	1595=1276
999=545	1310=1788	2001=1620
1010=2163	1320=1946	2006=2024
1020=1955	1335=2231	2010=1631
1070=2125	1350=968	2015=877
1110=1771	1385=2124	2020=941
1120=1786	1500=3100	2030=1540
1140=1277	1510=153	2040=2087
1160=1789	1520=3321	2080=1743
1230=1302	1530=153	2310=1363
1240=2224	1540=3473	2320=1662
1255=1788	1550=153	2330=1361
1265=1945	1560=2669	2350=1408
1285=1790	1570=366	2360=1556

77

```
2375=1443              9000=877
2400=444               9020=4338
2510=1874              9023=1666
3000=348               9025=1335
3020=2610              9040=917
3030=1039              9110=3410
3040=1036              9120=3964
3050=2793              9130=3410
3100=2129             11010=2737
3200=1511             11020=3310
3220=2634             11030=4206
4000=758              11040=1641
4020=1661             12010=4038
4050=356              12020=4045
4052=1171             12030=1373
4058=2776             20000=585
4060=3271             21000=3441
4062=3596             22000=1643
4064=835              22210=1643
4066=1503             22220=3177
4070=583              22230=2139
4100=750              22240=2139
4120=944              22250=3441
4130=2386             22260=366
4200=750              22270=3689
4220=949              22280=2958
4230=2385             22290=2960
6000=636              22300=3356
6002=2602             22310=3218
6030=348              22320=2700
6040=4327             22330=3232
6045=3085             23000=1226
6046=2308
6050=608              TOTAL= 243970
6060=1694
6065=1691
6090=585
7000=0
7010=3674
7020=143
7500=2856
7501=0
7502=964
7510=829
7540=143
7600=2473
7620=1957
8000=1205
8020=1130
8025=1082
8027=1082
8030=1242
8035=2450
8050=1205
8100=3363
```

Tank Ambush

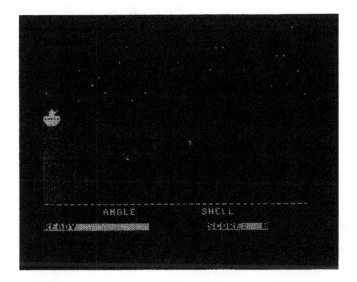

Lob bombs from your tank on the cliff onto the enemy tanks in the dark.

Hit 'space' for a flare or key in angle of elevation and shell (muzzle velocity) followed by 'space' to send a bomb.

VARIABLES

FL = Flare flag
CO = Collision flags
M   = Message
A   = Angle
SH = Shell
T   = Parameter for equations of motion
XI = Initial velocity in X direction
YI = Initial velocity in Y direction
LT = Last tank to move
RN = round number
SC = Score

1   REM TANK AMBUSH

> Build the tank, explosion and shell, set up video chip.

```
10     PRINT" [*] ";TAB(13);"TANK _ AMBUSH":PRINT" [*] [*] [*] [*] [*]
       [*] [*] _ _ _ _ _ _ _ _ _ _ HIT _ ANY _ KEY _ TO _
       START"
15     V=53248:POKE2040,192:POKE2041,193:POKE2042,193:POKE2043,19
       3:POKE2044,193
17     POKEV+39,15:POKEV+40,0:POKEV+41,0:POKEV+42,0:POKEV+43,0
19     POKEV+21,0:POKEV+16,0:FORI=12352TO12414:READQ:POKEI,Q:NEXT
       :RESTORE
21     FORI=12288TO12350:READQ:POKEI,Q:NEXT
22     POKE12297,0:POKE12300,0:POKE12290,16:POKE12293,48:POKE1229
       6,96:POKE12299,192
24     POKE12302,128
26     POKE2045,194:POKEV+44,7
28     FORI=12416TO12437STEP3:READQ:POKEI,Q:POKEI+1,0:POKEI+2,0:
       NEXT
30     FORI=12440TO12478:POKEI,0:NEXT
35     POKE53276,PEEK(53276)OR64:POKEV+45,1:POKEV+37,8:POKEV+38,7
       :POKE2046,195
37     FORI=12480TO12542:READQ:POKEI,Q:NEXT
40     GETX$:IFX$=""THEN40
```

> Print the cliff, tank and enemy tanks, set screen colours.

```
50     PRINT" [*] ":POKE53280,0:POKE53281,0
55     FORI=55296TO55375:POKEI,11:NEXT
56     FORI=1024TO1343:IFRND(0)<.05THENPOKEI,46
57     NEXT
58     FORI=55296TO55615:POKEI,3:NEXT
60     POKEV,23:POKEV+1,120:POKEV+21,1
65     FORI=1864TO1903:POKEI,45:POKEI+54272,3:NEXT
67     PRINT" [*] [*] [*] [*] [*] [*] [*] [*] [*] [*] [*] [*] [*] [*] [*]
       [*] [*] [*] [*] [*] [*] [*] _ _ _ _ _ _ _ _ _ ANGLE _ _
       _ _ _ _ _ _ _ SHELL";" [*] "
70     M$="READY _ _ _ _ _ _ _ _ _ _ ":GOSUB1000
71     POKEV+2,240:POKEV+3,INT(RND(1)*40+130):POKEV+16,PEEK(V+16)
       AND253
72     POKEV+4,0:POKEV+16,PEEK(V+16)OR28:POKEV+5,PEEK(V+3)-25
73     POKEV+6,25:POKEV+7,PEEK(V+3):POKEV+8,35:POKEV+9,PEEK(V+3)+
       30
74     POKEV+21,PEEK(V+21)OR30:LT=1
79     FORI=1464TO1824STEP40:FORJ=0TO6:POKEI+J,160:POKEI+J+54272,
       9:NEXT:NEXT
```

```
80    IF(PEEK(V+21)AND32)=ØORFL=1THEN95
85    GOSUB150
87    J=Ø:CO=PEEK(V+3Ø):IF(COAND32)=ØTHEN95
88    IF(COAND1)=1THEN95
89    FORI=1TO4:IF(COAND2^I)<>ØTHENJ=I
90    NEXT:IFJ=ØTHEN95
92    GOSUB3ØØ:IF(PEEK(V+21)AND3Ø)=ØTHEN5ØØ
95    GOSUB2ØØ
100   IF(PEEK(V+21)AND32)=32THEN85
102   GETX$:IFX$=""ORFL=1THEN8Ø
105   IFX$="   "THENM$="FLARE         ":GOSUB1ØØØ:FL=1:A=   /
      5:SH=9:GOSUB15Ø:GOTO8Ø
110   IFX$<"Ø"ORX$>"9"THEN1ØØ
115   K1=VAL(X$):POKE192Ø,K1+48
117   GETX$:IFX$=""THENGOSUB2ØØ:GOTO117
120   IFX$<"Ø"ORX$>"9"THEN117
122   A=1Ø*K1+VAL(X$):POKE1921,VAL(X$)+48:A=A*   /18Ø
136   GETX$:IFX$=""THENGOSUB2ØØ:GOTO136
138   IFX$<"Ø"ORX$>"9"THEN136
140   SH=VAL(X$):POKE1934,SH+48:POKE562Ø6,3
142   FL=Ø
145   GETX$:IFX$=""THENGOSUB2ØØ:GOTO145
147   IFX$="   "THENM$="FIRE          ":GOSUB1ØØØ:GOSUB15Ø:
      GOTO8Ø
149   GOTO145
```

```
150   T=T+4:XI=SH*COS(A)/1.5:YI=SH*SIN(A)/1.5
152   IF(PEEK(V+21)AND32)<>ØTHEN155
153   POKEV+1Ø,28:POKEV+16,PEEK(V+16)AND223:POKEV+11,122:POKEV+2
      1,PEEK(V+21)OR32
154   GOSUB1Ø2Ø
155   X=INT(28+T*XI)
160   Y=INT(122-T*YI+.Ø49*T*T)
162   IFX<1ØØRX>32ØRY<1ØØRY>215THENGOSUB4ØØ:RETURN
165   IFX>255THENPOKEV+1Ø,X-256:POKEV+16,PEEK(V+16)OR32:GOTO17Ø
168   POKEV+1Ø,X:POKEV+16,PEEK(V+16)AND223
170   POKEV+11,Y
175   IFFL=ØTHEN185
177   IFT>=3ØTHEN25Ø
185   RETURN
```

```
2ØØ   LT=LT+1:IFLT=5THENLT=1
```

81

```
210    IF(PEEK(V+21)AND2^LT)=ØTHENRETURN
215    K=PEEK(V+2*LT)+(2^(8-LT))*(PEEK(V+16)AND2^LT)
220    IFK<2560RK>261THEN225
222    POKEV+2*LT,K-6:POKEV+16,PEEK(V+16)AND(255-2^LT):GOTO230
225    POKEV+2*LT,PEEK(V+2*LT)-6
227    IFPEEK(V+2*LT)<55AND(PEEK(V+16)AND2^LT)=ØTHEN600
230    RETURN
```

> Launch the flare, keep it flying and illuminate the enemy tanks.

```
250    POKEV+21,PEEK(V+21)AND223:FORK1=1TO20:POKE53281,1:FORT=1TO
       20:NEXT
260    POKE53281,Ø:NEXT:M$="READY ▲ ▲ ▲ ":GOSUB1ØØØ:FL=Ø:T=Ø:
       POKE1920,32:POKE1921,32
270    POKE1934,32:RETURN
```

> Destroy enemy tank, call machine routine for sound and illuminate darkness.

```
300    POKEV+12,PEEK(V+1Ø):POKEV+13,PEEK(V+11)-5:POKEV+21,PEEK(V+
       21)AND223
305    POKE2Ø4Ø+J,195:POKE2Ø46,193:POKEV+28,PEEK(V+28)OR2^J
307    POKEV+28,PEEK(V+28)AND191:POKEV+39+J,1:POKEV+45,Ø
310    POKEV+21,PEEK(V+21)OR64:IF(PEEK(V+16)AND32)=32THENPOKEV+16
       ,PEEK(V+16)OR64
320    GOSUB1Ø2Ø:POKE53281,1:FORK=1TO5ØØ:NEXT:POKE53281,Ø:FORK=1
       TO2ØØ:NEXT
325    SC=SC+5Ø:POKEV+21,PEEK(V+21)AND(191-2^J):POKEV+3Ø,PEEK(V+3
       Ø)AND(191-2^J)
330    M$="READY ▲ ▲ ▲ ▲ ▲ ▲ ▲ ▲ ▲ ":
       GOSUB1ØØØ
335    POKE1920,32:POKE1921,32:POKE1934,32
340    POKEV+1Ø,28:POKEV+16,PEEK(V+16)AND223:POKEV+11,122:T=Ø
345    POKE2Ø4Ø+J,193:POKE2Ø46,195:POKEV+28,PEEK(V+28)AND(255-2^J
       )
347    POKEV+28,PEEK(V+28)OR64:POKEV+39+J,Ø:POKEV+45,1
350    RETURN
400    POKEV+12,PEEK(V+1Ø):POKEV+13,PEEK(V+11):POKEV+21,PEEK(V+21
       )AND223
410    POKEV+21,PEEK(V+21)OR64:IF(PEEK(V+16)AND32)=32THEN415
412    POKEV+16,PEEK(V+16)AND191:GOTO42Ø
415    POKEV+16,PEEK(V+16)OR64
420    GOSUB1Ø2Ø
425    POKEV+21,PEEK(V+21)AND191:M$="READY ▲ ▲ ▲ ▲ ▲ ▲
       ▲ ▲ ▲ ▲ ▲ ▲ ":GOSUB1ØØØ
427    POKE1920,32:POKE1921,32:POKE1934,32
430    POKEV+1Ø,28:POKEV+16,PEEK(V+16)AND223:POKEV+11,122:T=Ø:
       RETURN
```

```
500    RN=RN+1:IFRN>1THEN510
502    POKEV+2,210:POKEV+4,226:POKEV+6,251:POKEV+8,5:POKEV+16,
       PEEK(V+16)AND248
504    POKEV+16,PEEK(V+16)OR16
506    GOTO530
510    IFRN>2THEN520
512    POKEV+2,180:POKEV+4,196:POKEV+6,221:POKEV+8,231:POKEV+16,
       PEEK(V+16)AND232
516    GOTO530
520    POKEV+2,150-4*RN:POKEV+4,166-RN:POKEV+6,191-RN:POKEV+8,201
       -RN
522    POKEV+16,PEEK(V+16)AND232
530    POKEV+3,INT(RND(0)*40+130):POKEV+5,PEEK(V+3)-25:POKEV+7,
       PEEK(V+3)
535    POKEV+9,PEEK(V+3)+30
540    POKEV+21,PEEK(V+21)OR30:LT=1
550    GOTO80
```

```
600    PRINT" ▮▮ ▲ ▲ ▲ ▲ ▲ ▲ ▲ ▲ ▲ ▲ ▲ ▲ ▲ ▲ ▮▮
       ▮▮ GAME ▲ OVER ▮ ":PRINT:PRINT:POKEV+21,0
610    PRINT"YOUR ▲ SCORE ▲ IS ▲ ";SC
620    END
```

```
1000   PRINT" ▮▮ ▮▮ ▮▮ ▮▮ ▮▮ ▮▮ ▮▮ ▮▮ ▮▮ ▮▮ ▮▮ ▮▮ ▮▮ ▮▮
       ▮▮ ▮▮ ▮▮ ▮▮ ▮▮ ▮▮ ▮▮ ▮▮ ▮▮ ";M$;TAB(25);"SCORE: ▲ ";SC;" ▮
       ▮ "
1010   RETURN
1020   S=54272:FORL=0TO24:POKES+L,0:NEXT
1022   VL=54296:W=54276:AT=54277:H=54273:L=54272
1025   FORK=15TO0STEP-2:POKEVL,K:POKEW,129:POKEAT,15:POKEH,40
1030   POKEL,200:NEXT
1040   POKEW,0:POKEAT,0:RETURN
1050   RETURN
10000  DATA 0,60,0,0,60,0,0,255,0,255,255,0,255,255,0,0,255,0,0,2
       55,0,63,255,252
10010  DATA127,255,254,127,255,254,102,102,102,127,255,254,127,25
       5,254,63,255,252
10020  DATA31,255,248,15,255,240,7,255,224,3,255,192,0,0,0,0,0,0,0,
       0,0,0
10030  DATA24,60,60,126,126,60,60,24
10040  DATA36,27,32,0,64,4,8,137,2,0,6,64,174,39,172,3,92,137,35,
       190,192
```

83

```
10050 DATA13,127,62,67,255,192,40,255,64,32,255,109,45,255,0,0,2
      55,192,185
10060 DATA126,154,0,28,192,129,167,188,48,25,65,64,198,100,14,0,
      0,0,105
10070 DATA200,60,8,97
```

CHEXSUM

1=0	138=1571	415=1537
10=4974	140=2369	420=350
15=3933	142=380	425=3589
17=3588	145=2018	427=1750
19=3893	147=3157	430=3875
21=2103	149=525	500=1686
22=3967	150=3605	502=4669
24=636	152=1947	504=1539
26=1302	153=4953	506=532
28=3708	154=350	510=873
30=1761	155=1261	512=4802
35=4268	160=2268	516=532
37=2101	162=3083	520=4836
40=1195	165=4066	522=1572
50=1583	168=2372	530=4645
55=1838	170=655	535=1425
56=2540	175=862	540=2006
57=131	177=1039	550=480
58=1782	185=143	600=3420
60=1870	200=1921	610=1527
65=2618	210=2029	620=129
67=3221	215=3920	1000=2967
70=1750	220=1532	1010=143
71=4321	222=4301	1020=2254
72=3776	225=2057	1022=3236
73=4130	227=3607	1025=3255
74=2006	230=143	1030=638
79=4574	250=4183	1040=1018
80=2318	260=4468	1050=143
85=299	270=729	10000=4282
87=2748	300=4608	10010=4553
88=1142	305=3408	10020=3405
89=2564	307=3291	10030=1519
90=928	310=5042	10040=3563
92=2140	320=3819	10050=3851
95=294	325=5588	10060=3558
100=1774	330=1984	
102=1784	335=1750	10070=707
105=5059	340=3642	
110=1565	345=3831	TOTAL= 308042
115=1672	347=3262	
117=2021	350=143	
120=1570	400=4338	
122=3751	410=3540	
136=2023	412=2195	

Brick Buster

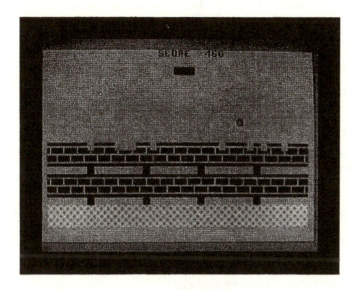

Blast your way through brick wall by moving your bat. The bat becomes shorter if you manage to get through.

LEFT: 'I'   RIGHT: 'P'

VARIABLES

DX = X direction (1 — positive, 255 — negative)
DY = Y direction
R,SC = Round, score

```
1     REM BRICK BUSTER
```

```
10    POKE53281,10:POKE53280,2:PRINT" ▥ ▣ ▲ ▲ ▲ ▲ ▲ ▲ ▲
      ▲ ▲ ▲ ▲ ▲ ▲ BRICK ▲ BUSTER"
15    V=53248:POKE2040,192:POKE2041,193:POKEV+39,0:POKEV+40,6
20    FORI=12288TO12311:POKEI,255:NEXT
25    FORI=12312TO12350:POKEI,0:NEXT
30    FORI=12352TO12373STEP3:READQ:POKEI,Q:POKEI+1,0:POKEI+2,0:
      NEXT
35    FORI=12376TO12414:POKEI,0:NEXT
40    FORI=49152TO49306:READQ:POKEI,Q:NEXT
50    FORI=54272TO54295:POKEI,0:NEXT
85    PRINT" ▩ ▩ ▩ ▩ ▩ ▩ ▩ ▩ ▩ ▩ ▩ ▩ ▩ ▲ ▲ ▲ ▲ ▲
      ▲ ▲ ▲ ▲ HIT ▲ ANY ▲ KEY ▲ TO ▲ START"
90    GETX$:IFX$=""THEN90
95    TI$="000000"
```

```
100   PRINT" ▥ ";:POKE53281,12:POKE53280,6
105   GOSUB1000:PRINT" ▩ ▩ ▩ ▩ ▩ ▩ ▩ ▩ ▩ ▩ ▩ ":GOSUB1100
107   C=160
110   K=INT(RND(1)*3+5):POKE1624+K,C:POKE1632+K,C:POKE1640+K,C:
      POKE1648+K,C
115   POKE55896+K,2:POKE55904+K,2:POKE55912+K,2:POKE55920+K,2
120   GOSUB1100:PRINT" ▩ ▬ ▥ ▲ ✖ ✖ ✖ ✖ ✖ ✖ ✖ ✖ ✖ ✖
      ✖ ✖ ✖ ✖ ✖ ✖ ✖ ✖ ✖ ✖ ✖ ✖ ✖ ✖ ✖ ✖ ✖ ✖
      ✖ ✖ ✖ ✖ ✖ ✖ ✖ ✖ ✖ ▲ ";
121   PRINT" ▥ ▲ ✖ ✖ ✖ ✖ ✖ ✖ ✖ ✖ ✖ ✖ ✖ ✖ ✖ ✖ ✖
      ✖ ✖ ✖ ✖ ✖ ✖ ✖ ✖ ✖ ✖ ✖ ✖ ✖ ✖ ✖ ✖ ✖ ✖
      ✖ ✖ ✖ ✖ ▲ ";
122   PRINT" ▥ ▲ ✖ ✖ ✖ ✖ ✖ ✖ ✖ ✖ ✖ ✖ ✖ ✖ ✖ ✖ ✖
      ✖ ✖ ✖ ✖ ✖ ✖ ✖ ✖ ✖ ✖ ✖ ✖ ✖ ✖ ✖ ✖ ✖ ✖
      ✖ ✖ ✖ ✖ ▲ ";
125   POKE1784+K,C:POKE1792+K,C:POKE1800+K,C:POKE1808+K,C
130   POKE56056+K,2:POKE56064+K,2:POKE56072+K,2:POKE56080+K,2
140   RN=RN+1:POKEV+2,28:POKEV,172:POKEV+16,0:POKEV+1,68:POKEV+3
      ,25:POKEV+21,3
145   DX=1:DY=4:SC=SC+500
150   POKEV+30,0:POKEV+31,0
160   IFRN=1THEN200
165   IFRN>4THEN200
170   IFRN=2THENFORI=12290TO12313STEP3:POKEI,240:NEXT:GOTO200
180   IFRN=3THENFORI=12290TO12313STEP3:POKEI,0:NEXT:GOTO200
185   FORI=12289TO12312STEP3:POKEI,240:NEXT
```

86

```
200    SYS(49152):SYS(49152):SYS(49152)
210    POKE178,DX:POKE179,DY:SYS(49231)
215    CO=PEEK(V+30):IF(COAND3)=3THENGOSUB400
220    POKE178,DX:POKE179,DY:SYS(49231)
225    CO=PEEK(V+30):IF(COAND3)=3THENGOSUB400
230    CL=PEEK(V+31):IF(CLAND2)=2THENGOSUB300
240    IFPEEK(V+3)<25THEN550
250    IFPEEK(V+3)>202THEN450
260    K=PEEK(V+2)+128*(PEEK(V+16)AND2):IFK>335ORK<23THENGOSUB500
270    GOSUB1000:GOTO200
```

```
300    R=INT((PEEK(V+3)-44)/8):C=INT((PEEK(V+2)+128*(PEEK(V+16)
       AND2)-19)/8)
305    PS=1024+40*R+C:IFPEEK(PS)<>32THEN320
307    IFPEEK(PS+1)=160THENPOKEPS+1,32:GOTO350
308    IFPEEK(PS+1)<>32THENPOKEPS+1,32:GOSUB1300:GOTO330
310    IFPEEK(PS-1)=160THENPOKEPS-1,32:GOTO350
311    IFPEEK(PS-1)=32THENRETURN
312    POKEPS-1,32:GOSUB1300:GOTO330
320    IFPEEK(PS)=160THEN350
325    POKEPS,32:GOSUB1300
330    DY=252:RETURN
```

```
350    POKEPS,32:SC=SC+50:GOSUB1300:GOSUB1000:RETURN
```

```
400    DF=PEEK(V)+256*(PEEK(V+16)AND1):BX=PEEK(V+2)+128*(PEEK(V+1
       6)AND2)
410    IFBX<=DFANDDX=1THENDX=255:GOTO445
415    IFDX=1THEN445
420    IFBX>=DF+16THENDX=1
445    DY=4:RETURN
450    PRINT" 🄻 ■ ▲ ▲ ▲ ▲ ▲ ▲ ▲ ▲ ▲ ▲ ▲ ▲ ▲
       ▲ NEW ▲ ROUND"
460    POKEV+21,0
465    FORT=1TO2000:NEXT
470    GOTO100
```

87

Buster hits sides chamber, so reset direction.

```
500    IFK<23THENDX=1:RETURN
520    DX=255:RETURN
```

Buster missed bat, flash screen, and call sound routine.

```
550    FORI=10TOINT(RND(1)*50+50):POKE53281,I:POKE53280,I
560    POKEVL,15:POKEW,129:POKEA,15:POKEH,I:POKEL,200
565    NEXT:POKEW,0:POKEA,0
570    POKE53280,0:POKE53281,0:PRINT" ▨ ▤ ▬ ▬ ▬ ▬ ▬
       ▬ ▬ ▬ ▬ ▬ ▬ GAME ▬ OVER!":PRINT
580    PRINT" ▨ ▨ ▨ ▨ ▨ ▨ ▨ ▨ ▬ ▬ ▬ ▬ ▬ ▬
       ▬ ▬ ▬ YOUR ▬ SCORE ▬ WAS ▬ ";INT(SC)
590    GETX$:IFX$=""THENEND
595    GOTO590
1000   PRINT" ▨ ▤ ▬ ▬ ▬ ▬ ▬ ▬ ▬ ▬ ▬ ▬
       ▬ ▬ ▨ SCORE ▬ ";INT(SC);CHR$(13);" ▢ ";
1005   SC=SC-TI/60 :TI$="000000"
1010   RETURN
1100   PRINT" ▨ ▨ ▬ ▨ ▼ ▬ ▼ ▬ ▼ ▬ ▼ ▬ ▼ ▬ ▼ ▬ ▼
       ▬ ▼ ▬ ▼ ▬ ▼ ▬ ▼ ▬ ▼ ▬ ▼ ▬
       ▼ ▬ ▼ ▬ ▼ ▬ ▤ ▬ ";
1105   PRINT" ▲ ▨ ▲ ▼ ▲ ▼ ▲ ▼ ▲ ▼ ▲ ▼ ▲ ▼ ▲ ▼
       ▲ ▼ ▲ ▼ ▲ ▼ ▲ ▼ ▲ ▼ ▲ ▼ ▲ ▼
       ▲ ▼ ▲ ▼ ▤ ▬ ";
1120   PRINT" ▲ ▨ ▬ ▲ ▬ ▲ ▬ ▲ ▬ ▲ ▬ ▲ ▬ ▲ ▬
       ▲ ▬ ▲ ▬ ▲ ▬ ▲ ▬ ▲ ▬ ▲ ▬ ▲ ▬
       ▬ ▲ ▬ ▲ ▤ ▬ ";
1130   RETURN
```

Push sound data into registers and make bloop sound.

```
1300   VL=54296:W=54276:A=54277:H=54273:L=54272
1305   FORX=15TO0STEP-4:POKEVL,X:POKEW,129:POKEA,15:POKEH,12:POKE
       L,32:NEXT
1310   POKEW,0:POKEA,0
1350   RETURN
10000  DATA61,126,255,255,255,255,126,61
10100  DATA165,197,133,181,201,33,208,41,173,16,208,41,1,240,21,1
       73,0,208,201
10110  DATA0,208,14,169,252,141,0,208,173,16,208,41,254,141,16,20
       8,96,206,0,208
10120  DATA206,0,208,206,0,208,206,0,208,96,201,41,208,251,238,0,
       208,238,0,208
10130  DATA238,0,208,238,0,208,173,0,208,208,234,173,16,208,9,1,1
       41,16,208,96
10200  DATA24,165,179,109,3,208,141,3,208,165,178,201,255,240,28,
       238,2,208
10210  DATA238,2,208,238,2,208,238,2,208,173,2,208,201,0,208,8,17
       3,16,208,9,2
```

88

```
10220 DATA141,16,208,96,173,16,208,41,2,240,13,173,2,208,208,8,1
     73,16,208,41,253
10230 DATA141,16,208,206,2,208,206,2,208,206,2,208,206,2,208,96
```

CHECKSUM

1=0	330=705
10=3823	350=2450
15=3354	400=4935
20=1877	410=2723
25=1765	415=878
30=3708	420=1687
35=1766	445=596
40=2106	450=2049
50=1770	460=616
85=2936	465=1031
90=1196	470=525
95=805	500=1275
100=1726	520=705
105=1356	550=3160
107=403	560=2502
110=4943	565=926
115=3503	570=3765
120=10072	580=2879
121=9189	590=1214
122=9189	595=538
125=3377	1000=3180
130=3498	1005=1999
140=5013	1010=143
145=1799	1100=8334
150=1332	1105=7576
160=870	1120=8189
165=869	1130=143
170=3467	1300=3125
180=3332	1305=3894
185=2106	1310=723
200=1762	1350=143
210=1758	10000=1774
215=2438	10100=4063
220=1758	10110=4296
225=2438	10120=4189
230=2436	10130=4108
240=1407	10200=3767
250=1462	10210=4058
260=4183	10220=4551
270=965	10230=3084
300=5347	
305=2945	TOTAL= 240833
307=2763	
308=3327	
310=2764	
311=1441	
312=1767	
320=1316	
325=908	

89

Alligator!

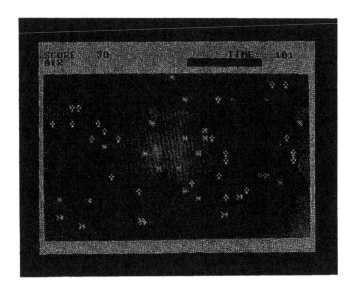

Move the alligator to right side of screen, ensuring that all yellow fish have been eaten. Beware of the black mines which explode if eaten, and watch the air guage in case alligator drowns (i.e. surface for air).

Must also beat overall time limit in order to get to a new round.

Scoring: exotic fish (red)   20
          yellow fish   150
          plants   10

Move: UP   — 'Q'
          DOWN — 'Z'
          RIGHT — 'P'

VARIABLES

NM   = No. of 'men'
AI,TM   = Air (initial), time left
R,SC   = Round, score
AR,AX   = Air used, alligator X co-ordinates
FL   = Flag for air guage

```
1       REM ALLIGATOR
```

Create alligator and yellow fish sprites and set variables.

```
10      PRINT" 🂠 _ _ _ _ _ _ _ _ _ _ _ 🂡 A
        LLIGATOR! ■ ":PRINT" 🂢 🂢 🂢 🂢 🂢 🂢 🂢 🂢 🂢 🂢 🂢 🂢 🂢
        🂢 🂢 ";
20      V=53248:POKE2040,192:POKE2041,194:POKE2042,194:POKE2043,19
        4:POKE2044,194
22      POKE2045,194:POKE2046,194:POKE2047,194
25      FORI=12288TO12350:READQ:POKEI,Q:POKEI+64,Q:NEXT
30      POKEV+39,0:POKEV+40,7:POKEV+41,7:POKEV+42,7:POKEV+43,7:
        POKEV+16,0
33      POKEV+44,7:POKEV+45,7:POKEV+46,7
35      FORI=12366TO12381STEP3:READQ:POKEI,Q:NEXT
40      FORI=12416TO12437STEP3:READQ:POKEI,Q:POKEI+1,0:POKEI+2,0:
        NEXT
45      FORI=12440TO12478:POKEI,0:NEXT
50      FORI=49152TO49262:READQ:POKEI,Q:NEXT
60      NM=4
70      FORI=54272TO54296:POKEI,0:NEXT
90      PRINT" _ _ _ _ _ _ _ _ _ _ _ HIT _ ANY _ KEY _ T
        O _ START"
95      GETX$:IFX$=""THEN95
97      GOSUB1300
```

Print ocean, alligator and yellow fish, set clock and colours.

```
100     POKEV+21,0:NM=NM-1:IFNM=0THEN600
102     PRINT" 🂠 ";:POKE53280,14:POKE53281,6
105     FORI=1024TO1143:POKEI,160:POKEI+54272,14:NEXT
110     FORI=1144TO1823:K=RND(1):IFK<.92THEN130
115     K=RND(1):IFK<.4THENPOKEI,42:POKEI+54272,10:GOTO130
117     IFK<.6THENPOKEI,81:POKEI+54272,0:GOTO130
120     POKEI,88:POKEI+54272,13
130     NEXT
135     POKEV,10:POKEV+1,150:POKEV+16,0:POKE178,1
140     AI=28-R:TM=0
144     FORI=1TO7
145     K1=INT(RND(1)*280+40):K2=INT(RND(0)*30+200)
147     IFK1>255THENPOKEV+16,PEEK(V+16)OR2^I:POKEV+2*I,K1-256:GOTO
        154
150     POKEV+2*I,K1:POKEV+16,PEEK(V+16)AND(255-2^I)
154     POKEV+2*I+1,K2
156     NEXT
157     R=R+1:GOSUB1100:POKE1545,32
160     POKEV+21,255:PRINT" 🂣 🂢 🂤 🂥 AIR"
170     POKEV+30,0
180     TI$="000000":GOSUB1000
```

Move alligator left, right, up and down.

```
200    SYS(49233):IFTM>120-2*RTHEN600
205    GOSUB1000:IFAR>=AITHEN700
210    AX=PEEK(V)+256*(PEEK(V+16)AND1)
220    IFPEEK(V+1)<67THENGOSUB400:GOTO230
225    FL=0
230    IFAX>327AND(PEEK(V+21)AND30)<>0THEN750
235    IF(PEEK(V+30)AND1)=1THENGOSUB500
240    K1=INT(AX/8)+40*INT((PEEK(V+1)-42)/8)+1024:IFPEEK(K1)=32
       THEN200
250    IFPEEK(K1)=42THENGOSUB450
260    IFPEEK(K1)=81THENGOSUB550
270    IFPEEK(K1)=88THENGOSUB300
280    GOTO200
```

Eat the plants, let the alligator breath and eat the fish.

```
300    SC=SC+10:POKEK1,32:GOSUB1000
310    RETURN
400    IFFL=1THEN420
410    TM=TM+INT(TI/60):TI$="000000":GOSUB1100:FL=1
420    RETURN
450    SC=SC+20:POKEK1,32:GOSUB1000
460    RETURN
```

Eat the yellow fish, increment the score and clear yellow fish.

```
500    F1=0
505    FORJ=1TO7:K2=PEEK(V+2*J)+(2^(8-J))*(PEEK(V+16)AND(2^J)):K3
       =PEEK(V+2*J+1)
507    GOSUB1000
510    K4=PEEK(V)+256*(PEEK(V+16)AND1)
512    IF(PEEK(V+21)AND(2^J))=0THEN540
515    IFK2-K4>=18ANDK2-K4<25ANDK3-PEEK(V+1)<8THENF1=J
540    NEXT:IFF1=0THENRETURN
545    IFF1=FBTHEN350
547    SC=SC+150:POKEV+21,PEEK(V+21)AND(255-2^F1):GOSUB1000
548    POKEV+30,0:RETURN
```

Alligator dead, call sound routine and print score.

```
550    GOSUB1300
580    GOTO100
600    POKEV+21,0:POKE53281,0:POKE53280,0:PRINT" ░ ▲ ▲ ▲ ▲
       ▲ ▲ ▲ ▲ ▲ ▲ ▲ ▲ ▲ ▲ ▲ ▲ ▲ GAME ▲ OVER"
```

```
610    PRINT" 🔲 🔲 🔲 🔲 ▲ ▲ ▲ ▲ ▲ ▲ ▲ ▲ ▲ ▲ ▲ ▲ YOUR
       ▲ SCORE ▲ WAS ▲ ";SC
620    GETX$:IFX$=""THENEND
630    GOTO620
```

Alligator drowned, start game again, decrement alligator count.

```
700    POKEV+21,0:POKE53281,0:PRINT" 🔲 🔲 ▲ ▲ ▲ ▲ ▲ ▲ ▲ ▲
       ▲ ▲ ▲ ▲ ALLIGATOR ▲ DROWNED"
710    FORT=1TO3000:NEXT
720    GOTO100
750    IF(PEEK(V+21)AND30)=0THEN100
760    PRINT" 🔲 🔲 ▲ ▲ ▲ ONE ▲ OR ▲ MORE ▲ YELLOW ▲ FISH ▲ REMAIN
       ING"
770    POKE53281,0:PRINT" 🔲 🔲 🔲 🔲 ▲ ▲ ▲ ▲ ▲ ▲ ▲
       ▲ ▲ ▲ LOSE ▲ ONE ▲ ALLIGATOR"
780    FORT=1TO3000:NEXT
790    GOTO100
```

Update the score, time left and air guage

```
1000   AR=INT(TI/60):POKE55340+AR,14
1005   FORI=1058TO1063:POKEI,160:NEXT
1010   PRINT" 🔲 🔲 🔲 SCORE ▲ ▲ ";SC;TAB(28);"TIME: ▲ ";120-2*R-
       TM-AR
1020   RETURN
1100   FORI=55340TO55340+AI:POKEI,0:NEXT
1110   RETURN
```

Generate sound and data for sprites.

```
1300   FORX=15TO0STEP-1:IFNM=4THEN1302
1301   POKE53281,X+100
1302   POKE54296,X:POKE54276,129:POKE54277,15
1305   POKE54278,128:POKE54273,X:POKE54272,200:NEXT
1310   POKE54276,0:POKE54277,0:RETURN
10000  DATA0,0,0,0,0,0,0,0,0,224,0,0,96,0,1,32,0,3,48,252,230,63,
       255,252
10010  DATA31,255,248,31,255,240,15,255,255,7,255,255,1,255,0,3,1
       22,0,6,6,0
10020  DATA6,6,0,0,3,0,0,1,128,0,0,0,0,0,0,0,0,0
10030  DATA0,0,224,240,240,255
10040  DATA0,128,198,111,63,111,198,128
10100  DATA165,197,201,41,208,39,173,16,208,41,1,240,7,173,0,208,
       201,74,176,24
10110  DATA24,173,0,208,105,6,141,0,208,173,0,208,201,6,176,8,173
       ,16,208,9,1,141
```

```
10120 DATA16,208,96,201,62,208,14,173,1,208,201,64,144,6,56,233,
      6,141,1,208,96
10130 DATA201,12,208,251,173,1,208,201,240,176,244,24,105,6,141,
      1,208,96,165,178
10140 DATA201,0,208,12,169,193,141,248,7,169,1,133,178,76,0,192,
      169,192,141,248
10150 DATA7,169,0,133,178,76,0,192
```

CHECKSUM

1=0	240=4845	1301=911
10=3297	250=1358	1302=2005
20=3937	260=1353	1305=2291
22=1952	270=1355	1310=1383
25=2887	280=525	10000=3505
30=4304	300=1719	10010=3831
33=2032	310=143	10020=2128
35=2333	400=860	10030=1157
40=3708	410=3278	10040=1695
45=1761	420=143	10100=4247
50=2107	450=1719	10110=4411
60=389	460=143	10120=4362
70=1769	500=353	10130=4550
90=2367	505=6264	10140=4450
95=1196	507=348	10150=1477
97=348	510=2258	
100=2400	512=2043	TOTAL= 205151
102=1726	515=4038	
105=2739	540=1006	
110=2747	545=928	
115=3320	547=3742	
117=2551	548=818	
120=1311	550=348	
130=131	580=525	
135=2387	600=4208	
140=1173	610=2392	
144=656	620=1214	
145=3252	630=531	
147=4649	700=4326	
150=3301	710=1032	
154=1125	720=525	
156=131	750=1759	
157=1626	760=3467	
160=1553	770=3374	
170=617	780=1032	
180=1221	790=525	
200=2118	1000=2091	
205=1580	1005=1748	
210=2284	1010=3794	
220=2172	1020=143	
225=380	1100=2119	
230=2705	1110=143	
235=1852	1300=2119	

Road Patrol

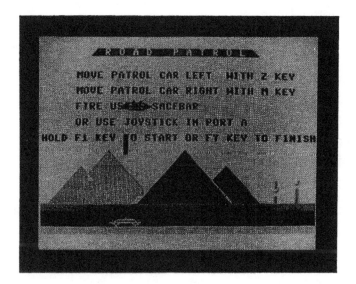

During the year 2033 there was high UFO activity and thus all patrol cars were fitted with laser guns, however the laser beams were as yet unable to penetrate the UFO force field.

Unfortunately, earth had not developed a force field which was permanent and every 20 hits from a laser ray dissipated some of the force field energy which could only withstand 100 direct hits.

As Commander of patrol car C64 it is your duty to patrol a desert road where there have been sightings of a UFO. It is your duty to fire rapidly at the UFO to try and break the force field even though it is believed impossible.

VARIABLES

V   = Sprite register

SS = Sound register

CC = Patrol Car column

CR = Patrol Car row

CX = Patrol Car horizontal increment

CY = Patrol Car vertical increment

SC = UFO column

SR = UFO row

SX = UFO horizontal increment

SY = UFO vertical increment

JY = Joystick value

GS = Game start flag ($\emptyset$ = NO, 1 = YES)

HC = Number of hits on Patrol Car

HS = Number of hits on UFO

HH = Highest number of hits on UFO

SE = UFO expansion value

```
0      REM ROAD PATROL
```

Call print the back ground and set up the sprites, move patrol.

```
10     GOTO1000
20     REM   JOYSTICK ROUTINE
25     JY=PEEK(56320):IFJY=255THENA$="":RETURN
30     IF(JYAND16)=0THENA$=" ▲ ":RETURN
35     IF(JYAND4)=0THENA$="Z":RETURN
40     IF(JYAND8)=0THENA$="M":RETURN
45     A$="":RETURN
200    IFGS=1THEN220
210    GETA$:IFA$=" ▀ "THENGOSUB2000
220    POKEV,SC:POKEV+1,SR
240    POKEV+2,CC:POKEV+3,CR
250    GETA$:IFA$=""THENGOSUB20:IFA$=""THEN500
255    IFGS=1THENIFA$=" ▐▌ "THENSYS65535
260    IFA$="Z"THENCX=-14:CC=CC+CX:GOTO350
265    IFA$="M"THENCX=14:CC=CC+CX:GOTO350
270    IFA$<>" ▲ "THEN500
275    POKEV+41,2:POKEV+21,PEEK(V+21)OR4
280    POKESS+24,15:POKESS+1,18
285    FORI=CR-20TOSR-4STEP-16:POKEV+4,CC+12:POKEV+5,I
290    IFPEEK(V+30)AND1=1THENPOKEV+39,7:FORT=1TO20:NEXT:GOTO315
300    NEXT
310    GOTO325
315    IFGS=0THEN325
320    IFSE=3THENHS=HS+1:PRINT" 🄢 🄤 🄤 🄤 🄤 🄤 🄤 🄤 🄤 🄤 🄤
       🄤 🄤 🄤 🄤 🄤 🄤 🄤 🄤 🄤 🄤 🄤 ■ 🄡 "SPC(36)HS
322    IFSE=2THENHS=HS+2:PRINT" 🄢 🄤 🄤 🄤 🄤 🄤 🄤 🄤 🄤 🄤
       🄤 🄤 🄤 🄤 🄤 🄤 🄤 🄤 🄤 🄤 🄤 ■ 🄡 "SPC(36)HS
325    POKESS+1,40
330    POKEV+21,3:POKEV+39,0
340    IFHS>4THENGOTO2500
345    GOTO500
350    IFCC<60THENCC=60
360    IFCC>240THENCC=240
380    GOTO240
```

Move the spaceship around the screen, ship fires missile.

```
500    SC=SC+SX
510    IFSC<20THENSC=20:SX=-SX:SY=(INT(RND(.)*9)+8)*(1-(INT(RND(.
       )*3)))
520    IFSC>240THENSC=240:SX=-SX:SY=(INT(RND(.)*9)+8)*(1-(INT(RND
       (.)*3)))
530    SR=SR+SY:POKESS+24,SR/12
540    IFSR>180THENSR=180:SY=-SY:GOTO600
550    IFSR>30THEN600
560    SR=30:SY=-SY
```

97

```
570   IFRND(.)>.25THEN600
575   IFSE=3THENSE=2:GOTO590
580   SE=3
590   POKEV+29,SE:GOTO600
600   REM SAUCER FIRE
610   IFSC<CC-10ORSC>CC+10THEN220
620   POKEV+41,0:POKEV+21,PEEK(V+21)OR4
640   POKESS,240:POKESS+1,176
660   FORI=SR+24TO220STEP16:POKEV+4,SC+14:POKEV+5,I
680   IFPEEK(V+30)AND2=2THENPOKEV+40,7:FORT=1TO20:NEXT:GOTO730
700   NEXT
720   GOTO750
```

Move the spaceship missile make UFO sound.

```
730   IFGS=0THEN750
740   IFSE=3THENHC=HC+1: PRINT"[S] [Q] [Q] [Q] [Q] [Q] [Q] [Q] [Q] [Q] [Q]
      [Q] [Q] [Q] [Q] [Q] [Q] [Q] [Q] [Q] [Q] [Q] [Q] ▬ [R]"HC
745   IFSE=2THENHC=HC+2: PRINT"[S] [Q] [Q] [Q] [Q] [Q] [Q] [Q] [Q] [Q] [Q]
      [Q] [Q] [Q] [Q] [Q] [Q] [Q] [Q] [Q] [Q] [Q] [Q] ▬ [R]"HC
750   POKESS,0:POKESS+1,40
760   POKEV+21,PEEK(V+21)AND(255-2^2)
770   POKEV+40,INT((119-HC)/20)
780   IFHC>99THEN2100
790   GOTO200
800   REM UFO SOUND
810   FORI=SSTOSS+23:POKEI,0:NEXT:POKESS+24,5
820   POKESS+5,17:POKESS+6,218:POKESS,0:POKESS+1,40:POKESS+2,70:
      POKESS+3,6
830   POKESS+12,17:POKESS+13,218:POKESS+7,0:POKESS+8,40:POKESS+9
      ,175:POKESS+10,15
840   POKESS+4,65:POKESS+11,65
850   RETURN
```

Print the background, make sprites define variables.

```
1000  REM GAME SCREEN
1020  POKE53280,3:POKE53281,3
1060  PRINT"[C] [Q] [Q] [Q] [Q] [Q] [Q] [Q] [Q] [Q] [Q] [Q] [Q] [Q] [Q] [Q] [Q]
      [C]";
1080  PRINT"▲ ▲ ▲ ▲ ▲ ▲ ▲ ▲ ▲ [R] ◤ ◥ ▬ ▲ ▲   ▲
      ▲ ▲ ▲ ▲ ▲ [R] [E] ◤ ◥ "
1100  PRINT"▲ ▲ ▲ ▲ ▲ ▲ ▲ ▲ [R] [C] ◤ ▲ ▲ ◥ ▬ ▲ ▲
      ▲ ▲ ▲ ▲ ▲ [R] [E] ◤ ▲ ▲ ◥ "
1120  PRINT"▲ ▲ ▲ ▲ ▲ [R] [C] ◤ ◥ ◤ ▲ ▲ ▲ ▲ ◥ ▬ ▲
      ▲ ▲ ▲ ▲ [R] [E] ◤ ▲ ▲ ▲ ▲ ◥ ▬ ▲ ▲ [R] ◤ ◥ "
1140  PRINT"▲ ▲ ▲ ▲ [R] [C] ◤ ▲ ▲ ▬ ◥ [R] ▲ ▲ ▲ ▲ ▲
      ◥ ▬ ▲ ▲ ▲ [R] [E] ◤ ▲ ▲ ▲ ▲ ▲ ▲ ▲ ◥ ◤ ▲ ▲ ◥ "
1160  PRINT"▲ ▲ ▲ [R] [C] ◤ ▲ ▲ ▲ ▲ ▲ ▲ ▲ ▲ ▲ ▲ ◥
      ▬ ▲ [R] [E] ◤ ▲ ▲ ▲ ▲ ▲ ▲ ▲ ▲ ▲ ╲ ▲ ▲ ▲ ◥ ▬
      ▲ ▲ ▲ ▲ [I] ▌ ▲ ▲ [I] ╯ "
```

```
1180    PRINT"                                              
                                                  
                              "
1200    PRINT"                                              
                                                  
                              "
1220    PRINT"                                              
                                                  
                              ";
1240    PRINT"                                              
                              ";
1260    PRINT"                                              
                              ";
1280    PRINT"                                              
                              ";
1300    PRINT"                          R  O  A  D  
                  P  A  T  R  O  L        "
1320    PRINT"             MOVE  PATROL  CAR  LEFT  
          WITH  Z  KEY"
1330    PRINT"           MOVE  PATROL  CAR  RIGHT  WITH
          M  KEY"
1340    PRINT"           FIRE  USING  SPACEBAR"
1360    PRINT"           OR  USE  JOYSTICK  IN  PORT  
        A"
1370    PRINT"    HOLD  F1  KEY  TO  START  OR  F7  KEY
          TO  FINISH"
1500    REM INITIAL LOCATIONS
1510    POKE650,128:V=53248:SS=54272:SE=3:GOSUB5000
1520    POKE2040,13:POKE2041,14:POKE2042,15
1530    POKEV+21,3:POKEV+39,0:POKEV+40,6:POKEV+29,SE
1550    CR=216:CC=INT(RND(.)*200)+40
1560    SR=INT(RND(.)*90)+40
1580    SC=INT(RND(.)*230)+20
1600    SX=INT((RND(.)*9)+8)*(1-(INT(RND(.)*3))):IFSX=0THEN1600
1620    SY=INT((RND(.)*9)+8)*(1-(INT(RND(.)*3)))
1640    GOSUB800:GOTO200
2000    REM BLANK TITLE SCREEN
2020    GS=1:B$="                    ":B$=B$+B$:B$=B$+B$
        :B$=B$+B$:B$=B$+B$
2040    PRINT"    "B$B$B$
2060    RETURN
```

> The patrol car is destroyed, prompt player for another game.

```
2100    REM PATROL CAR DESTROYED
2120    PRINT"                                           
                    "SPC(INT(CC/8));
2130    POKEV+21,0:POKESS+4,0:POKESS+11,0:POKESS+12,75:POKESS+13,1
        8:POKESS+24,15
2140    FORI=1TO4:PRINT"          ";:FORT=1TO80:NEXT:PRINT"  
              ";:POKESS+11,129
```

99

```
2150    FORT=1TO100:NEXT:NEXT:POKESS+11,0
2160    IFHS>HHTHENHH=HS
2170    PRINT:PRINT" ▢ ▢ ▢ ▢ ◨ ◨ ◨ ◨ ◨ ◨ ◨ ◨ ◨ ◨ ◨ ◪
        ◩HIGHEST ▲ HITS ▲ ON ▲ UFO:"HH
2180    PRINT" ◪ ◨ ◨ ◨ ◨ ◨ ◨ ◨ ◨ ◨ ◨ ◨ ◨ ◨ ◪ ANOTHER ▲
        GAME(Y/N)"
2200    GETA$:IFA$="Y"THENHS=0:HC=0:RESTORE:GS=0:GOTO1000
2220    IFA$<>"N"THEN2200
2230    SYS65535
```

> The UFO was destroyed and data for patrol and spaceship.

```
2500    REM UFO DESTROYED
2520    POKESS+4,0:POKESS+11,0:POKESS+5,78:POKESS+6,22:POKESS+24,1
        5:POKESS+4,129
2540    FORI=1TO15:POKEV+39,I:FORT=1TO100:NEXT:NEXT:POKESS+4,0
2560    POKEV+21,2
2570    PRINT" ▨ ◖ ◖ ◖ ◖ ◖ ◖ ◖ ◖ ◖ ◖ ◖ ◖ ◖ ◖ ◖ ◖
        ◖ ◖ ◖ ◖ "
2580    GOTO2160
5000    REM UFO,PATROL CAR & FIRE DATA
5020    FORI=0TO191:READA:POKE(832+I),A:NEXT:RETURN
5040    DATA0,0,0,0,0,0,0,0,0,0,0,0,0,0,34,0,0,34,0,0,255,0
5060    DATA3,60,192,6,0,96,31,255,248,31,255,248,6,0,96,3,255,192
        ,0,255,0
5080    DATA0,0,0,0,0,0,0,0,0,0,0,0,0,0,0,0,0,0,0,0,0,0,0,0
5100    DATA0,0,0,0,0,0,0,0,0,0,0,0,0,0,0,0,0,0,0,0,0,0,0,0
5120    DATA0,24,0,0,24,0,17,255,136,11,255,208,6,0,96,31,255,248,
        63,255,252
5140    DATA13,129,176,7,0,224,2,0,64,0,0,0,0,0,0,0,0,0,0,0
5160    DATA0,60,0,0,60,0,0,60,0,0,60,0,0,60,0,0,60,0,0,60,0,0,60,
        0,0,60,0,0,60,0
5180    DATA0,60,0,0,60,0,0,60,0,0,60,0,0,60,0,0,60,0,0,60,0,0,60,
        0,0,60,0,0,60,0
5200    DATA0,60,0,0
```

CHEXSUM

0=0	270=1085	380=525
10=579	275=2203	500=836
20=0	280=1576	510=5144
25=2473	285=3657	520=5278
30=1770	290=3805	530=2096
35=1761	300=131	540=2816
40=1753	310=527	550=939
45=564	315=869	560=1232
200=865	320=3369	570=1168
210=1535	322=3371	575=1719
220=1216	325=701	580=388
240=1413	330=1331	590=1355
250=2286	340=1317	600=0
255=1972	345=529	610=2237
260=3022	350=1191	620=2203
265=2826	360=1315	640=1378

```
660=3284          2140=5599
680=3801          2150=1978
700=131           2160=1300
720=530           2170=3511
730=868           2180=2039
740=2981          2200=3386
745=2983          2220=1181
750=1205          2230=431
760=2159          2500=0
770=1742          2520=4962
780=984           2540=3496
790=525           2560=616
800=0             2570=762
810=2608          2580=582
820=4596          5000=0
830=5160          5020=2404
840=1581          5040=2563
850=143           5060=3610
1000=0            5080=2436
1020=1175         5100=2638
1060=994          5120=3805
1080=2058         5140=2593
1100=2147         5160=4361
1120=2995
1140=2860
1160=3865
1180=3529         5180=4361
1200=3777         5200=537
1220=2483
1240=2308         TOTAL= 257898
1260=2308
1280=2380
1300=2701
1320=3189
1330=3133
1340=2008
1360=2436
1370=3596
1500=0
1510=2797
1520=1732
1530=2914
1550=2168
1560=1518
1580=1558
1600=4209
1620=3100
1640=912
2000=0
2020=4844
2040=589
2060=143
2100=0
2120=1796
2130=4918
```

Snakepit

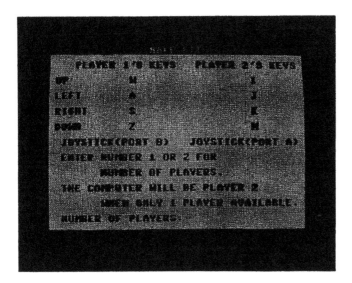

Pit two snakes against each other to make one bite the other's tail.

You can play an opponent or the computer, using the keyboard or joysticks. Do not run into the wall, do not bite your own tail or turn back on yourself. You must try and block the other snake's path so he runs into your tail.

Seven bites of the tail determines the winner of each game.

Do not hold keys down or the joystick in a fixed position; the snake will run in one direction until a new direction given.

VARIABLES

CO = Colour offset address and sound register

JL = Left joystick (Port B) Value

JR = Right joystick (Port A) Value

XI = Left snake X direction increment

YI = Left snake Y direction increment

X2 = Right snake X direction increment

Y2 = Right snake Y direction increment

PI = Screen location of left snake

P2 = Screen location of right snake

N = Number of players

F = Speed variable

SI = Left snake score

S2 = Right snake score

```
1       REM    SNAKEPIT
2       CO=54272:GOTO2000
5       REM    GET DIRECTION
6       IFN=1THEN8
7       IFJL<>0THEN18
```

Scan the joystick port, if pressed then move snake.

```
8       JL=PEEK(56321)
10      JL=15-(JLAND15)
12      IFJL=0THEN18
14      IFJL=1THENX1=0:Y1=-1:GOTO100
15      IFJL=2THENX1=0:Y1=1:GOTO100
16      IFJL=8THENX1=1:Y1=0:GOTO100
17      IFJL=4THENX1=-1:Y1=0:GOTO100
18      JL=0:JR=PEEK(56320)
19      JR=15-(JRAND15)
20      IFJR=0THEN50
21      IFJR=1THENX2=0:Y2=-1:GOTO100
22      IFJR=2THENX2=0:Y2=1:GOTO100
23      IFJR=8THENX2=1:Y2=0:GOTO100
24      IFJR=4THENX2=-1:Y2=0:GOTO100
50      GETA$:IFA$=""THEN100
55      IFA$="I"THENX2=0:Y2=-1:GOTO100
60      IFA$="W"THENX1=0:Y1=-1:GOTO100
65      IFA$="M"THENX2=0:Y2=1:GOTO100
70      IFA$="Z"THENX1=0:Y1=1:GOTO100
75      IFA$="K"THENX2=1:Y2=0:GOTO100
80      IFA$="S"THENX1=1:Y1=0:GOTO100
85      IFA$="J"THENX2=-1:Y2=0:GOTO100
90      IFA$="A"THENX1=-1:Y1=0:GOTO100
```

Plot the players snake and the other players snake.

```
100     REM PLOT PLAYER POSITION
120     P1=P1+X1+(Y1*40):P=P1:S=1:GOSUB200
130     IFS=0THEN2380
135     IFN=1THENGOSUB600
140     P2=P2+X2+(Y2*40):P=P2:S=2:GOSUB200
150     IFS=0THEN2380
160     POKEP1,81:POKEP1+CO,2
180     POKEP2,87:POKEP2+CO,5
190     FORT=1TOF*F+F*20:NEXT:GOTO5
200     REM CHECK FOR HIT
220     IFPEEK(P)=32THENRETURN
230     FORI=4TO0STEP-1:POKE53280,I:GOSUB500
240     POKEP,81:POKEP+54272,S*3-1:FORT=1TO60:NEXT
250     POKEP,81:POKEP+54272,3:NEXT
260     IFS=1THENS2=S2+1:S=0
270     IFS=2THENS1=S1+1:S=0
```

```
280    FORT=1TO200:NEXT
290    IFS1<7ANDS2<7THENRETURN
300    REM WINNERS ROUTINE
320    GOSUB1000:PRINT" ▤ ▨ ▧ ▥ PLAYER ▲ 1: ▲ ▲ ▥ ▥ ▥ ▥
       ▥ ▥ ▥ ▥ ▥ ▥ ▥ ▥ ▥ ▥ ▥ ▥ ▤ PLAYER ▲ 2: ▲ ▲ "
340    PRINT" ▤ ▥ ▨ "SPC(10)S1SPC(24)" ▤ "S2
350    IFS1<S2THENN=2:PRINT" ▤ ▨ ▤ "
360    IFS2<S1THENN=1:PRINT" ▤ ▨ ▥ "
390    PRINT" ▥ ▥ ▥ ▥ ▥ ▥ ▥ ▥ ▥ ▥ ▥ ▥ ▥ ▥ ▥ ▥ ▥ ▨ W
       INNER....PLAYER ▲ ";
400    PRINTN
420    PRINT" ▥ ▥ ▥ ▥ ▥ ▥ ▥ ▥ ▥ ▥ ▥ ▥ ▥ ▥ ▥ ▥ ▥ ▥ ANOT
       HER ▲ GAME? ▲ (Y/N)"
430    GET A$:IFA$="Y"THENRUN
440    IFA$<>"N"THEN430
450    SYS65535
460    END
```

> Generate sound, the computer makes its move, set screen colours.

```
500    REM SOUND
510    POKECO+6,240:POKECO+4,17
520    POKECO+1,34:POKECO,75
530    FORT=1TO100:NEXT
540    POKECO+1,0:POKECO,0
550    POKECO+4,33:POKECO+1,6:POKECO,206
560    FORT=1TO200:NEXT
570    POKECO+1,0:POKECO,0
590    RETURN
600    REM COMPUTERS MOVE
620    IFPEEK(P2+X2+Y2*40)=32ANDRND(.)<.85THENRETURN
650    XN=X2:YN=Y2:Y2=0
655    X2=1-(INT(RND(.)*3)):IFX2=0THEN655
660    X=PEEK(P2+X2+Y2*40):IFX=32THENIFX2=1THENA$="K":RETURN
680    IFX=32THENIFX2=-1THENA$="J":RETURN
700    X2=0
710    Y2=1:X=PEEK(P2+X2+Y2*40):IFX=32THENA$="M":RETURN
720    Y2=-1:X=PEEK(P2+X2+Y2*40):IFX=32THENA$="I":RETURN
740    X2=XN:Y2=YN
760    RETURN
1000   POKE53280,0:POKE53281,3
1010   PRINT" ▥ ▨ ▪ ▲ ▲ ▲ ▲ ▲ ▲ ▲ ▲ ▲ ▲ ▲ ▲ ▲ ▲ ▲
       ▲ SNAKE ▲ PIT ▲ ▲ ▲ ▲ ▲ ▲ ▲ ▲ ▲ ▲ ▲ ▲ ▲
       ▲ ▲ "
1020   FORI=1TO22:PRINT" ▮▮ ▨ ▲ ▲ ":NEXT
1030   PRINT" ▨ ▮▮ ▲ ▲ ▲ ▲ ▲ ▲ ▲ ▲ ▲ ▲ ▲ ▲
       ▲ ▲ ▲ ▲ ▲ ▲ ▲ ▲ ▲ ▲ ▲ ▲
       ▲ ▲ ▲ ▲ ▲ ▲ ▤ "
1040   POKE2023,160:POKE56295,0
1050   RETURN
```

105

```
2000    GOSUB1000
2080    PRINT" ◼ ◼ ◼ ◼ ◼ PLAYER ▲ 1'S ▲ KEYS ▲ ▲ ▲ PLAYER ▲
        2'S ▲ KEYS"
2100    PRINT" ◼ ◼ UP"SPC(9)"W"SPC(17)"I"
2120    PRINT" ◼ ◼ LEFT"SPC(7)"A"SPC(17)"J"
2140    PRINT" ◼ ◼ RIGHT"SPC(6)"S"SPC(17)"K"
2160    PRINT" ◼ ◼ DOWN"SPC(7)"Z"SPC(17)"M"
2200    PRINT" ◼ ◼ ◼ JOYSTICK(PORT ▲ B) ▲ ▲ ▲ JOYSTICK(PORT ▲
        A)"
2240    PRINT" ◼ ◼ ◼ ENTER ▲ NUMBER ▲ 1 ▲ OR ▲ 2 ▲ FOR"
2250    PRINT" ◼ ◼ ◼ ◼ ◼ ◼ ◼ ◼ NUMBER ▲ OF ▲ PLAYERS."
2260    PRINT" ◼ ◼ ◼ THE ▲ COMPUTER ▲ WILL ▲ BE ▲ PLAYER ▲ 2"
2270    PRINT" ◼ ◼ ◼ ◼ ◼ ◼ ◼ ◼ ◼ WHEN ▲ ONLY ▲ 1 ▲ PLAYER
        ▲ AVAILABLE."
2280    PRINT" ◼ ◼ ◼ NUMBER ▲ OF ▲ PLAYERS: ▲ ";
2290    PRINT" ◻ ▲ ◼ ";:FORT=1TO80:NEXT
2300    GETA$:IFA$="1"ORA$="2"THEN2325
2320    PRINT" ◼ ▲ ◼ ";:FORT=1TO80:NEXT:GOTO2290
2325    N=VAL(A$)
2330    PRINT" ◼ ◻ ◻ ◻ ◻ ◻ ◻ ◻ ◻ ◻ ◻ ◻ ◻ ◻ ◻ ◻
        ◻ ◻ ◻ ◻ ◻ ◻ ◼ ◼ ENTER ▲ SPEED ▲ (1:FAST ▲ - ▲ 9:SLO
        W) ▲ ";:GOTO2340
2334    PRINT" ◻ ▲ ◼ ";:FORT=1TO80:NEXT
2336    PRINT" ◼ ▲ ◼ ";:FORT=1TO80:NEXT
2340    GETA$:IFA$<"1"ORA$>"9"THEN2334
2360    F=VAL(A$):GOSUB60000
2380    GOSUB1000:PRINT" ◼ ◻ ◼ ◼ PLAYER ▲ 1: ▲ ▲ ◼ ◼ ◼ ◼
        ◼ ◼ ◼ ◼ ◼ ◼ ◼ ◼ ◼ ◼ PLAYER ▲ 2: ▲ ▲ "
2390    PRINT" ◼ ◼ ◻ "SPC(10)S1SPC(24)" ◼ "S2
2400    REM SET RANDOM WALLS
2420    NW=INT(RND(.)*4):PRINT" ◼ ";
2430    IFNW=0THEN2600
2440    FORI=1TONW
2460    FORJ=1TORND((.)*6)+3
2480    PRINT:NEXT
2500    PRINTSPC((RND(.)*8)+8):FORK=1TORND(.)*16+8:PRINT" ◼ ◻ ▲
        ";:NEXT
2540    NEXT
2600    REM SET INITIAL POSITIONS
2620    P1=1106:P2=1141:X1=0:X2=0:Y1=1:Y2=1:S=9:POKE198,0
2630    IFN=2THEN2640
2640    FORI=COTOCO+24:POKEI,0:NEXT
2650    POKECO+24,15:POKECO+4,0
2660    GOTO20
60000   FORI=828TO853:READA:POKEI,A:NEXT:SYS828:RETURN
60010   DATA120,169,73,141,20,3,169,3,141,21,3,88,96,169,1,141,139
        ,2,169,0
60020   DATA141,140,2,76,49,234
```

CHECKSUM

1=0	400=231	2360=1149
2=1283	420=2193	2380=3312
5=0	430=1263	2390=1402
6=678	440=1124	2400=0
7=991	450=431	2420=1576
8=905	460=129	2430=938
10=1151	500=0	2440=766
12=805	510=1520	2460=1487
14=2339	520=1228	2480=342
15=2174	530=975	2500=3752
16=2181	540=1101	2540=131
17=2341	550=2015	2600=0
18=1413	560=974	2620=3937
19=1169	570=1101	2630=843
20=809	590=143	2640=1741
21=2346	600=0	2650=1466
22=2181	620=3073	2660=472
23=2188	650=1521	60000=2461
24=2345	655=2441	60010=3632
50=1212	660=3915	60020=1157
55=2419	680=2285	
60=2428	700=370	TOTAL= 200236
65=2220	710=3666	
70=2236	720=3858	
75=2221	740=1061	
80=2230	760=143	
85=2393	1000=1172	
90=2386	1010=2724	
100=0	1020=1495	
120=2745	1030=2316	
130=842	1040=1211	
135=927	1050=143	
140=2752	2000=348	
150=842	2080=3003	
160=1252	2100=1460	
180=1251	2120=1604	
190=2201	2140=1719	
200=0	2160=1619	
220=1117	2200=3196	
230=2101	2240=2075	
240=2866	2250=2004	
250=1481	2260=2652	
260=1727	2270=3023	
270=1729	2280=1854	
280=974	2290=1534	
290=1398	2300=1967	
300=0	2320=2365	
320=3312	2325=654	
340=1402	2330=4427	
350=1493	2334=1534	
360=1493	2336=1680	
390=2208	2340=1975	

Detonator

Position the space ship within firing range of the hollowed sections of the three mountains and detonate the small bombs in these sections. The idea is to drop the bomb sitting on top of each mountain as far as possible into the mountain in order to blow it up.

However, if you touch any of the mountains, you blow up and the game is over. Engine malfunctions become more common as game proceeds.

CONTROLS

'Q', 'Z'   : up, down
'I', 'P'   : left, right
space bar   : fire

VARIABLES

VL,W,A,HI,LW	= sound effects
DB(I,J)	= "doomsday bomb" I's position (J)
PEEK(178)	= direction of ship
LV	= level of bomb
BD	= bomb to drop
SC,R	= score, round
RW,C	= row, column
SP	= starting position for blankout

```
1    REM DETONATOR
10   POKE53280,0:POKE53281,0:PRINT" ▚ ▲ ▲ ▲ ▲ ▲ ▲
     ▲ ▲ ▲ ▲ ▲ ▲ ▲ ▤ DETONATOR":PRINT" ▨ ▨ ▨ ▨ ▨ ▨
     ▨ ▨ ▨ ▨ "
15   V=53248:POKEV+21,0:POKEV+16,0:POKE2040,192:POKE2041,193:
     POKEV+39,6
20   POKEV+40,0:FORI=12288TO12350:READQ:POKEI,Q:NEXT
30   FORI=12352TO12357:POKEI,255:NEXT
35   FORI=12358TO12414:POKEI,0:NEXT
50   FORI=49152TO49287:READQ:POKEI,Q:NEXT
60   VL=54296:W=54276:A=54277:HI=54273:LW=54272
70   FORI=LWTOLW+24:POKEI,0:NEXT
90   PRINT" ▲ ▲ ▲ ▲ ▲ ▲ ▲ ▲ ▲ ◣ HIT ▲ ANY ▲ KEY ▲ T
     O ▲ START"
95   GETX$:IFX$=""THEN95
100  POKE53281,12:R=R+1:PRINT" ▚ ▨ ▨ ▨ ▨ ▨ ▲ ▲ ▲
     ▲ ▲ ▲ ▲ ▤ ● ▲ ▲ ▲ ▲ ▲ ▲ ▲ ▲ ▲ ▲
     ▲ ● ▲ ▲ ▲ ▲ ▲ ▲ ▲ ▲ ▲ ▲ ▲ ● ▥ ";
101  POKE53280,9
102  PRINT" ▲ ▲ ▲ ▲ ▲ ▲ ▲ ▲ ▨ ◤ ▲ ◥ ▰ ▲ ▲ ▲ ▲
     ▲ ▲ ▲ ▲ ▲ ▲ ▨ ◤ ▲ ▰ ▲ ▲ ▲ ▲ ▲
     ▲ ▲ ▲ ▲ ▲ ▨ ◤ ▲ ▰ ";
104  PRINT" ▲ ▲ ▲ ▲ ▲ ▲ ▲ ▨ ▲ ▰ ▨+▥ ▨ ▲ ▰ ▲
     ▲ ▲ ▲ ▲ ▲ ▲ ▲ ▨ ▲ ▰ ▨+▥ ▨ ▲ ▰
     ▲ ▲ ▲ ▲ ▲ ▲ ▲ ▨ ▲ ▰ ▨+▥ ";
106  PRINT" ▲ ▲ ▲ ▲ ▲ ▲ ▨ ▲ ▰ ▲ ▲ ▰ ▲
     ▲ ▲ ▲ ▲ ▲ ▨ ▲ ▲ ▰ ▲ ▲
     ▲ ▲ ▲ ▲ ▨ ▲ ▲ ▰ ";
108  PRINT" ▲ ▲ ▲ ▲ ▲ ▲ ▨ ◤ ▲ ▲ ▲ ◥ ▰ ▲ ▲ ▲
     ▲ ▲ ▲ ▲ ▲ ▨ ◤ ▲ DETONATOR ▲ ◥ ▰ ▲ ▲ ▲
     ▲ ▲ ▲ ▲ ▨ ◤ ▲ ▲ ▰ ";
110  PRINT" ▲ ▲ ▲ ▲ ▲ ▲ ▨ ▲ ▰ ▨+▥ ▲ ▨ ▲ ▰
     ▲ ▲ ▲ ▲ ▲ ▲ ▨ ▲ ▰ ▨+▥ ▲ ▨ ▲
     ▰ ▲ ▲ ▲ ▲ ▲ ▨ ▲ ▲ ▨+▥ ";
112  PRINT" ▲ ▲ ▲ ▲ ▲ ▲ ▨ ▲ ▲ ▰ ▲ ▲
     ▲ ▲ ▲ ▲ ▨ ▲ ▲ ▰ ▲ ▲
     ▲ ▲ ▲ ▨ ▲ ▲ ▰ ";
114  PRINT" ▲ ▲ ▲ ▲ ▨ ◤ ▲ ▲ ▲ ◥ ▰ ▲
     ▲ ▲ ▲ ▨ ◤ ▲ ▲ ▲ ◥ ▰ ▲
     ▲ ▲ ▨ ◤ ▲ ▲ ▲ ▰ ";
116  PRINT" ▲ ▲ ▲ ▲ ▲ ▨ ▲ ▰ ▲ ▲ ▨+▥ ▲ ▲ ▨ ▲
     ▰ ▲ ▲ ▲ ▲ ▲ ▨ ▲ ▰ ▲ ▲ ▨+▥ ▲ ▲ ▨
     ▲ ▰ ▲ ▲ ▲ ▲ ▨ ▲ ▰ ▲ ▲ ▨+▥ ";
118  PRINT" ▲ ▲ ▲ ▲ ▨ ▲ ▲ ▲ ▲ ▲ ▰ ▲ ▲
     ▲ ▲ ▲ ▨ ▲ ▲ ▲ ▲ ▰ ▲ ▲
     ▲ ▲ ▨ ▲ ▲ ▲ ▰ ";
120  PRINT" ▲ ▲ ▲ ▲ ▲ ▨ ◤ ▲ ▲ ▲ ◥ ▰ ▲ ▲
     ▲ ▲ ▲ ▨ ◤ ▲ ▲ ▲ ◥ ▰ ▲ ▲
     ▲ ▲ ▨ ◤ ▲ ▲ ▲ ▰ ";
```

```
122  PRINT"  ▲  ▲  ▲  ▲  ▲  🄻  ▲  ■  ▲  ▲  ▲  🄴 + 🄵  ▲  ▲  ▲  🄻
        ▲  ■  ▲  ▲  ▲  ▲  ▲  ▲  🄻  ▲  ■  ▲  ▲  ▲  🄴 + 🄵  ▲  ▲  ▲
        🄻  ▲  ■  ▲  ▲  ▲  ▲  ▲  🄻  ▲  ■  ▲  ▲  ▲  🄴 + 🄵 ";
124  PRINT"  ▲  ▲  ▲  ▲  ▲  🄻  ▲  ▲  ▲  ▲  ▲  ▲  ▲  ▲  ▲  ■  ▲  ▲
        ▲  ▲  ▲  ▲  🄻  ▲  ▲  ▲  ▲  ▲  ▲  ▲  ▲  ■  ▲  ▲
        ▲  ▲  ▲  🄻  ▲  ▲  ▲  ▲  ▲  ■ ";
126  PRINT"  ▲  ▲  ▲  🄻  ◤  ▲  ▲  ▲  ▲  ▲  ▲  ▲  ▲  ◥  ■
        ▲  ▲  ▲  🄻  ◤  ▲  ▲  ▲  ▲  ▲  ▲  ▲  ◥  ■  ▲  ▲
        🄻  ◤  ▲  ▲  🄻  ▲  ▲  ◥  ■ ";
128  PRINT"  ▲  ▲  ▲  🄻  ▲  ■  ▲  ▲  ▲  ▲  🄴 + 🄵  ▲  ▲  ▲
        🄻  ▲  ■  ▲  ▲  ▲  🄻  ▲  ■  ▲  ▲  ▲  🄴 + 🄵  ▲  ▲
        ▲  🄻  ▲  ■  ▲  ▲  ▲  🄻  ▲  ■  ▲  ▲  ▲  🄴 + 🄵 ";
130  PRINT"  ▲  ▲  ▲  ▲  🄻  ▲  ▲  ▲  ▲  ▲  ▲  ▲  ▲  ■
        ▲  ▲  ▲  🄻  ▲  ▲  ▲  ▲  ▲  ▲  ▲  ■
        ▲  🄻  ▲  ▲  ▲  ▲  ■ ";
132  PRINT"  🄻  ◥  ■  ▲  ▲  🄻  ◤  ▲  ■  ▲  ▲  ▲  🄴 + 🄵  ▲
        ▲  ▲  🄻  ▲  ◥  ■  ▲  ▲  🄻  ◤  ▲  ■  ▲  ▲  ▲  🄴 + 🄵  ▲
        ▲  ▲  🄻  ▲  ◥  ■  ▲  ▲  🄻  ◤  ▲  ■  ▲  ▲  ▲  🄴 + 🄵
        ";
134  PRINT"  🄻  ▲  ▲  ▲  ▲  ▲  ▲  ▲  ▲  ▲  ▲  ▲  ▲  ▲  ▲
        ▲  ▲  ▲  ▲  ▲  ▲  ▲  ▲  ▲  ▲  ▲  ▲  ▲  ▲  ▲
        ▲  ▲  ▲  ▲  ▲  ■ ";
```

> Move the spaceship round the mountain and keep direction.

```
140  GOSUB1000:POKEV,25:POKEV+1,55:POKEV+21,1:POKEV+16,0
150  DB(1,1)=1233:DB(2,1)=1248:DB(3,1)=1263
160  POKEV+31,0
200  SYS(49152):IFPEEK(179)=1THENGOSUB300
205  LM=3*R:IFRND(1)*100<LMTHENI=INT(RND(1)*3+1):POKE178,I
210  IFPEEK(1273)=32ANDPEEK(1233)<>32THENBD=1:GOTO500
215  IFPEEK(1288)=32ANDPEEK(1248)<>32THENBD=2:GOTO500
220  IFPEEK(1303)=32ANDPEEK(1263)<>32THENBD=3:GOTO500
230  IF(PEEK(V+31)AND1)=0THEN200
240  GOTO700
```

> Fire laser at interior of mountain check if a detonation.

```
300  XP=PEEK(V)+256*(PEEK(V+16)AND1)+16
310  IFXP>255THENPOKEV+16,PEEK(V+16)OR2:POKEV+2,XP-256:GOTO320
315  POKEV+16,PEEK(V+16)AND253:POKEV+2,XP
320  POKEV+3,PEEK(V+1)+5:POKEV+21,3
330  REM NOISE
340  RW=INT((PEEK(V+3)-54)/8):C=INT(XP/8):I=1024+40*RW+C:KL=
     PEEK(I)
345  IFPEEK(I)=32ANDPEEK(I-1)=160THENGOSUB400:GOTO350
347  IFPEEK(I)=43ANDPEEK(I-1)=160THENGOSUB400
350  POKEV+21,1:RETURN
400  IFC<10THENC=9:GOTO420
405  IFC<25THENC=24:GOTO420
410  C=39
```

111

```
420    POKEVL,15:POKELW,220:POKEHI,68:POKEW,129:POKEA,15
430    POKE984+40*RW+C,32:POKE1024+40*RW+C,32:POKE1064+40*RW+C,32
440    FORTM=1TO10:NEXT:POKEA,0:POKEW,0:RETURN
```

> Drop the bomb, from top of mountain down the tube, blast mountain.

```
500    LV=0
505    POKEDB(BD,1),32:DB(BD,1)=DB(BD,1)+40:IFPEEK(DB(BD,1))<>32
       THEN600
510    POKEDB(BD,1),81:POKEDB(BD,1)+54272,2:LV=LV+1:SC=SC+LV:
       GOSUB1000:GOTO505
```

> Ship is destroyed, call explosion.

```
600    POKEVL,15:POKEW,129:POKEA,15:POKELW,200:IFBD=3THEN650
602    IFBD=1THENSP=1264:GOTO605
603    SP=1279
605    FORI=SP+40*LVTOSPSTEP-40:FORJ=4TO14
610    POKEI+J,32:POKE53281,J:POKEHI,INT(RND(1)*20+2):NEXT:NEXT
620    POKE53281,12:POKEVL,0
630    IFPEEK(1233)=32ANDPEEK(1248)=32ANDPEEK(1263)=32THEN100
640    GOTO200
650    FORI=1298+40*LVTO1298STEP-40:FORJ=0TO6
660    POKEI+J,32:POKE53281,J:POKEHI,INT(RND(1)*20+2):NEXT:NEXT
670    POKE53281,12:POKEVL,0
680    GOTO630
700    FORI=LWTOLW+24:POKEI,0:NEXT
705    FORI=15TO0STEP-1:POKE12288+INT(RND(1)*60),0:POKE12288+INT(
       RND(1)*60),1
710    POKEVL,I:POKEW,129:POKEA,15:POKEHI,40:POKELW,200:NEXT
720    POKEV+21,0
```

> Game score is updated, data for spaceship and machine code routine.

```
800    PRINT" ";:POKE53281,0:POKE53280,0
810    PRINT"                                        GAME
        OVER                                   "
820    PRINT"                             YOUR   SCORE   WAS
        ";SC
830    GETX$:IFX$=""THENEND
840    GOTO830
1000   PRINT"
                                                   SCORE:   ";SC;
1010   RETURN
10000  DATA0,28,0,0,62,0,0,127,0,0,201,0,0,201,0,0,255,0,31,255,2
       48,63,255,252
10010  DATA127,255,254,255,255,255,127,255,254,63,255,252,31,255,
       248,7,255,224
```

```
10020 DATA7,255,224,1,255,128,0,255,0,0,0,0,0,0,0,0,0,0,0,0,0
10100 DATA165,197,133,180,169,0,133,179,165,180,201,60,208,4,169
      ,1,133,179,165
10110 DATA180,201,62,208,4,169,1,133,178,165,180,201,12,208,4,16
      9,2,133,178,165
10120 DATA180,201,33,208,4,169,3,133,178,165,180,201,41,208,4,16
      9,4,133,178,165
10130 DATA178,201,1,208,10,173,1,208,206,1,208,206,1,208,96,201,
      2,208,10,173,1
10140 DATA208,238,1,208,238,1,208,96,201,3,208,22,206,0,208,206,
      0,208,173,0,208
10150 DATA201,254,144,8,173,16,208,41,254,141,16,208,96,238,0,20
      8,238,0,208,173
10160 DATA0,208,201,2,176,8,173,16,208,9,1,141,16,208,96
```

CHECKSUM

1=0	215=3394	710=2859
10=4515	220=3374	720=616
15=4111	230=1690	800=1652
20=2823	240=529	810=2352
30=1872	300=2605	820=2170
35=1760	310=4145	830=1214
50=2106	315=2354	840=536
60=3352	320=2065	1000=2505
70=1778	330=0	1010=143
90=2481	340=5427	10000=4129
95=1196	345=3067	10010=4211
100=4897	347=2413	10020=2926
101=530	350=817	10100=4370
102=3481	400=1591	10110=4444
104=3970	405=1649	10120=4446
106=2758	410=357	10130=4295
108=3526	420=2681	10140=4394
110=3922	430=4542	10150=4392
112=2742	440=2039	10160=2698
114=3523	500=394	
116=3922	505=4463	TOTAL= 245726
118=2740	510=5381	
120=3520	600=3079	
122=3874	602=1890	
124=2740	603=570	
126=3521	605=2859	
128=3874	610=3400	
130=2742	620=1087	
132=5092	630=3330	
134=2342	640=525	
140=2964	650=2942	
150=2629	660=3400	
160=617	670=1087	
200=1944	680=532	
205=4057	700=1778	
210=3369	705=4628	

Letterbox

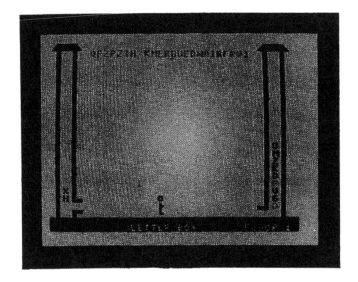

Catch the falling letters and post them in the letter box on the left. If you do not catch them they will go into the dead letter box on the right. If you fill the good letter box before the dead letter box then you will proceed to the next of the five floors. However, should the dead letter box be filled first then you will go back to the previous floor. The letters fall faster for each higher floor.

The mailman can be moved left and right with the left and right cursor keys prior to the letter falling. When the letter is falling the mailman can only be moved right by pressing the key that matches the letter that is falling. To move the mailman left, use the same key simultaneously with the shift key.

The game can be finished at any time by pressing the function 7 (seven) key.

VARIABLES

A$ (24) = Random letter table

A$ (0) = Used for mailman movement with cursor key

C$ = Colour table

LM$ = Left facing mailman

RM$ = Right facing mailman

LV = Floor level

S = Sound register

SL = Good letter stack (number from top)

SR = Missed letter stack (number from top)

X1 = Horizontal location of mailman

DX = Direction of mailman

N = Number of dropped letters
    Number of bells/buzzes to sound

K = Row number of dropped letter

M$ = Key pressed

M = ASC value of pressed key

K1 = Screen location for stacking letters

F = Colour of dropped letter

```
5      REM LETTER BOX
```

> Define variables, put letters in table, print the mailman.

```
20     DN$=" ▨ ▨ ▨ ▨ ▨ ▨ ▨ ▨ ▨ ▨ ▨ ▨ ▨ ▨ ▨ ▨
       ▨ ▨ ▨ ▨ ▨ ▨ ▨ "
30     BL$=" ▬ ▨ ▨ ▨ ▨ ▨   ▲ ▲ ▲ ▲ ▲ ▲ ▲
       ▲ ▲ ▲ ▲ "
40     RT$=" ▨ ▨ ▨ ▨ ▨ ▨ ▨ ▨ ▨ ▨ ▨ ▨ ▨ ▨ ▨ ▨
       ▨ ▨ ▨ ▨ ▨ ▨ ▨ ▨ ▨ ▨ ▨ ▨ ▨ ▨ ▨ ▨ ▨ ▨
       ▨ ▨ ▨ ▨ "
50     DIMA$(24):A$(0)=" ▨ ":C$=" ▨ ◤ ▨ ▨ ▨ ▨ ▨ ▨ "
60     LM$=" ▨ ● ▄ ▨ ▮▮ ▮▮ ◄ ▄ ▨ ▮▮ ▮▮ ◄ ▄ ":RM$=" ▨ ▄
       ● ▨ ▮▮ ▮▮ ▄ ► ▨ ▮▮ ▮▮ ▄ ► ":LV=1:POKE650,128:S=54272
100    SL=20:SR=21:X1=INT(RND(.)*8)+10:DX=1
110    IFLV<1THENLV=1
120    IFLV>5THENLV=5
140    GOSUB1000
160    FORL=1TO24:A$(L)=CHR$(INT(RND(.)*26+65)):NEXT
180    PRINTLEFT$(DN$,21)RIGHT$(RT$,X1)RM$;
190    E=INT(RND(.)*4)+1:F=E+6-LV
200    FORJ=ETOF:PRINT" ▨ ▨ ▨ ▨ ▨ ▨   ▲ ▲ ▲ ▲ ▲ ▲
       ▲ ▲ ▲ ▲ ▲ ▲ ▲ ▲ ▲ ▲ ▲ ▲ "
220    N=0:FORI=1TO24
```

> Drop letters randomly, move the letters round the screen.

```
230    GOSUB1500
240    PRINT" ▨ ▨ "MID$(C$,J,1)TAB(I+5)A$(I);
260    NEXT:NEXT
280    PRINT" ▨ ";:N=INT(RND(.)*24)+1
300    FORK=1TO22
310    PRINTLEFT$(DN$,K)TAB(5+N)" ▄ ▨ ▮▮ "MID$(C$,F,1)A$(N)" ▮▮ "
       ;
320    FORT=1TO85-(LV*12):NEXT:GOSUB1500
330    IFSL=0THENLV=LV+1:N=SR:GOSUB2000:GOTO100
340    IFK=23THEN160
350    NEXT
360    FORT=4+NTO32
370    IFT=X1THENGOSUB1580:T=T+1:GOTO400
380    PRINTTAB(T)" ▄ "MID$(C$,F)A$(N):PRINT" ▢ ";
```

> Moved missed letter into dead letter stack, sound buzzer.

```
400    NEXT
410    GOSUB5000
420    IFSR=0THENLV=LV-1:N=SL:GOSUB2500:GOTO100
450    GOTO160
```

116

```
1000    POKE53280,1:POKE53281,1:PRINT" ▉ "
1020    PRINT" ▉ ▉ ▉ ▉ ▲ ▲ ▲ ▲ ◀ ▬ ▲ ▲ ▲ ▲ ▲ ▲
        ▲ ▲ ▲ ▲ ▲ ▲ ▲ ▲ ▲ ▲ ▲ ▲ ▲ ▉
        ✿ ▉ ▲ ▲ ▲ ◀ "
1040    FORI=1TO22
1050    PRINT" ▉ ▉ ▉ ▉ ▉ ▉ ▬ ▲ ▲ ▲ ▲ ▲ ▲ ▲ ▲
        ▲ ▲ ▲ ▲ ▲ ▲ ▲ ▲ ▲ ▲ ▲ ▲ ▲ ▉
        ▉ ▉ ▉ ▬ "
1060    NEXT
1240    PRINT" ▉ ▬ ▲ ▲ ▲ ▲ ▲ ▲ ▲ ▲ ▲ ▲ ▲ ▲ ▲ ▲
        ▲ ▲ ▲ ▲ ▲ ▲ ▲ ▲ ▲ ▲ ▲ ▲
        ▲ ▲ "
1250    PRINT" ▉ ▬ ▲ ▲ ▲ ▲ ▲ ▲ ▲ ▲ ▲ ▲ ▲ LETTER ▲ B
        OX ▲ ▲ ▲ ▲ ▲ ▲ FLOOR ▲ ▲ ▲ ▉▉ ▉▉ ▉▉ "LV" ▉ "
1260    PRINTLEFT$(DN$,21)" ▉▉ ▉▉ ▉▉ ▉▉ ▬ ▉ ▉▉ ▉▉ ▲ ▉ ▉ ▬ ";
1270    PRINTLEFT$(BL$,29)" ▢ ▉▉ ▉▉ ▬ "
1280    RETURN
1500    REM MOVE MAILMAN
1520    GETM$:IFM$=""THEN1600
1530    IFM$=" ▉▉ "THENPRINT" ▉ ":END
1540    IFM$=A$(N)THENMM$=RM$:DX=1:GOTO1580
1550    M=ASC(M$):M=M-128
1560    IFM=ASC(A$(N)+CHR$(0))THENMM$=LM$:DX=-1:GOTO1580
1570    M$="":GOTO1600
1580    PRINTLEFT$(DN$,21)RIGHT$(RT$,X1)MM$;
1590    X1=X1+DX:IFX1<5THENX1=5
1595    IFX1>29THENX1=29
```

> Move mailman, letter went to good stack, sound bell and buzzer.

```
1600    IFK<20ORK>22THENRETURN
1630    IFDX=-1AND(X1<(N+3)ORX1>(N+5))THENRETURN
1640    IFDX=1AND(X1<(N+4)ORX1>(N+6))THENRETURN
1650    FORT=5+NTO5STEP-1
1655    PRINTLEFT$(DN$,22)TAB(T)MID$(C$,F)A$(N)" ▢ "LM$
1660    NEXT
1670    FORT=5TO2STEP-1
1680    PRINTLEFT$(DN$,22)TAB(T)MID$(C$,F)A$(N)" ▲ "
1690    NEXT
1700    PRINTLEFT$(DN$,22)TAB(5)" ▢ "LM$
1750    REM GOT LETTER STACK
1760    POKE56138,F+1
1770    FORK1=1026+SL*40TO1026+20*40STEP40
1780    POKEK1,PEEK(K1+40):POKEK1+54272,PEEK(K1+54312)
1790    NEXT
1800    POKEK1,32:POKEK1+54272,F+1:SL=SL-1
1820    N=1:GOSUB2000:K=23:X1=5:RETURN
2000    REM BELL SOUND
2020    FORL=0TO20:POKES+L,0:NEXT
2040    POKES+1,30:POKES+5,9:POKES+15,30:POKES+24,15
```

117

```
2060    FORL=1TON:POKES+4,29
2080    FORT=1TO300:NEXT:POKES+4,0
2100    NEXT:RETURN
2500    REM BUZZ SOUND
2520    FORL=0TO20:POKES+L,0:NEXT
2540    POKES+1,179:POKES+5,69:POKES+15,13:POKES+24,15
2560    FORL=1TON:POKES+4,29
2580    FORT=1TO300:NEXT:POKES+4,0
2600    NEXT:RETURN
5000    REM MISSED LETTER STACK
5010    POKE56209,F+1
5020    FORK1=1057+SR*40TO1057+21*40STEP40
5040    POKEK1,PEEK(K1+40):POKEK1+54272,PEEK(K1+54312)
5050    NEXT
5060    POKEK1,32:POKEK1+54272,F+1:SR=SR-1
5080    N=1:GOSUB2500:RETURN
```

CHECKSUM

5=0	420=3062	1690=131
20=1061	450=527	1700=1565
30=2317	1000=1643	1750=0
40=2115	1020=3171	1760=786
50=2588	1040=710	1770=2592
60=5870	1050=2957	1780=2856
100=3110	1060=131	1790=131
110=1126	1240=2111	1800=2505
120=1128	1250=3765	1820=1836
140=348	1260=1859	2000=0
160=3090	1270=1529	2020=1583
180=1826	1280=143	2040=2815
190=2327	1500=0	2060=1398
200=2418	1520=1297	2080=1634
220=1116	1530=1435	2100=332
230=352	1540=2708	2500=0
240=1888	1550=1421	2520=1583
260=320	1560=3728	2540=2926
280=1767	1570=1050	2560=1398
300=710	1580=1833	2580=1634
310=3059	1590=1946	2600=332
320=2093	1595=1197	5000=0
330=3044	1600=1380	5010=786
340=843	1630=3050	5020=2611
350=131	1640=2853	5040=2856
360=984	1650=1327	5050=131
370=2388	1655=2576	5060=2493
380=1981	1660=131	5080=934
400=131	1670=1069	
410=352	1680=2229	TOTAL= 141169

Crash Barrier

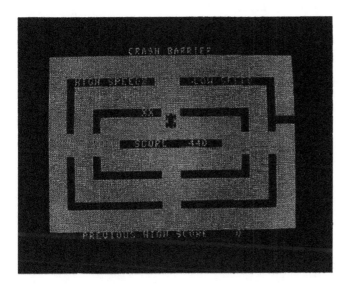

Test your skiill as a high speed driver. Race around the track swapping lanes whenever you feel like it. Use the A, W, D & Z keys to steer and press the X key to swap speeds — High speed to low speed and low speed to high speed.

Your car is red at low speed and green at high speed.

You will gain more points by keeping the keys depressed and you get higher points for high speed.

Do not crash into the walls and beware of the crash barriers that appear suddenly in front of you. You have 8 cars to demolish!

VARIABLES

HS = High score
SC = Score
G1 = Number of cars used
MS = Sound register
V   = Sprite register
DX = Horizontal increment/decrement
DY = Vertical increment/decrement
X1 = Horizontal location of car sprite
Y1 = Vertical location of car sprite
S1 = Speed
K   = Key value

```
10     REM  CRASH BARRIER
```

Build the racing car, position it at start, clear score.

```
40     FORN=0TO191:READA:POKE832+N,A:NEXT:MS=54272
50     GOSUB1000
60     PRINT" ▩ ▨ ▪ ▨ ▨ ▨ ▨ ▨ ▨ ▨ ▨ ▨ ▲ ▲ ▲ ▲ CRAS
       H ▲ BARRIER ▲ ▲ ▲ ▲ ▲ "
70     PRINT" ▩ ▨ ▨ ▨ ▨ ▨ ▨ ▨ ▨ ▨ ▨ ▨ ▨ ▨ ▨ ▨ ▨
       ▨ ▨ ▨ ▨ ▨ ▨ ▨ ▨ ▨ ▨ ▨ ▨ ▨ ▨ ▨ ▩ ▪ ▲ ▲
       ▲ ▲ ▲ "
80     PRINT" ▨ ▨ ▨ ▨ ▨ ▨ ▨ ▨ ▨ ▨ ▨ ▨ ▨ ▨ ▨ ▨ ▨ ▨
       ▨ ▨ ▨ ▨ ▨ ▨ ▨ ▨ ▨ ▨ ▨ ▨ ▨ ▨ ▨ ▨ ▨ ▨
       ▨ ▨ ▩ ▪ ";HS" ▩ ":G1=0:SC=0
100    POKEMS+4,0:POKEMS+24,10:POKEMS+5,102:POKEMS+6,255:POKEMS,1
       5:POKEMS+1,1
110    DX=0:DY=0:V=53248:X1=32:Y1=60:S1=8
120    POKEV,X1:POKEV+1,Y1:POKEV+16,0
130    POKE2040,13:POKEV+39,2:POKEV+21,1:POKEV+31,0
140    WAIT197,60,1:POKEMS+4,129
180    IFSC<0THENSC=0
190    PRINT" ▩ ▨ ▨ ▨ ▨ ▨ ▨ ▨ ▨ ▨ ▨ ▨ ▨ ▨ ▨ ▨ ▨
       ▨ ▨ ▨ ▨ ▨ ▨ ▨ ▨ ▨ ▨ ▨ ▩ ▪ "SPC(6-
       LEN(STR$(SC)))SC
```

Check keyboard, move car in current direction, add to score.

```
200    K=PEEK(197):IFK=64THENSC=SC+1:GOTO350
201    IFK<>23THEN204
202    IFS1=8THENS1=14:POKEV+39,5:POKEMS+24,15:GOTO260
203    IFS1=14THENS1=8:POKEV+39,2:POKEMS+24,10:GOTO260
204    IFK=9THENDX=0:DY=-S1:DR=0:POKE2040,13:GOTO260
206    IFK=18THENDX=S1:DY=0:DR=1:POKE2040,14:GOTO260
208    IFK=12THENDX=0:DY=S1:DR=1:POKE2040,13:GOTO260
210    IFK=10THENDX=-S1:DY=0:DR=0:POKE2040,14
260    SC=SC+S1
350    X1=X1+DX:Y1=Y1+DY
360    IFPEEK(V+16)=0ANDX1<24THENX1=24
365    IFPEEK(V+16)=0ANDX1>255THENX1=1:POKEV+16,3:GOTO500
370    IFPEEK(V+16)=3ANDX1>56THENX1=56
372    IFPEEK(V+16)=3ANDX1<1THENX1=255:POKEV+16,0:GOTO500
380    IFY1<50THENY1=50
390    IFY1>228THENY1=228
500    POKEV,X1:POKEV+1,Y1
510    IFRND(.)<.15THENGOSUB1500
515    IFRND(.)<.15THENGOSUB1600
518    IFRND(.)<.15THENGOSUB1700
520    IFPEEK(V+31)=0THEN180
522    POKEMS+6,0
525    POKEMS+24,15:POKEMS+4,0:POKEMS+1,72:POKEMS,179:POKEMS+5,14
       0:POKEMS+4,129
```

```
530    POKE198,0
532    POKE2041,15:POKEV+21,2:POKEV+40,2:POKEV+2,X1:POKEV+3,Y1
535    FORT=1TO800:NEXT:POKEMS+4,0
540    SC=SC-100:G1=G1+1:IFSC<0THENSC=0
```

> Game has ended, prompt for another, set highest score.

```
545    PRINT" ▨ ◩ ◩ ◩ ◩ ◩ ◩ ◩ ◩ ◩ ◩ ◩ ◩ ▨ ▨ ▨ ▨
       ▨ ▨ ▨ ▨ ▨ ▨ ▨ ▨ ▨ ▨ ▨ ▨ ▨ ▨ ▨ ▨ ◪ ■ "SPC(6-
       LEN(STR$(SC)))SC
550    PRINT" ▨ ◩ ◩ ◩ ◩ ◩ ◩ ◩ ◩ ◩ ▨ ▨ ▨ ▨ ▨ ▨ ▨
       ◪ ■ "SPC(G1)" ▲ "
560    IFG1<8THEN100
580    PRINT" ▨ ▨ ▨ ▨ ▨ ▨ ▨ ▨ ▨ ▨ ■ ANOTHER ▲ GAM
       E ▲ (Y/N)":FORT=1TO70:NEXT
590    PRINT" ▨ ▨ ▨ ▨ ▨ ▨ ▨ ▨ ▨ ▨ ▨ ◪ ■ ANOTHER ▲
       GAME ▲ (Y/N)":FORT=1TO70:NEXT
600    GETA$:IFA$=""THEN580
620    IFA$="N"THENPRINT" ◱ ":END
640    IFSC>HSTHENHS=SC
650    GOTO60
```

> Print car racetrack, previous high score.

```
1000   POKE53280,6:POKE53281,3
1020   PRINT" ◱ ■ ";
1030   PRINT" ◪ ▲ ▲ ▲ ▲ ▲ ▲ ▲ ▲ ▲ ▲ ▲ ▲ ▲
       ▲ ▲ ▲ ▲ ◧ ▲ ■ ";
1040   PRINT" ◪ ■ ▲ ■ ▲ ▲ ▲ ▲ ▲ ▲ ▲ ▲ ▲ ▲
       ▲ ▲ ▲ ▲ ▲ ◪ ▲ ◧ ▲ ■ ";
1050   PRINT" ◪ ■ ▲ ▲ ▲ ▲ ▲ ▲ ▲ ▲ ▲ ▲ ▲ ▲
       ▲ ▲ ▲ ◪ ■ ▲ ◧ ▲ ■ ";
1060   PRINT" ◪ ■ ▲ ▲ ■ ▲ ▲ ▲ ▲ ▲ ▲ ▲ ▲ ▲
       ▲ ▲ ▲ ◪ ▲ ◧ ▲ ■ ";
1070   PRINT" ◪ ■ ▲ ■ ▲ ▲ ▲ ◪ ■ ▲ HIGH ▲ SPEED ▨ ▲ ■
       ▲ ■ ▲ ▲ ▲ ▲ ◪ ■ ▲ LOW ▲ SPEED ◪ ▲ ■ ▲ ▲ ■
       ▲ ▲ ▲ ◪ ■ ▲ ◧ ▲ ■ ";
1080   PRINT" ◪ ■ ▲ ■ ▲ ▲ ▲ ◪ ▲ ■ ▲ ▲ ▲
       ▲ ▲ ◪ ▲ ■ ▲ ▲ ◪ ▲ ◧ ▲ ■ ";
1090   PRINT" ◪ ■ ▲ ■ ▲ ▲ ▲ ◪ ■ ▲ ■ ▲ ▲ ▲ ▲
       ▲ ▲ ▲ ◪ ■ ▲ ■ ▲ ▲ ▲ ◪ ■ ▲ ◧ ▲ ■ ";
1100   PRINT" ◪ ■ ▲ ■ ▲ ▲ ◪ ▲ ■ ▲ ▲
       ▲ ▲ ◪ ▲ ■ ▲ ▲ ◪ ▲ ◧ ▲ ■ ";
1110   PRINT" ◪ ■ ▲ ■ ▲ ◪ ▲ ▲ ◪ ■ ▲ ■ ▲ ◪ ▲ ▲ ◪
       ■ ▲ XXXXXXX ▲ ■ ▲ ▲ ◪ ▲
       ▲ ■ ▲ ◪ ▲ ◪ ▲ ■ ▲ ◪ ▲ ▲ ◪ ■ ▲ ◧ ▲
       ■ ";
```

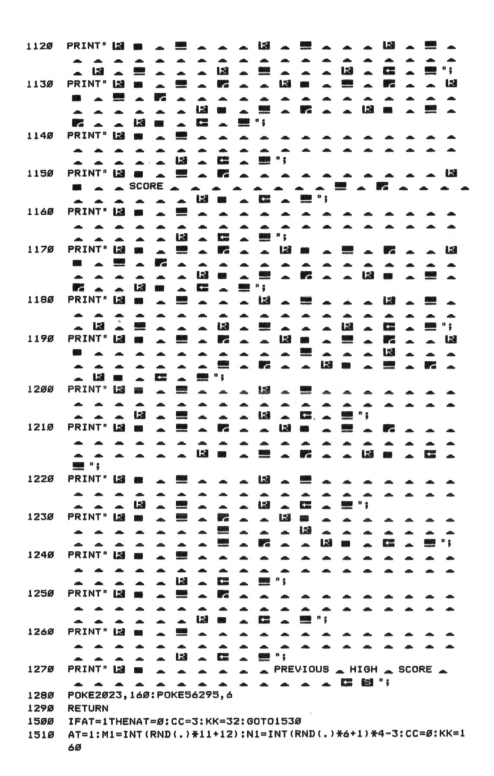

```
1120  PRINT"  [graphics]  ";
1130  PRINT"  [graphics]  ";
1140  PRINT"  [graphics]  ";
1150  PRINT"  [graphics] SCORE [graphics] ";
1160  PRINT"  [graphics]  ";
1170  PRINT"  [graphics]  ";
1180  PRINT"  [graphics]  ";
1190  PRINT"  [graphics]  ";
1200  PRINT"  [graphics]  ";
1210  PRINT"  [graphics]  ";
1220  PRINT"  [graphics]  ";
1230  PRINT"  [graphics]  ";
1240  PRINT"  [graphics]  ";
1250  PRINT"  [graphics]  ";
1260  PRINT"  [graphics]  ";
1270  PRINT"  [graphics] PREVIOUS  HIGH  SCORE  [graphics] ";
1280  POKE2023,160:POKE56295,6
1290  RETURN
1500  IFAT=1THENAT=0:CC=3:KK=32:GOTO1530
1510  AT=1:M1=INT(RND(.)*11+12):N1=INT(RND(.)*6+1)*4-3:CC=0:KK=1
      60
```

123

```
1520    P1=1024+M1+N1*40
1530    FORI=P1TOP1+80STEP40
1540    POKEI,KK:POKEI+54272,CC
1550    NEXT
1560    RETURN
1600    IFTA=1THENTA=0:CC=3:KK=32:GOTO1630
1610    TA=1:M2=INT(RND(.)*2+1)*4-3:N2=INT(RND(.)*11)+7:CC=0:KK=16
        0
1620    P2=1024+M2+N2*40
1630    FORI=P2TOP2+2
1640    POKEI,KK:POKEI+54272,CC
1650    NEXT
1660    RETURN
1700    IFTT=1THENTT=0:CC=3:KK=32:GOTO1730
1710    TT=1:M3=INT(RND(.)*2+8)*4-1:N3=INT(RND(.)*11)+7:CC=0:KK=16
        0
1720    P3=1024+M3+N3*40
1730    FORI=P3TOP3+2
1740    POKEI,KK:POKEI+54272,CC
1750    NEXT
1760    RETURN
```

> Data for the four positions of the car and explosion.

```
2000    DATA0,0,0,0,0,0,0,0,0,0,24,0,3,60,192,3,126,192,3,255,192,
        3,126,192,3,126,192
2010    DATA0,126,0,0,126,0,0,126,0,3,126,192,3,126,192,3,255,192,
        3,126,192,3,60,192
2020    DATA0,24,0,0,0,0,0,0,0,0,0,0,0
2030    DATA0,0,0,0,0,0,0,0,0,0,0,0,0,0,0
2040    DATA7,195,224,7,195,224,1,0,128,7,255,224,31,255,248,31,25
        5,248,7,255,224
2050    DATA1,0,128,7,195,224,7,195,224,0,0,0,0,0,0,0,0,0,0,0,0,0,
        0,0,0,0,0,0
3000    DATA32,140,64,140,96,140,32,60,64,92,96,124
3010    DATA168,60,168,92,168,124,255,60,255,92,240,124
3020    DATA49,60,17,92,240,124,49,140,17,140,240,140
3030    DATA49,220,17,188,240,156,255,220,255,188,240,156
3040    DATA168,220,168,188,168,156,32,220,64,188,96,156
3050    DATA32,140,64,140,96,140
3060    DATA99,0,0,0,0,8,0,2,8,8,0,8,32,0,42,128,0,174,160,2,239,1
        28,42,255,160
3070    DATA11,255,224,2,255,224,2,255,128,2,190,0,8,186,128,0,184
        ,32,0,40,0
3080    DATA0,32,0,32,32,0,0,0,128,2,0,2,0,0,0,0,0,0
```

CHEXSUM

10=0	1040=2771	2050=3895
40=2838	1050=2962	3000=2303
50=348	1060=2771	3010=2528
60=2193	1070=5081	3020=2410
70=1694	1080=3221	3030=2664
80=3312	1090=3757	3040=2620
100=4656	1100=3221	3050=1216
110=2954	1110=5437	3060=4217
120=1880	1120=3647	3070=3818
130=2684	1130=5599	3080=2311
140=1411	1140=2771	
180=1099	1150=3833	TOTAL= 281527
190=3034	1160=2771	
200=2880	1170=5599	
201=1028	1180=3647	
202=3343	1190=5165	
203=3325	1200=3221	
204=3485	1210=4269	
206=3358	1220=3221	
208=3350	1230=3855	
210=2915	1240=2771	
260=805	1250=3131	
350=1700	1260=2771	
360=2282	1270=3037	
365=3655	1280=1215	
370=2283	1290=143	
372=3648	1500=2814	
380=1193	1510=5086	
390=1331	1520=1427	
500=1167	1530=1414	
510=1373	1540=1414	
515=1375	1550=131	
518=1375	1560=143	
520=1392	1600=2809	
522=643	1610=5009	
525=4831	1620=1427	
530=420	1630=1062	
532=3536	1640=1414	
535=1710	1650=131	
540=2841	1660=143	
545=3034	1700=2849	
550=1439	1710=5036	
560=840	1720=1429	
580=3312	1730=1063	
590=3332	1740=1414	
600=1212	1750=131	
620=1359	1760=143	
640=1320	2000=4848	
650=476	2010=4762	
1000=1178	2020=1546	
1020=584	2030=1719	
1030=2406	2040=4455	

Laser Battle

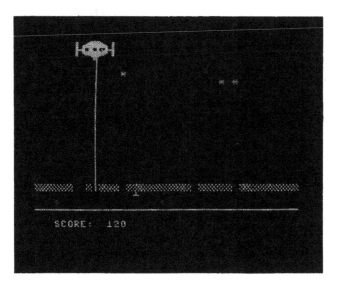

Defend three nuclear reactors by zapping aliens with your laser. The aliens must first destroy part of your bunker before they can shoot behind it.

CONTROLS

'I'	– left
'P'	– right
'space'	– fire

VARIABLES

NM   = Number of men left

PH   = Phase of guard ships (positioning, firing, retreating)

PG   = Column of player's laser gun

SH   = Ship hit

GS (I,J) = Guard ship number I, column, row, stopped, J=1, J=2, J=3

FG   = Guard ship firing gun

MC   = Mother ship's column

SC   = Score

```
1       REM LASER BATTLE
```

> Define variables, build sprites, wait to start game.

```
5       FORS=54272T054296:POKES,0:NEXT
10      POKE53280,6:POKE53281,13:PRINT" ⬛ ■ ━ ━ ━ ━ ━ ━ ━
        ━ ━ ━ ━ ━ ━ ▲ LASER ▲ BATTLE"
15      PRINT" 🔲 🔲 🔲 🔲 🔲 🔲 🔲 🔲 🔲 🔲 🔲 ━ ━ ━ ━
        ━ ━ ━ ━ HIT ━ ANY ━ KEY ━ TO ━ START"
17      NM=3:V=53248:POKEV+21,0:POKE2040,192:POKEV+39,3:POKEV,0:
        POKEV+37,7
20      POKEV+38,8:POKEV+1,0:POKEV+16,0:POKEV+29,1
22      FORI=12288T012350:READQ:POKEI,Q:NEXT
24      FORI=12352T012414:J=INT(2^(RND(0)*7))-1:POKEI,J:NEXT
30      FORI=49157T049244:READQ:POKEI,Q:NEXT
45      GETX$:IFX$=""THEN45
50      PRINT" ⬛ ";:POKE53280,0:POKE53281,0
52      FORI=1704T01823:POKEI,102:NEXT
54      FORI=1904T01943:POKEI,64:POKEI+54272,7:NEXT
56      POKE1867,90:POKE1883,90:POKE1900,90:POKE56139,2:POKE56155,
        2:POKE56172,2
58      PG=19:POKE1843,113:GOSUB1000
```

> Controlling logic, move laser gun, launch and move mother ship.

```
60      X=PEEK(197):IFX=60THENGOSUB150
62      IFX=33ORX=41THENGOSUB100
63      IFPH=2THENGOSUB400
65      IFPH=0THENGOSUB220:GOTO70
67      GOSUB250
70      X=PEEK(197):IFX=60THENGOSUB150
72      IFX=33ORX=41THENGOSUB100
73      IFRND(1)<.01ANDPH=1THENPH=2
75      IFPH=0THEN80
77      IFRND(1)<.80RPH=2THEN80
78      GOSUB190
80      IFPEEK(1824+PG)<>113THEN500
90      GOTO60
100     IFPG=0ANDX=33THENRETURN
105     IFPG=39ANDX=41THENRETURN
110     IFX=33THENI=-1:GOTO120
115     I=1
120     POKEPG+1824,32:PG=PG+I:POKEPG+1824,113:POKEPG+56096,3:
        RETURN
```

> Fire players laser, guard ships laser, generate laser sound.

```
150     POKE49152,PG:POKE49154,18:POKE49202,66:POKE49217,1
152     POKE54296,15:POKE54277,190:POKE54276,17
153     POKE54273,17:POKE54272,37:POKE54278,248
```

127

```
155  SH=Ø:J=Ø:FORI=1TO4:IFGS(I,1)=PGTHENJ=I
156  NEXT
157  IFJ<>ØTHENSP=GS(J,2):POKE49153,SP:SH=2:GOTO165
160  M=PEEK(V)+256*(PEEK(V+16)AND1):P=PG*8+23
162  IFM<P-22OR M>P-18 OR PEEK(V+21)=ØTHENSP=Ø:POKE49153,SP:
     GOTO165
163  SH=1:SP=2:POKE49153,SP
165  SYS(49157)
170  POKE49202,32:POKE49217,Ø:POKE49153,SP
175  SYS(49157)
177  IFSH=1THENGOSUB300
178  IFSH=2THENGOSUB350
180  POKE54276,Ø:RETURN
190  IFGS(1,1)=ØANDGS(2,1)=ØANDGS(3,1)=ØANDGS(4,1)=ØTHENRETURN
191  POKE49152,PG:POKE49154,18:POKE49202,66:POKE49217,1:POKE542
     96,15
192  POKE54277,190:POKE54276,17:FG=FG+1:IFFG=5THENFG=1
193  IFGS(FG,1)=ØTHEN192
194  POKE49152,GS(FG,1):POKE49153,GS(FG,2)+1:POKE49217,1:POKE49
     202,66
196  IFPEEK(1784+GS(FG,1))=102THENPOKE49154,20:GOTO200
197  IFGS(FG,1)=PGTHENPOKE49154,21:GOTO200
198  K=GS(FG,1):IFK=3ORK=190RK=36THENPOKE49154,22:SYS(49157):
     GOTO500
199  POKE49154,20
200  SYS(49157)
202  X=PEEK(197):IFX=42ORX=50THENGOSUB100
206  POKE49202,32:POKE49217,Ø:POKE49153,GS(FG,2)+1
208  SYS(49157)
210  POKE54276,Ø:RETURN
```

> Position the guard ship, move the mother ship and fire her gun.

```
220  IFGS(1,1)<>ØTHEN225
221  I=INT(RND(1)*39+1):IFI=GS(2,1)ORI=GS(3,1)ORI=GS(4,1)THEN22
     1
222  GS(1,1)=I:GS(1,2)=Ø:POKE1024+I,42:POKE55296+I,7:RETURN
225  IFGS(2,1)<>ØTHEN230
226  I=INT(RND(1)*39+1):IFI=GS(1,1)ORI=GS(3,1)ORI=GS(4,1)THEN22
     6
227  GS(2,1)=I:GS(2,2)=Ø:POKE1024+I,42:POKE55296+I,7:RETURN
230  IFGS(3,1)<>ØTHEN235
231  I=INT(RND(1)*39+1):IFI=GS(1,1)ORI=GS(2,1)ORI=GS(4,1)THEN23
     1
232  GS(3,1)=I:GS(3,2)=Ø:POKE1024+I,42:POKE55296+I,7:RETURN
235  IFGS(4,1)<>ØTHEN240
236  I=INT(RND(1)*39+1):IFI=GS(1,1)ORI=GS(2,1)ORI=GS(3,1)THEN23
     6
237  GS(4,1)=I:GS(4,2)=Ø:POKE1024+I,42:POKE55296+I,7:RETURN
240  IFGS(1,3)=1ANDGS(2,3)=1ANDGS(3,3)=1ANDGS(4,3)=1THENPH=1:
     RETURN
242  I=INT(RND(1)*4+1):IFGS(I,3)=1THEN242
243  POKEGS(I,1)+40*GS(I,2)+1024,32:GS(I,2)=GS(I,2)+1
244  POKEGS(I,1)+40*GS(I,2)+1024,42:POKEGS(I,1)+40*GS(I,2)+5529
     6,7
```

128

```
246    IFRND(1)<.30RGS(I,2)>=10THENGS(I,3)=1
248    RETURN
250    IFPEEK(V+21)<>0THEN255
252    IFRND(1)<.95THENRETURN
253    MC=2:POKEV,25:POKEV+1,50:POKEV+21,1:POKEV+16,0:RETURN
255    IFPEEK(V)=253THENPOKEV,0:POKEV+16,1:GOTO260
257    POKEV,PEEK(V)+3
260    IFPEEK(V)>=50ANDPEEK(V+16)=1THENPOKEV+21,0:RETURN
263    I=PEEK(V)+256*(PEEK(V+16)AND1):MC=INT((I-23)/8)+3
265    IFRND(1)<.55THENRETURN
270    IFMC<>GS(1,1)ANDMC<>GS(2,1)ANDMC<>GS(3,1)ANDMC<>GS(4,1)
       THENGOSUB280
275    RETURN
280    POKE54296,15:POKE54276,129:POKE54277,15:POKE54273,40:POKE5
       4272,200
282    POKE49152,MC:POKE49153,2:POKE49217,1:POKE49202,66
284    IFPEEK(1784+MC)=102THENPOKE49154,20:GOTO290
287    IFMC=PGTHENPOKE49154,21:GOTO290
288    IFMC=30RMC=190RMC=36THENPOKE49154,22:SYS(49157):GOTO500
289    POKE49154,20
290    SYS(49157)
292    X=PEEK(197):IFX=420RX=50THENGOSUB100
296    POKE49202,32:POKE49217,0:POKE49153,2
298    SYS(49157)
299    POKE54276,0:RETURN
300    SC=SC+50:GOSUB1000:POKEV+39,7:POKE2040,193:GOSUB700:POKE54
       296,0
310    FORT=1TO500:NEXT
315    POKEV+21,0:POKEV+39,3:POKE2040,192
340    RETURN
```

Explode the guard ship and send guard ships running.

```
350    POKE1024+GS(J,1)+GS(J,2)*40,102:POKEGS(J,1)+GS(J,2)*40+552
       96,8
355    SC=SC+10:GOSUB1000
356    FORT=1TO100:NEXT
357    POKE1024+GS(J,1)+GS(J,2)*40,32:GS(J,1)=0
360    RETURN
400    IFGS(1,1)<>0ORGS(2,1)<>0ORGS(3,1)<>0ORGS(4,1)<>0THEN405
402    FORI=1TO4:GS(I,3)=0:NEXT:PH=0:RETURN
405    I=INT(RND(1)*4+1):IFGS(I,1)=0THEN405
407    POKE1024+GS(I,1)+GS(I,2)*40,32:IFGS(I,2)>0THENGS(I,2)=GS(I
       ,2)-1
410    POKE1024+GS(I,1)+GS(I,2)*40,42:POKEGS(I,1)+GS(I,2)*40+5529
       6,7
412    IFGS(I,2)=0THENPOKE1024+GS(I,1),32:GS(I,1)=0
415    RETURN
```

Start a new round, print men left and title.

```
500    IFPEEK(1824+PG)=113THEN560
502    POKEV+40,0:POKEV+28,2
```

129

```
504     POKE2041,193:K=PG*8+15:IFK>255THENPOKEV+2,K-256:POKEV+16,2
        :GOTO506
505     POKEV+16,PEEK(V+16)AND253:POKEV+2,K
506     POKEV+3,200:POKEV+21,3:GOSUB700
508     POKE54276,0:POKE54277,0
509     FORT=1TO1000:NEXT:POKE2040,192:POKEV+21,0:POKEV+39,3:POKE5
        4296,0
510     POKE53280,6:POKE53281,13:PRINT" ▟ ■ ▲ ▲ ▲ ▲ ▲ ▲
        ▲ ▲ ▲ ▲ LASER ▲ BATTLE":PRINT
515     NM=NM-1:IFNM=0THEN600
520     PRINT"YOU ▲ HAVE ▲ ";NM;" ▲ MEN ▲ LEFT":PRINT
530     FORT=1TO3000:NEXT
535     FORI=1TO4:GS(I,1)=0:NEXT:PH=0
550     GOTO50
560     FORI=1TO3:POKE53280,INT(RND(1)*10)+23:GOSUB700:NEXT:POKEV+
        21,0
565     POKE53280,6:POKE53281,13:PRINT" ▟ ■ ▲ ▲ ▲ ▲ ▲ ▲
        ▲ ▲ ▲ ▲ ▲ ▲ LASER ▲ BATTLE":PRINT
570     GOTO515
```

> Print scores, generate explosion, and update the scores.

```
600     PRINT" ▲ ▲ ▲ ▲ ▲ ▲ ▲ ▲ ▲ ▲ ▲ ▲ ▲ ▲ GAME
        ▲ OVER":PRINT
620     PRINT"YOUR ▲ SCORE ▲ WAS ▲ ";SC
625     POKEV+21,0:POKE54296,0
630     GETX$:IFX$=""THENEND
640     GOTO630
700     FORX=15TO0STEP-1:POKE54296,X:POKE54276,129
705     POKE54277,15:POKE54273,40:POKE54272,200:NEXT
710     RETURN
1000    PRINT" ▦ ▣ ▣ ▣ ▣ ▣ ▣ ▣ ▣ ▣ ▣ ▣ ▣ ▣ ▣ ▣ ▣
        ▣ ▣ ▣ ▣ ▣ ▣ ▣ ▣ ▲ ▲ ▲ ◣ SCORE: ▲ ";SC;" ▨ "
1005    RETURN
```

> Data for mother ship, your laser gun and explosion.

```
10000 DATA0,126,0,192,255,3,193,255,131,195,255,195,199,255,227,
      207,255,243
10010 DATA207,255,243,207,255,243,204,230,51,252,230,63,252,230,
      63,207,255,243
10020 DATA207,255,243,207,255,243,199,255,227,195,255,195,192,12
      7,3
10030 DATA0,62,0,0,28,0,0,28,0,0,28,0
10100 DATA24,173,0,192,133,178,169,4,133,179,173,1,192,141,3,192
      ,169,0,205,3
10110 DATA192,240,19,206,3,192,24,165,178,105,40,133,178,165,179
      ,105,0,133,179
10120 DATA76,21,192,160,0,169,93,145,178,24,165,178,133,180,165,
      179,105,212
10130 DATA133,181,169,1,145,180,238,1,192,24,165,178,105,40,133,
      178,165,179,105
10140 DATA0,133,179,173,1,192,205,2,192,208,211,96
```

CHECKSUM

1=0	194=3718	340=143
5=1771	196=3134	350=4462
10=3856	197=2411	355=1216
15=2911	198=4476	356=975
17=4446	199=586	357=2900
20=2737	200=521	360=143
22=2103	202=2390	400=4531
24=3728	206=2584	402=2293
30=2110	208=521	405=2635
45=1195	210=728	407=4776
50=1651	220=1328	410=4376
52=1741	221=4535	412=3030
54=2623	222=3427	415=143
56=3651	225=1331	500=1698
58=1546	226=4542	502=1328
60=1809	227=3427	504=4863
62=1603	230=1331	505=2268
63=1018	231=4536	506=1762
65=1581	232=3429	508=1166
67=298	235=1328	509=3812
70=1809	236=4539	510=4104
72=1603	237=3425	515=1662
73=1979	240=4338	520=2259
75=817	242=2639	530=1032
77=1642	243=3598	535=2074
78=303	244=4378	550=476
80=1878	246=2794	560=3852
90=476	248=143	565=4104
100=1418	250=1584	570=530
105=1481	252=1133	600=1934
110=1793	253=3224	620=1614
115=302	255=2759	625=1239
120=4051	257=889	630=1214
150=2602	260=3153	640=532
152=2035	263=3886	700=2549
153=2023	265=1137	705=2246
155=3182	270=5186	710=143
156=131	275=143	1000=2308
157=3461	280=3480	1005=143
160=3282	282=2522	10000=4000
162=4789	284=2781	10010=4300
163=1613	287=2038	10020=3338
165=521	288=3851	10030=1606
170=1965	289=586	10100=4057
175=521	290=521	10110=4340
177=1016	292=2390	10120=3979
178=1022	296=1841	10130=4449
180=728	298=521	10140=2365
190=3787	299=728	
191=3324	300=3678	TOTAL= 344703
192=3449	310=975	
193=1231	315=1979	

Attack of the Vogons

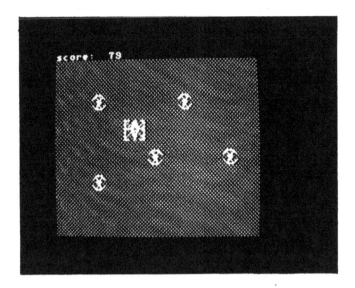

Escape from VOGON territory and avoid collisions. When your ship is yellow (achieved by pressing space bar) it can withstand a collision.

Game ends when you collide while not being 'armed' for collision.

VARIABLES

R,SC	= Round, score
NC	= Number of collisions
LX,PC	= Last, current player's X co-ords.
MC	= Maximum number collisions allowed
VL,A,W,HI,LW	= Sound
PEEK(177) − PEEK(183)	= VOGON directions

```
1      REM VOGON ATTACK
```

> Build sprites, vogons and spaceship, poke machine code into memory.

```
10     POKE53281,0:POKE53280,0:PRINT" 🖳 🔲 ▲ ▲ ▲ ▲ ▲ ▲
       ▲ ▲ ▲ ATTACK ▲ OF ▲ THE ▲ VOGONS"
15     PRINT" 🔲 🔲 🔲 🔲 🔲 🔲 🔲 🔲 🔲 🔲 🔲 🔲 🔲 "
20     V=53248:POKEV+39,14:FORI=1TO7:POKEV+39+I,10:NEXT:POKEV+37,
       8:POKEV+38,1
25     POKE2040,192:FORI=1TO7:POKE2040+I,193:NEXT:POKEV+28,0:POKE
       V+23,0:POKEV+29,0
30     FORI=12288TO12350:READQ:POKEI,Q:NEXT
40     FORI=12352TO12397STEP3:READQ,K:POKEI,Q:POKEI+1,K:POKEI+2,0
       :NEXT
45     FORI=12400TO12414:POKEI,0:NEXT
60     FORI=49152TO49411:READQ:POKEI,Q:NEXT
70     VL=54296:W=54276:A=54277:HI=54273:LW=54272
90     PRINT" ▲ ▲ ▲ ▲ ▲ ▲ ▲ ▲ ▲ ▲HIT ▲ ANY ▲ KEY ▲ TO
       ▲ BEGIN"
95     GETX$:IFX$=""THEN95
97     PRINT" 🖳 ";
98     FORI=1064TO1944STEP40:FORJ=0TO29:POKEI+J,102:POKEI+J+54272
       ,11:NEXT:NEXT
```

> Controller logic, move vogons round the screen and player.

```
100    R=R+1:IFR>6THENR=6
110    NC=0:LX=29:MC=1
150    PRINT" 🔲 🔳 ";
190    POKEV+21,255:POKEV+2,170:POKEV+3,220:POKEV+4,180:POKEV+5,1
       50
192    POKEV+6,170:POKEV+7,50:POKEV+8,50:POKEV+9,220:POKEV+10,70:
       POKEV+11,220
194    POKEV+12,10:POKEV+13,150:POKEV+14,70:POKEV+15,50
195    POKEV+16,64:POKEV,30:POKEV+1,150:POKE167,1:GOSUB1000:POKEV
       +30,0
199    POKE177,4:POKE178,2:POKE179,3:POKE180,4:POKE181,1:POKE182,
       2:POKE183,3
200    FORI=1TOR/3:SYS(49152):NEXT
210    GOSUB1000
220    IFRND(1)<.5THENPOKE167,INT(RND(1)*7+1):SYS(49349)
230    IFPX>330THEN100
235    IFPX<20THENPOKEV,20
240    K=PEEK(197):IFK=60ANDNC<MCTHENPOKEV+39,7
250    CO=PEEK(V+30):IF(COAND1)=0THEN200
```

Blow up enemy ship, remove from board, blow up player, finish game.

```
300    IF(PEEK(V+39)AND15)<>7THEN500
305    FORI=LWTOLW+24:POKEI,0:NEXT
310    FORX=15TO0STEP-1:POKEVL,X:POKEW,129:POKEA,15:POKEHI,20+X:
       POKELW,200:NEXT
330    POKEV+21,PEEK(V+21)AND(255-(COAND254)):POKEV+30,0
340    POKEV+39,3:NC=NC+1
350    GOTO200
500    POKEV+28,1:POKEV+23,1:POKEV+29,1
502    FORI=LWTOLW+24:POKEI,0:NEXT
505    FORI=1TO50:J=INT(RND(1)*120-80):IFJ<0THENJ=0
506    POKEHI,10+I:POKELW,200
507    POKE12288+INT(RND(0)*63),J:POKEVL,(60-I)/10+9:POKEW,129:
       POKEA,15
509    NEXT
510    PRINT" ▨ ▚ ▲ ▲ ▲ ▲ ▲ ▲ ▲ ▲ ▲
       ▲ ▲ GAME ▲ OVER":PRINT" ▨ ▨ ▨ ▨ ▨ ▨ ▨ ▨ ▨ "
512    FORI=LWTOLW+24:POKEI,0:NEXT
520    PRINT" ▲ ▲ ▲ ▲ ▲ ▲ ▲ ▲ ▲ ▲ YOUR ▲ SCORE ▲ W
       AS ▲ ";SC
530    POKEV+21,0
540    GETX$:IFX$=""THENEND
550    GOTO540
```

Update the score periodically and data for sprites and sound.

```
1000   PX=PEEK(V)+256*(PEEK(V+16)AND1):IFPX>LXTHENSC=SC+PX-LX:LX=
       PX
1010   PRINT"SCORE: ▲ ";SC;" ▨ ";
1020   RETURN
10000  DATA252,28,63,252,62,63,224,62,3,208,127,7,200,127,11,196,
       255,147
10010  DATA194,247,163,225,247,199,255,247,255,255,193,255,224,24
       7,135,192,247
10020  DATA131,192,247,131,193,127,67,194,62,35,196,62,19,200,62,
       11,208,28,7
10030  DATA224,28,7,252,28,63,252,28,63
10050  DATA15,240,31,248,56,28,124,62,198,99,131,193,7,224,15,240
       ,7,224,3,192
10060  DATA131,193,195,195,102,102,60,60,31,248,15,240
```

Data for moving sprites round the screen.

```
10100  DATA169,0,133,184,230,184,166,184,189,130,192,133,169,165,
       184,10,133
10110  DATA170,32,30,192,165,184,201,7,208,233,76,138,192,166,184
       ,189,176,0
```

134

```
10120 DATA201,1,208,14,230,170,166,170,189,0,208,56,233,6,157,0,
      208,96,201,2
10130 DATA208,31,166,170,189,0,208,56,233,6,157,0,208,201,252,14
      ,4,236,169,255
10140 DATA56,229,169,133,171,173,16,208,37,171,141,16,208,96,201
      ,3,208,14,230
10150 DATA170,166,170,189,0,208,24,105,6,157,0,208,96,166,170,18
      9,0,208,24
10160 DATA105,6,157,0,208,201,6,176,240,173,16,208,5,169,141,16,
      208,96,1,2,4
10170 DATA8,16,32,64,128,169,0,133,184,169,1,133,169,169,0,133,1
      70,165,197,201
10180 DATA62,208,7,169,1,133,176,76,30,192,201,33,208,7,169,2,13
      3,176,76,30,192
10190 DATA201,12,208,7,169,3,133,176,76,30,192,201,41,208,7,169,
      4,133,176,76,30
10200 DATA192,96
10300 DATA165,167,10,170,232,189,0,208,205,1,208,176,25,202,189,
      0,200,205,0
10310 DATA208,176,8,166,167,169,3,157,176,0,96,166,167,169,2,157
      ,176,0,96
10320 DATA202,189,0,208,205,0,208,176,8,166,167,169,4,157,176,0,
      96,166,167
10330 DATA169,1,157,176,0,96
```

CHECKSUM

1=0	235=1190	10020=3989
10=4453	240=2856	10030=1703
15=568	250=2271	10050=4091
20=4914	300=1952	10060=2530
25=4798	305=1778	10100=3876
30=2103	310=4513	10110=3834
40=3891	330=3218	10120=4080
45=1759	340=1418	10130=4206
60=2104	350=525	10140=4215
70=3352	500=2054	10150=3875
90=2301	502=1778	10160=4076
95=1196	505=3400	10170=4343
97=435	506=1309	10180=4424
98=4705	507=4272	10190=4449
100=1635	509=131	10200=458
110=1385	510=2937	10300=3967
150=471	512=1778	10310=3771
190=3853	520=2268	10320=3868
192=4575	530=616	10330=1129
194=3029	540=1214	
195=3643	550=529	TOTAL= 188269
199=3467	1000=5422	
200=1740	1010=1190	
210=348	1020=143	
220=3091	10000=3580	
230=1007	10010=4220	

Interceptor

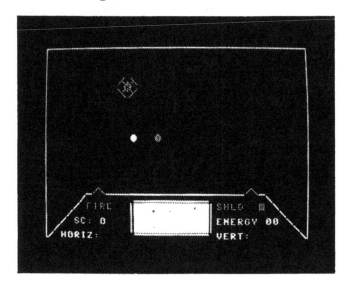

The task is to prevent the alien ships from landing. To fire, select horizontal and vertical co-ordinates (both $0-99$) and then press the space bar.

The game ends if the aliens land or if you run out of energy.

Scoring: mother ship is 100 points, other ships 50 points.

VARIABLES

SX,SY	= Strike point X,Y co-ords.
HT	= Sprite hit flag
H,VT	= Horizontal, vertical co-ords.
E	= Energy
SC,R	= Score, round
VL,W,A,HI,LW	= Sound effects
TE	= Energy parameter for calls to 'PRINT ENERGY'
F	= Sprite that is firing
TM	= Effectively a time measurement for period that selected enemy ship has been visible
CN	= Count to determine where player is up to in keying in co-ordinates
XD,YD	= X, Y differences
M1,M2,C1,C2	= Gradients, Y-intercepts

```
1     REM INTERCEPTOR
```

Create the alien ship and missiles, set screen colours and define variables.

```
10    POKE53281,7:POKE53280,0:PRINT" ▙ ";TAB(14);" ▬ INTERCEPTOR
      ":PRINT" ▨ ▨ ▨ ▨ ▨ ▨ ▨ ▨ ▨ ▨ ▨ ▨ ▨ "
15    V=53248:POKE2040,192:POKE2041,193:POKE2042,193:POKE2043,19
      3:POKE2044,194
20    POKE2045,194:POKE2046,195:POKE2047,192:POKEV+40,0:POKEV+41
      ,0:POKEV+42,2
25    POKEV+43,11:POKEV+44,11:POKEV+45,3
30    FORI=12288TO12309STEP3:READQ:POKEI,Q:POKEI+1,0:POKEI+2,0:
      NEXT
35    FORI=12312TO12350:POKEI,0:NEXT
40    FORI=12352TO12358STEP3:READQ:POKEI,Q:POKEI+1,0:POKEI+2,0:
      NEXT
45    FORI=12361TO12414:POKEI,0:NEXT
50    FORI=12416TO12478:READQ:POKEI,Q:NEXT
60    FORI=12480TO12542:READQ:POKEI,Q:NEXT
65    POKEV+27,129
70    VL=54296:W=54276:A=54277:HI=54273:LW=54272
90    PRINT" ▲ ▲ ▲ ▲ ▲ ▲ ▲ ▲ ▲ ▲ ▲ HIT ▲ ANY ▲ KEY ▲ T
      O ▲ START"
95    GETX$:IFX$=""THEN95
```

Draw the screen, messages to player and radar screen.

```
100   R=R+1:PRINT" ▙ ";:POKE53281,0
105   FORI=1024TO1984STEP40:POKEI,106:POKEI+54272,12:POKEI+39,11
      6:POKEI+54311,12
107   NEXT
110   FORI=1025TO1062:POKEI,119:POKEI+54272,12:NEXT
115   FORI=1790TO1985STEP39:POKEI,78:POKEI+54272,12:NEXT
120   FORI=1817TO2022STEP41:POKEI,77:POKEI+54272,12:NEXT
125   POKE1752,78:POKE56024,2:POKE1774,78:POKE56046,2:POKE1753,7
      7:POKE56025,2
127   POKE1775,77:POKE56047,2
130   POKE1751,111:POKE56023,12:POKE1776,111:POKE56048,12
135   FORI=1754TO1773:POKEI,111:POKEI+54272,12:NEXT
140   FORI=1838TO1958STEP40:FORJ=0TO10:POKEI+J,160:POKEI+J+54272
      ,13:NEXT:NEXT
145   FORI=1798TO1808:POKEI,82:POKEI+54272,12:NEXT
150   FORI=1998TO2008:POKEI,69:POKEI+54272,12:NEXT
155   FORI=1837TO1957STEP40:POKEI,72:POKEI+54272,12:POKEI+12,84:
      POKEI+54284,12
157   NEXT
160   PRINT" ▧ ▨ ▨ ▨ ▨ ▨ ▨ ▨ ▨ ▨ ▨ ▨ ▨ ▨ ▨ ▨ ▨
      ▨ ▨ ▨ ▨ ▮ ▮ ▮ ▮ ▮ ▮ ▮ ▮ ▮ ▨FIRE ▮ ▮ ▮ ▮ ▮ ▮
      ▮ ▮ ▮ ▮ ▮ ▮ ▮ ▮ ▮ ▮SHLD"
165   PRINT" ▨ ▨ ▨ ▣ ▮ ▮ ▮ ▮HORIZ: ▮ ▮ ▮ ▮ ▮ ▮ ▮ ▮
      ▮ ▮ ▮ ▮ ▮ ▮ ▮ ▮ ▮VERT: ▢ ▢ ◈ ▮▮ ▮▮ ▮▮ ▮▮ ▮▮ ▮▮ENE
      RGY"
```

```
167    K1=INT(RND(1)*20):K2=INT(RND(1)*20):K3=INT(RND(1)*20)
170    POKEV+2,135+K1:POKEV+4,223-K2
173    POKEV+6,170+K3:POKEV+3,209+R*2:POKEV+5,209+R*2
175    POKEV+7,209+R*2:POKEV+21,14
180    POKEV+8,25+4*K1:POKEV+10,77-4*K2:POKEV+12,170+K3
183    POKEV+9,50+8*R:POKEV+11,50+8*R:POKEV+13,50+8*R
185    POKEV+16,32:POKE56266,7:POKE56267,7:POKE56289,7:POKE56290,
       7
190    E=E+55-5*R:TE=E:GOSUB1000:POKE56209,3:POKE56210,3:POKE5612
       8,2
193    POKE56108,3
195    GOTO730
```

> Input the vertical and horizontal co-ordinates, launch and move alien.

```
200    GOTO600
205    IFRND(1)<.6THEN209
206    IFF<>0THENTM=TM+1:IFTM>10ANDPEEK(V+2*F+1)>80THEN500
207    IFF=0THENF=INT(RND(1)*3+4):TM=0:IF(PEEK(V+21)AND2^(F-3))=0
       THENF=0:GOTO209
208    POKEV+21,PEEK(V+21)OR2^F
209    GETX$:IFX$="  "AND(CN=0ORCN=2)THEN400
210    IFPEEK(V+9)>189 OR PEEK(V+11)>189 OR PEEK(V+13)>189 OR E<=
       0 THEN800
215    IFX$=""THEN200
220    IFX$<"0" OR X$>"9" THEN200
225    CN=CN+1
230    IFCN=1THENPOKE1994,VAL(X$)+48:K=10*VAL(X$):GOTO200
235    IFCN=2THENPOKE1995,VAL(X$)+48:H=K+VAL(X$):GOTO200
240    IFCN=3THENPOKE2017,VAL(X$)+48:L=10*VAL(X$):GOTO200
245    CN=0:POKE2018,VAL(X$)+48:VT=L+VAL(X$):GOTO200
```

> Check if alien has been hit by your missiles.

```
250    POKE1836,32:IFHT=0THENSC=SC+100:GOTO700
255    IFHT=4ORHT=5THENSC=SC+50:GOTO700
260    GOTO200
400    E=E-5:TE=E:GOSUB1000:CN=0:SX=INT(3.162*H+23):SY=INT(185-1.
       374*VT)
403    POKE1836,160
405    HT=0:FORI=4TO6:YD=PEEK(V+2*I+1)-SY+10:IFYD<0THENYD=-YD
410    XD=PEEK(V+2*I)+2^(8-I)*(PEEK(V+16)AND(2^I))-SX+12:IFXD<0
       THENXD=-XD
415    IFXD<15ANDYD<15THENHT=I
420    NEXT:POKEV+21,PEEK(V+21)OR129
422    IF(PEEK(V+21)AND2^(HT-3))=0THENHT=0
425    IFSX=91THENSX=86
427    IFSX=268THENSX=272
430    M1=(SY-193)/(SX-91):M2=(SY-193)/(SX-268):C1=193-M1*91:C2=1
       93-M2*268
435    FORY=193TOSY STEP-3
```

```
440     POKEV+1,Y:X=INT((Y-C1)/M1)
445     IFX>255THENPOKEV+16,PEEK(V+16)OR1:POKEV,X-256:GOTO450
447     POKEV+16,PEEK(V+16)AND254:POKEV,X
450     K1=193-Y:K2=39:GOSUB480
455     POKEV+15,Y:X=INT((Y-C2)/M2)
460     IFX>255THENPOKEV+16,PEEK(V+16)OR128:POKEV+14 ,X-256:GOTO046
        5
463     POKEV+16,PEEK(V+16)AND127:POKEV+14,X
465     K2=46:GOSUB480
470     NEXT:POKEV+21,PEEK(V+21)AND126:GOTO250
480     IFK1<8THENPOKEV+K2,7:RETURN
482     IFK1<15THENPOKEV+K2,1:RETURN
484     IFK1<30THENPOKEV+K2,3:RETURN
486     IFK1<45THENPOKEV+K2,15:RETURN
488     IFK1<55THENPOKEV+K2,12:RETURN
490     POKEV+K2,11:RETURN
```

Enemy fires missile at base, move the missile.

```
500     TE=0:GOSUB1000:POKE1856,160:B=0:IFE<20THENB=1
505     EX=PEEK(V+2*F)+(2^(8-F))*(PEEK(V+16)AND2^F):EY=PEEK(V+2*F+
        1)
510     IFEX=150THENPOKEV+2*F,154:EX=154
515     IFEX=209THENPOKEV+2*F,205:EX=205
520     M1=(EY-193)/(EX-150):M2=(EY-193)/(EX-209):C1=193-M1*150:C2
        =193-M2*209
525     POKEV+21,PEEK(V+21)OR129:FORY=EYTO193STEP3
530     POKEV+1,Y:X=INT((Y-C1)/M1)
535     IFX>255THENPOKEV+16,PEEK(V+16)OR1:POKEV,X-256:GOTO540
537     POKEV+16,PEEK(V+16)AND254:POKEV,X
540     K1=193-Y:K2=39:GOSUB480
545     POKEV+15,Y:X=INT((Y-C2)/M2)
550     IFX>255THENPOKEV+16,PEEK(V+16)OR128:POKEV+14 ,X-256:GOTO55
        5
553     POKEV+16,PEEK(V+16)AND127:POKEV+14,X
555     K2=46:GOSUB480
560     NEXT:POKEV+21,PEEK(V+21)AND(126-2^F):F=0:POKE1856,32:E=E-
        INT(RND(1)*5+10)
565     TE=E:GOSUB1000:GOSUB1100:GOTO200
```

Plot the enemy on the screen and reset any previous dots.

```
600     IFRND(1)<.7THEN205
602     I=INT(RND(1)*3+1):D=RND(1):IF(PEEK(V+21)AND2^I)=0THEN600
605     IFD<.4THENPOKEV+2*I+1,PEEK(V+2*I+1)+1:POKEV+2*I+7,PEEK(V+2
        *I+7)+4:GOTO205
610     IFPEEK(V+2*I)<167THEN620
615     POKEV+2*I,PEEK(V+I*2)-1:J=PEEK(V+I*2+6)+(2^(5-I))*(PEEK(V+
        16)AND2^(I+3))
616     IFJ>=256ANDJ<=259THEN618
617     POKEV+2*I+6,PEEK(V+2*I+6)-4:GOTO205
```

140

```
618    POKEV+16,PEEK(V+16)AND(255-2^(I+3)):POKEV+2*I+6,J-4:GOTO20
       5
620    POKEV+2*I,PEEK(V+I*2)+1:J=PEEK(V+I*2+6)+(2^(5-I))*(PEEK(V+
       16)AND2^(I+3))
622    IFJ>=252ANDJ<=255THEN626
624    POKEV+2*I+6,PEEK(V+2*I+6)+4:GOTO205
626    POKEV+16,PEEK(V+16)OR(2^(I+3)):POKEV+2*I+6,J+4:GOTO205
```

> Destroy the enemy ship, print the current score, restart game.

```
700    POKEV+21,PEEK(V+21)OR2^HT:POKEV+39+HT,3
705    FORI=15TO0STEP-1:POKEVL,I:POKEW,129:POKEA,15:POKEHI,6:POKE
       LW,100:NEXT
710    POKEW,0:POKEA,0:POKEVL,0
720    POKEV+21,PEEK(V+21)AND(255-2^HT-2^(HT-3)):IFHT=FTHENF=0
725    POKEV+39+HT,11:IFHT=6THENPOKEV+45,3
730    PRINT" 🅂 🄴 🄴 🄴 🄴 🄴 🄴 🄴 🄴 🄴 🄴 🄴
       🄴 🄴 🄴 🄴 🄴 🄴 🄴 🄴 ⋉ SC:";SC;
735    IFHT=6THENE=E+10:TE=E:GOSUB1000
740    IF(PEEK(V+21)AND13)=0THEN100
750    GOTO200
```

> Print score, end game, generate sound effects and dab for sprites.

```
800    POKEV+21,0:PRINT" 🄻🄸 🄼🄸 ▲ ▲ ▲ ▲ ▲
       ▲ ▲ ▲ ▲ ▲ GAME ▲ OVER":PRINT" 🄴 🄴 🄴 🄴 🄴 🄴 🄴 🄴 🄴
       🄴 🄴 "
810    PRINT" ▲ ▲ ▲ ▲ ▲ ▲ ▲ ▲ ▲ ▲ YOUR ▲ SCORE ▲ W
       AS ▲ ▲ ";SC
820    END
1000   IFTE>99THENTE=99:E=99
1002   IFTE<0THENTE=0
1005   I=INT(TE/10):J=TE-10*I:POKE1937,I+48:POKE1938,J+48
1010   RETURN
1100   FORI=15TO0STEP-1:POKE53281,I+50:POKE53280,I+50:POKEVL,I:
       POKEW,129:POKEA,15
1115   POKEHI,50:POKELW,190:NEXT
1120   POKEW,0:POKEA,0:POKE53281,0:POKE53280,0:RETURN
10000  DATA60,126,255,255,255,255,126,60
10010  DATA64,224,64
10020  DATA1,129,128,3,0,192,6,0,96,14,0,48,27,24,120,49,188,204,
       96,255,134
10030  DATA192,255,3,129,219,129,3,231,192,129,231,129,192,219,3,
       96,255,6
10040  DATA49,189,140,27,24,216,14,0,112,6,0,96,3,0,192,1,129,128
       ,0,195,0,0,102,0
10050  DATA1,0,128,3,0,192,6,60,96,12,255,48,25,255,152,51,255,20
       4,103,255,230
10060  DATA199,255,227,207,255,243,255,255,255,255,255,255,255,25
       5,255,207,255,243
10070  DATA199,255,227,103,255,231,51,255,204,25,255,152,12,255,4
       8,6,60,96
10080  DATA3,0,192,1,0,128
```

141

CHECKSUM

1=0	215=867	555=791
10=4628	220=1566	560=5250
15=3935	225=703	565=1893
20=4212	230=3635	600=1113
25=2142	235=3608	602=4159
30=3711	240=3637	605=6293
35=1765	245=3422	610=1688
40=3705	250=2849	615=6280
45=1761	255=2783	616=1885
50=2100	260=525	617=3033
60=2101	400=5387	618=4670
65=733	403=591	620=6279
70=3352	405=5128	622=1883
90=2367	410=6175	624=3032
95=1196	415=1854	626=4340
100=1710	420=1775	700=2942
105=4630	422=2666	705=4116
107=131	425=1265	710=1220
110=2742	427=1397	720=4509
115=2981	430=6441	725=2482
120=2974	435=1320	730=1693
125=3665	440=2070	735=2258
127=1169	445=3726	740=1762
130=2599	447=2026	750=525
135=2743	450=1629	800=3840
140=4713	455=2133	810=2361
145=2688	460=4161	820=129
150=2703	463=2320	1000=1690
155=4534	465=791	1002=1108
157=131	470=2426	1005=3870
160=2808	480=1538	1010=143
165=4288	482=1613	1100=4776
167=3838	484=1614	1115=1285
170=2083	486=1672	1120=2177
173=3574	488=1672	10000=1773
175=1946	490=901	10010=617
180=3681	500=3028	10020=3842
183=3719	505=5387	10030=3639
185=3190	510=2357	10040=4530
190=3926	515=2359	10050=4191
193=535	520=6484	10060=4691
195=532	525=2868	10070=3747
200=529	530=2070	10080=940
205=1112	535=3725	
206=4232	537=2026	TOTAL= 384420
207=5721	540=1629	
208=1760	545=2133	
209=2571	550=4160	
210=4677	553=2320	

Breakin

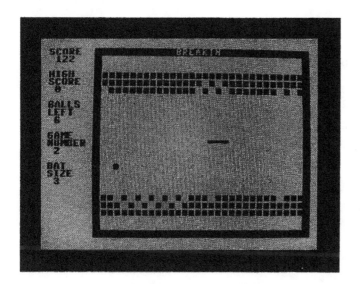

In this game you score 1 point for each brick you knock out of the wall. A bonus is awarded at the start of each game and every multiple of 100 points gained refreshes the brick wall. You are given 9 balls for each game and you lose a ball each time it gets past your bat. The bat can be moved left and right with the 'Z' and 'M' keys. There are 3 different game versions and two bat sizes for your own selection. Selecting Bat 2 gives 200 bonus points. Selecting Bat 3 gives 100 bonus points.

VARIABLES

SC = Start address of screen

CB = Colour offset value and base address for voice 1 sound

GM = Game number

BS = Bat size

GS = Game score

HS = High score

FF = Voice 1 control register value

BV = Vertical position of bat

BH = Horizontal position of bat

BY = Vertical position of ball

BX = Horizontal position of ball

BA = Screen position of ball

DX = Horizontal movement value for ball

DY = Vertical movement value for ball

SW = Switch to allow screen refresh

```
5      REM  BREAKIN
```

Define variables

```
10     DN$=" ▤ ▨ ▨ ▨ ▨ ▨ ▨ ▨ ▨ ▨ ▨ ▨ ▨ ▨ ▨ ▨ ▨ ▨
       ▨ ▨ ▨ ▨ ▨ ▨ ▨ ▨ ▨ ▨ ◪ ◪ ◪ ◪ ◪ ◪ ◪ ◪ ◪ ◪
       ◪ ◪ ◪ ◪ ◪ ◪ ◪ ◪ ◪ ◪ ◪ ◪ ◪ ◪ ◪ ◪ ◪ ◪ ◪ ◪
       ◪ ◪ ◪ ◪ ◪ ◪ ◪ ◪ ◪ "
20     SC=1024:NB=9:CB=54272:FORI=0TO24:POKECB+I,0:NEXT:GOTO2000
40     FORI=0TO24:POKECB+I,0:NEXT:GOTO100
```

Make noise when ball hits bat

```
50     REM  SOUND ROUTINE
60     POKECB+24,15:POKECB+4,0:POKECB+6,222
70     POKECB+4,FF:POKECB+1,18:POKECB,9
80     FORT=1TO5:NEXT
90     POKECB,0:POKECB+1,0:RETURN
```

Move the ball and the bat around the screen.

```
1000   REM  MOVE BAT
1020   A=PEEK(197):IFA=64THEN1220
1050   PRINTLEFT$(DN$,BV)RIGHT$(DN$,BH);:FORI=1TOBS:PRINT" ▲ ";:
       NEXT
1060   BH=BH+((A=12)-(A=36))*2
1070   IFBH<8THENBH=8
1080   IFBH>38-BSTHENBH=38-BS
1090   PRINTLEFT$(DN$,BV)RIGHT$(DN$,BH);:FORI=1TOBS:PRINT" ▬ ▬ "
       ;:NEXT:
1200   REM  CHECK BOUNDARY HIT
1220   BX=BX+DX:BY=BY+DY:FF=21
1230   IFBX<9THENDX=-DX:GOSUB50:GOTO1520
1240   IFBX>36THENDX=-DX:GOSUB50:GOTO1520
1250   IFBY<1THENBY=1:DY=-DY:GOSUB50:GOTO1520
1260   IFBY>23THENBY=23:DY=-DY:GOSUB50
```

Test if ball hit brick or bat change the ball direction

```
1500   REM CHECK BAT/BRCK HIT & PRINT BALL
1520   POKEBA,32:BA=SC+BY*40+BX
1530   IFPEEK(BA)=120THENBA=B1:DY=-DY:FF=133:GOSUB50:GOTO1000
1540   IFPEEK(BA)=207THENDY=-DY:FF=35:GOSUB50:GS=GS+1:PRINT" ▤
       ▬ ◪ "GS
1550   POKEBA,81:POKEBA+CB,0
```

145

```
1560  REM CHECK FOR MISSED BALL
1570  IFGM=1ANDBY>22ANDDY=-1THENNB=NB-1:PRINT" ▨ ▨ ▨ ▨ ▨ ▨
      ▨ ▨ ▨ ▨ ■ "NB
1580  IFGM<>1ANDBY=12THENNB=NB-1:PRINT" ▨ ▨ ▨ ▨ ▨ ▨ ▨ ▨
      ▨ ▨ ■ "NB
1590  IFNB<1THEN5000
1600  IFINT(GS/100)-(GS/100)<>0THEN1000
1610  ONGMGOSUB2650,2700,2800
```

```
2000  REM TITLE SCREEN
2020  POKE53281,3:POKE53280,3:PRINT" ▨ ▨ ▨ ▨ ▨ ■ ▲ ▲ ▲
      ▲ ▲ ▲ ▲ ▲ ▲ ▲ ▲ ▲ ▲ ● "
2030  FORT=1TO100:NEXT
2040  PRINT" ▨ ▨ ▨ ▨ ▨ ▨ ▨ ▲ ▲ ▲ ▲ ▲ ▲
      ▲ ▲ ▲ ▲ ▲ ● ■ ● ▤ ● "
2050  FORT=1TO100:NEXT
2060  PRINT" ▨ ▨ ▨ ▨ ▨ ▨ ▨ ▨ ▲ ▲ ▲ ▲ ▲ ▲
      ▲ ▲ ▲ ▲ ● ▲ ■ ● ▲ ▤ ● "
2070  FORT=1TO100:NEXT
2080  PRINT" ▨ ▨ ▨ ▨ ▨ ▨ ▨ ▨ ▤ ▲ ▲ ▲ ▲ ▲ ▲
      ▲ ▲ ▲ ▲ ● ▤ ● ▲ ■ ● ▲ ▤ ● ▤ ● "
2090  FORT=1TO100:NEXT
2100  PRINT" ▨ ▨ ▨ ▨ ▨ ▨ ▨ ▨ ▤ ▲ ▲ ▲ ▲ ▲
      ▲ ▲ ▲ ▲ ▲ ● ▲ ▤ ● ▲ ■ ● ▲ ▤ ● ▲ ▤
      ● "
2110  FORT=1TO100:NEXT
2120  PRINT" ▨ ▨ ▨ ▨ ▨ ▨ ▨ ▨ ▨ ▨ ▤ ▲ ▲ ▲ ▲
      ▲ ▲ ▲ ▲ ● ▤ ● ▲ ▤ ● ▲ ■ ● ▲ ▤ ●
      ▲ ▤ ● ◎ ● "
2130  FORT=1TO100:NEXT
2140  PRINT" ▨ ▨ ▨ ▨ ▨ ▨ ▨ ▨ ▨ ▨ ▨ ▤ ▲ ▲ ▲ ▲
      ▲ ▲ ● ▲ ▤ ● ▲ ▤ ● ▲ ■ ● ▲ ▤
      ● ▲ ▤ ● ▲ ◎ ● "
2150  FORT=1TO200:NEXT:FF=35:GOSUB50
2160  PRINT" ▨ ▨ ▨ ▨ ▨ ▨ ▨ ▨ ▨ ▨ ▨ ▤ ▲ ▲ ▲ ▲
      ▲ ▲ ▲ ▲ ▲ B ▲ ▤ ● ▲ ▤ ● ▲ ■ ● ▲ ▤ ●
      ▲ ▤ ● ▲ ◎ ● "
2170  FORT=1TO200:NEXT:FF=21:GOSUB50
2180  PRINT" ▨ ▨ ▨ ▨ ▨ ▨ ▨ ▨ ▨ ▨ ▨ ▨ ▤ ▲ ▲ ▲
      ▲ ▲ ▲ ▲ ▲ B ▲ ▤ R ▲ ▤ ● ▲ ■ ● ▲ ▤ ● ▲
      ▤ ● ▲ ◎ ● "
2190  FORT=1TO200:NEXT:FF=35:GOSUB50
2200  PRINT" ▨ ▨ ▨ ▨ ▨ ▨ ▨ ▨ ▨ ▨ ▤ ▲ ▲ ▲ ▲
      ▲ ▲ ▲ ▲ ▲ B ▲ ▤ R ▲ ▤ E ▲ ■ ● ▲ ▤ ● ▲
      ▤ ● ▲ ◎ ● "
2210  FORT=1TO200:NEXT:FF=21:GOSUB50
2220  PRINT" ▨ ▨ ▨ ▨ ▨ ▨ ▨ ▨ ▨ ▨ ▨ ▨ ▤ ▲ ▲ ▲
      ▲ ▲ ▲ ▲ ▲ B ▲ ▤ R ▲ ▤ E ▲ ■ A ▲ ▤ ● ▲ ▤
      ● ▲ ◎ ● "
```

146

```
2230    FORT=1TO200:NEXT:FF=35:GOSUB50
2240    PRINT"▓ ▨ ▨ ▨ ▨ ▨ ▨ ▨ ▨ ▨ ▨ ▨ ▨ ▣ ▲ ▲ ▲ ▲
        ▲ ▲ ▲ ▲ ▲ ▲ ▲B ▲ ▛R ▲ ◪E ▲ ■ A ▲ ▟K ▲ ▰ ●
        ▲ ◙ ● "
2250    FORT=1TO200:NEXT:FF=21:GOSUB50
2260    PRINT"▓ ▨ ▨ ▨ ▨ ▨ ▨ ▨ ▨ ▨ ▨ ▨ ▨ ▣ ▲ ▲ ▲ ▲
        ▲ ▲ ▲ ▲ ▲ ▲ ▲B ▲ ▛R ▲ ◪E ▲ ■ A ▲ ▟K ▲ ▰ I
        ▲ ◙ ● "
2270    FORT=1TO200:NEXT:FF=35:GOSUB50
2280    PRINT"▓ ▨ ▨ ▨ ▨ ▨ ▨ ▨ ▨ ▨ ▨ ▨ ▨ ▣ ▲ ▲ ▲ ▲
        ▲ ▲ ▲ ▲ ▲ ▲ ▲B ▲ ▛R ▲ ◪E ▲ ■ A ▲ ▟K ▲ ▰ I
        ▲ ◙ N "
2290    FORT=1TO200:NEXT:FF=21:PRINT" ▨ ▨ "
2300    GOSUB50
```

> Print difficulty level, bat size and other player information.

```
2400    PRINT" ■ ▲ ▲ ▲ ▲ ▲ ▲ ▲ ▲ ▧ SELECT ▲ GAME ▲ NUMBER
        (1-3)":FORT=1TO90:NEXT
2410    PRINT" ◻ ▬ ▲ ▲ ▲ ▲ ▲ ▲ ▲ ▲ SELECT ▲ GAME ▲ NUMBER
        (1-3)";:FORT=1TO90:NEXT
2420    GETGM$:IFGM$<"1"THENPRINT:PRINT" ◻ ";:GOTO2300
2430    IFGM$>"3"THENPRINT:PRINT" ◻ ";:GOTO2300
2440    GM=VAL(GM$):PRINT" ▲ "GM:PRINT:FF=35
2450    GOSUB50
2460    PRINT" ■ ▲ ▲ ▲ ▲ ▲ ▲ ▲ ▲ ▧ SELECT ▲ BAT ▲ SIZE
        (2-3)":FORT=1TO90:NEXT
2470    PRINT" ◻ ▬ ▲ ▲ ▲ ▲ ▲ ▲ ▲ ▲ SELECT ▲ BAT ▲ SIZE
        (2-3)";:FORT=1TO90:NEXT
2480    GETBS$:IFBS$<"2"THENPRINT:PRINT" ◻ ";:GOTO2450
2490    IFBS$>"3"THENPRINT:PRINT" ◻ ";:GOTO2450
2500    BS=VAL(BS$):PRINT" ▲ "BS
2510    NB=9:GS=100*(4-BS)
2570    FORT=1TO500:NEXT
```

> Print breakin court

```
2580    PRINT"▓ ■ ▲ ▲ ▲ ▲ ▲ ▲ ▲ ▧ ▲ ▲ ▲ ▲ ▲ ▲
        ▲ ▲ ▲ ▲ ▲ BREAKIN ▲ ▲ ▲ ▲ ▲ ▲ ▲ ▲
        ▲ "
2590    FORI=1TO23:PRINT" ▲ ▲ ▲ ▲ ▲ ▲ ▲ ▧ ▲ ▬ ▲ ▲ ▲
        ▲ ▲ ▲ ▲ ▲ ▲ ▲ ▲ ▲ ▧ ▲ ":NEXT
2600    PRINT" ■ ▲ ▲ ▲ ▲ ▲ ▲ ▲ ▧ ▲ ▲ ▲ ▲ ▲ ▲ ▲ ▲
        ▲ ▲ ▲ ▲ ▲ ▨ "
2610    PRINT" ▨ SCORE":PRINTGS:PRINT" ▨ HIGH":PRINT"SCORE":PRINTH
        S:PRINT" ▨ BALLS"
2620    PRINT"LEFT":PRINTNB:PRINT" ▨ GAME":PRINT"NUMBER":PRINTGM
2630    PRINT" ▨ BAT":PRINT"SIZE":PRINTBS
2640    ONGMGOTO2650,2700,2800
```

147

```
2650   REM    GAME 1
2655   PRINT" ▨ ▨ ▨ ▨ "
2660   FORJ=1TO4:PRINT" ▨ ▨ ▨ ▨ ▨ ▨ ▨ ▨ ▨ ◪ ▛ ▛ ▛ ▛ ▛
       ▛ ▛ ▛ ▛ ▛ ▛ ▛ ▛ ▛ ▛ ▛ ▛ ▛ ▛
       ▛ ▛ ▛ ▛ ▛ ▛ ":NEXT
2665   IFGS>ØTHENGS=GS+1
2666   IFSW>ØTHEN1000
2670   SW=1:BV=21:BH=17:BY=15:BX=18:BA=SC+BY*4Ø+BX:DX=-1:DY=-1
2680   GOTO1Ø5Ø
2700   REM GAME2
2710   PRINT" ▨ ▨ ▨ ▨ "
2720   FORJ=1TO3:PRINT" ▨ ▨ ▨ ▨ ▨ ▨ ▨ ▨ ▨ ◪ ▛ ▛ ▛ ▛ ▛
       ▛ ▛ ▛ ▛ ▛ ▛ ▛ ▛ ▛ ▛ ▛ ▛ ▛ ▛ ▛
       ▛ ▛ ▛ ▛ ▛ ▛ ":NEXT
2730   PRINT" ▨ ▨ ▨ ▨ ▨ ▨ ▨ ▨ ▨ ▨ ▨ ▨ "
2740   FORJ=1TO3:PRINT" ▨ ▨ ▨ ▨ ▨ ▨ ▨ ▨ ▨ ◪ ▛ ▛ ▛ ▛ ▛
       ▛ ▛ ▛ ▛ ▛ ▛ ▛ ▛ ▛ ▛ ▛ ▛ ▛ ▛ ▛
       ▛ ▛ ▛ ▛ ▛ ▛ ":NEXT
2745   IFGS>ØTHENGS=GS+1
2746   IFSW>ØTHEN1000
2750   SW=1:BV=13:BH=2Ø:BY=1Ø:BX=21:BA=SC+BY*4Ø+BX:DX=1:DY=-1
2760   GOTO1Ø5Ø
2800   REM GAME3
2810   PRINT" ▨ ▨ ▨ "
2820   FORI=ØTO8:PRINT" ▨ ▨ ▨ ▨ ▨ ▨ ▨ ▨ ▨ ▨ ";:FORJ=9-I
       TO1STEP-1:PRINT" ◪ ▤ ▛ ";:NEXT
2830   PRINTSPC(I*2+8);:FORJ=9-ITO1STEP-1:PRINT" ▛ ";:NEXT:PRINT:
       NEXT:PRINT
2850   FORI=ØTO8:PRINT" ▨ ▨ ▨ ▨ ▨ ▨ ▨ ▨ ▨ ▨ ";:FORJ=1TOI
       +1:PRINT" ◪ ▤ ▛ ";:NEXT
2860   PRINTSPC(((8-I)*2)+8);:FORJ=1TOI+1:PRINT" ▛ ";:NEXT:PRINT:
       NEXT:PRINT" ▨ "
2865   IFGS>ØTHENGS=GS+1
2866   IFSW>ØTHEN1000
2870   SW=1:BV=13:BH=16:BY=9:BX=24:BA=SC+BY*4Ø+BX:DX=1:DY=-1
2880   GOTO1Ø5Ø
```

```
5000   REM END GAME
5020   PRINT" ▨ ▨ ▨ ▨ ▨ ▨ ▨ ▨ ▨ ▨ ▨ ▨ ▨ ▨ ▨ ▨ ▨
       ▨ ▨ ▨ ▨ ▨ ▨ ▨ ▁ ▁ ▁ ▁ ANOTHER ▁ GAME(Y/N)"
5030   GETA$
5050   IFA$="N"THENPRINT" ▨ ":END
5060   IFA$<>"Y"THEN5Ø3Ø
5070   IFGS>HSTHENHS=GS
5080   SW=Ø:GOTO228Ø
```

148

CHECKSUM

```
        5=0            2190=1821         2830=3941
       10=3709         2200=3676         2850=3397
       20=4262         2210=1817         2860=4143
       40=2260         2220=3532         2865=1448
       50=0            2230=1821         2866=936
       60=2318         2240=3396         2870=5463
       70=1977         2250=1817         2880=579
       80=868          2260=3252         5000=0
       90=1284         2270=1821         5020=2726
     1000=0            2280=3110         5030=267
     1020=1658         2290=1853         5050=1359
     1050=3210         2300=247          5060=1205
     1060=2108         2400=3625         5070=1328
     1070=1079         2410=3827         5080=1072
     1080=1914         2420=2653
     1090=3604         2430=2178         TOTAL= 257594
     1200=0            2440=2072
     1220=2291         2450=247
     1230=2388         2460=3391
     1240=2427         2470=3593
     1250=2906         2480=2674
     1260=2332         2490=2176
     1500=0            2500=1325
     1520=2008         2510=1644
     1530=4003         2570=975
     1540=4413         2580=2593
     1550=1254         2590=3324
     1560=0            2600=2264
     1570=4078         2610=3959
     1580=3307         2620=2957
     1590=913          2630=1488
     1600=2512         2640=1440
     1610=1207         2650=0
     2000=0            2655=317
     2020=2899         2660=8437
     2030=975          2665=1448
     2040=2337         2666=936
     2050=975          2670=5699
     2060=2495         2680=579
     2070=975          2700=0
     2080=3037         2710=317
     2090=975          2720=8438
     2100=3147         2730=534
     2110=975          2740=8438
     2120=3941         2745=1448
     2130=975          2746=936
     2140=4073         2750=5500
     2150=1821         2760=579
     2160=3945         2800=0
     2170=1817         2810=286
     2180=3816         2820=3802
```

Tanc

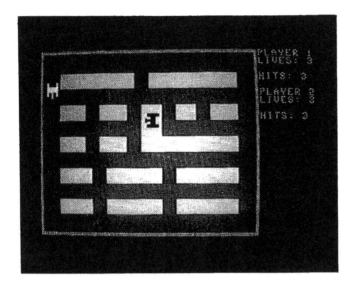

This game is a two player tank game. You need two joysticks to play. Each player has 3 tanks. If a tank is hit 3 times it is destroyed. Avoid the mud because it slows down your progress.

```
Ø       REM TANC
```

Build four versions of tank and set screen colours.

```
10      REM INITIALIZE
20      POKE53280,2:POKE56,60:POKE52,60:CLR:PRINT" ▧ "
30      FORI=15360TO15360+256:READA:POKEI,A:NEXTI
40      FORI=15616TO15680:POKEI,Ø:NEXTI
50      POKE15647,24:SH=244:POKE2042,SH:POKE2043,SH:L1=3:P1=L1:L2=
        L1:H1=L1
60      POKE53269,3:SE=240:POKE53248,27:POKE53249,217:POKE2040,SE:
        AB=1:AC=1
65      POKE53288,1:SP=243:POKE53250,251:POKE53251,53:POKE2041,SP
66      PRINT" ▧ ▬ ▬ ▬ ▬ ▬ ▬ ▬ ▬ ▬ ▬ ▬ ▬ ▬ ▬ ▬ ▬ ▬
        ▬ ▬ ▬ ▬ ▬ ▬ ▬ ▬ ▬ ▬ ▬ ▬ ▬ ▬ ▪ "
67      FORI=ØTO21:PRINT" ▮ ▲ ▲ ▲ ▲ ▲ ▲ ▲ ▲ ▲ ▲ ▲ ▲ ▲ ▲ ▲ ▲ ▲ ▲ ▧
        ▮ ":NEXTI
68      PRINT" ▧ ▪ ▬ ▬ ▬ ▬ ▬ ▬ ▬ ▬ ▬ ▬ ▬ ▬ ▬ ▬ ▬ ▬ ▬
        ▬ ▬ ▬ ▬ ▬ ▬ ▬ ▬ ▬ ▬ ▬ ▬ ▧ ▪ "
69      GOSUB90
```

Print maze on screen and main logic loop.

```
70      GOSUB200
71      IFAB=ØTHENGOSUB830
72      IFAC=ØTHENGOSUB1030
75      GOSUB400
76      SS=PEEK(53278):SB=PEEK(53279)
77      IF(SSAND6)=6THEN2500
78      IF(SSAND9)=9THEN2000
80      GOTO70
90      PRINT" ▧ ▨ ▨ ▨ ▨ ▨ ▨ ▨ ▨ ▨ ▨ ▨ ▨ ▨ ▨ ▨
        ▨ ▨ ▨ ▨ ▨ ▨ ▨ ▨ ▨ ▨ ▨ ▨ ▨ ▨ ▨ ▨PLAYER ▲ 1"
        ;
91      PRINT" ▨ ▨ ▨ ▨ ▨ ▨ ▨ ▨ ▨ ▨ ▨ ▨ ▨ ▨ ▨ ▨
        ▨ ▨ ▨ ▨ ▨ ▨ ▨ ▨ ▨ ▨ ▨ ▨ ▨ ▨ ▨LIVES:";P1
92      PRINT" ▨ ▨ ▨ ▨ ▨ ▨ ▨ ▨ ▨ ▨ ▨ ▨ ▨ ▨ ▨ ▨
        ▨ ▨ ▨ ▨ ▨ ▨ ▨ ▨ ▨ ▨ ▨ ▨ ▨ ▨ ▨HITS:";H1
93      PRINT" ▨ ▨ ▨ ▨ ▨ ▨ ▨ ▨ ▨ ▨ ▨ ▨ ▨ ▨ ▨ ▨
        ▨ ▨ ▨ ▨ ▨ ▨ ▨ ▨ ▨ ▨ ▨ ▨ ▨ ▨ ▨PLAYER ▲ 2";
94      PRINT" ▨ ▨ ▨ ▨ ▨ ▨ ▨ ▨ ▨ ▨ ▨ ▨ ▨ ▨ ▨ ▨
        ▨ ▨ ▨ ▨ ▨ ▨ ▨ ▨ ▨ ▨ ▨ ▨ ▨ ▨ ▨LIVES:";L1
95      PRINT" ▨ ▨ ▨ ▨ ▨ ▨ ▨ ▨ ▨ ▨ ▨ ▨ ▨ ▨ ▨ ▨
        ▨ ▨ ▨ ▨ ▨ ▨ ▨ ▨ ▨ ▨ ▨ ▨ ▨ ▨ ▨HITS:";L2
96      PRINT" ▧ ▨ ▨ ▨ ▨ ▨ ▨ ▧ ▪ ▲ ▲ ▲ ▲ ▲ ▲ ▲
        ▨ ▨ ▨ ▨ ▨ ▨ ▨ ▨ ▨ ▨ ";
97      PRINT" ▨ ▨ ▨ ▧ ▪ ▲ ▲ ▲ ▲ ▲ ▲ ▲ ▨
        ▨ ▲ ▲ ▲ ▲ ▲ ▲ ▲ ▲ ▲ ▨ ▨ ▨ ▨ ▨
        ▨ ▨ ▨ ▨ ▨ ▨ ";
```

```
98    PRINT"[graphics]";

100   PRINT"[graphics]";

101   PRINT"[graphics]";

102   PRINT"[graphics]";

103   PRINT"[graphics]";

104   PRINT"[graphics]";

108   PRINT"[graphics]";

109   PRINT"[graphics]";

110   PRINT"[graphics]";

111   PRINT"[graphics]";

180   POKE53287,1:POKE53288,0
181   A=PEEK(53278):A=PEEK(53279):SS=0:SB=0
190   RETURN
```

Input player one and player two joystick movement, move tank.

```
200   REM JOYSTICK CONTROL
203   IF(SBAND1)=1THENS1=1:GOTO210
205   S1=4
210   IFNOTPEEK(56320)AND1THENSE=240:GOTO242
220   IFNOTPEEK(56320)AND2THENSE=241:GOTO244
230   IFNOTPEEK(56320)AND4THENSE=243:GOTO246
235   IFNOTPEEK(56320)AND8THENSE=242:GOTO246
240   IFNOTPEEK(56320)AND16THENGOTO700
241   RETURN
242   IFPEEK(53249)>49THENPOKE53249,PEEK(53249)-S1:GOTO300
244   IFPEEK(53249)<219THENPOKE53249,PEEK(53249)+S1:GOTO300
245   GOTO242
246   IFPEEK(53248)<253THENPOKE53248,PEEK(53248)+S1:GOTO300
248   IFPEEK(53248)>24THENPOKE53248,PEEK(53248)-S1:GOTO300
249   GOTO246
300   POKE2040,SE
310   IFNOTPEEK(56320)AND16THENGOTO700
```

152

```
350     RETURN
400     REM JOYSTICK CONTROL PL2
402     IF(SBAND2)=2THENS2=1:GOTO410
405     S2=4
410     IFNOTPEEK(56321)AND1THENSP=240:GOTO442
420     IFNOTPEEK(56321)AND2THENSP=241:GOTO444
430     IFNOTPEEK(56321)AND4THENSP=243:GOTO448
435     IFNOTPEEK(56321)AND8THENSP=242:GOTO446
440     IFNOTPEEK(56321)AND16THEN900
441     RETURN
442     IFPEEK(53251)>49THENPOKE53251,PEEK(53251)-S2:GOTO600
444     IFPEEK(53251)<219THENPOKE53251,PEEK(53251)+S2:GOTO600
445     GOTO442
446     IFPEEK(53250)<253THENPOKE53250,PEEK(53250)+S2:GOTO600
448     IFPEEK(53250)>24THENPOKE53250,PEEK(53250)-S2:GOTO600
449     GOTO446
600     POKE2041,SP
610     IFNOTPEEK(56321)AND16THEN900
650     RETURN
```

> Player one has fired gun, keep the shell moving, check for bang.

```
700     IFAB=0THEN830
705     AB=0:SC=5:SK=SE
710     POKE53252,PEEK(53248):POKE53253,PEEK(53249)
720     IFSE=240THEN743
730     IFSE=241THEN745
740     IFSE=242THEN747
741     IFPEEK(53252)<20THEN870
742     GOTO750
743     IFPEEK(53253)<20THEN870
744     GOTO760
745     IFPEEK(53253)>235THEN870
746     GOTO770
747     IFPEEK(53252)>235THEN870
748     GOTO780
750     POKE53252,PEEK(53252)-10:GOTO790
760     POKE53253,PEEK(53253)-10:GOTO790
770     POKE53253,PEEK(53253)+10:GOTO790
780     POKE53252,PEEK(53252)+10
790     IFSC=5THENPOKE53269,PEEK(53269)OR4
800     SC=SC-1:IFSC=0THEN870
820     RETURN
830     IFSK=240THEN743
840     IFSK=241THEN745
850     IFSK=242THEN747
860     IFSK=243THEN741
870     POKE53269,PEEK(53269)AND251:AB=1
890     RETURN
```

> Player two has fired gun, move shell and check for bang.

```
900     IFAC=0THEN1030
905     AC=0:SD=5:SL=SP
910     POKE53254,PEEK(53250):POKE53255,PEEK(53251)
920     IFSP=240THEN943
930     IFSP=241THEN945
940     IFSP=242THEN947
941     IFPEEK(53254)<20THEN1070
942     GOTO950
943     IFPEEK(53255)<20THEN1070
944     GOTO960
945     IFPEEK(53255)>235THEN1070
946     GOTO970
947     IFPEEK(53254)>235THEN1070
948     GOTO980
950     POKE53254,PEEK(53254)-10:GOTO990
960     POKE53255,PEEK(53255)-10:GOTO990
970     POKE53255,PEEK(53255)+10:GOTO990
980     POKE53254,PEEK(53254)+10
990     IFSD=5THENPOKE53269,PEEK(53269)OR8
1000    SD=SD-1:IFSD=0THEN1070
1020    RETURN
1030    IFSL=240THEN943
1040    IFSL=241THEN945
1050    IFSL=242THEN947
1060    IFSL=243THEN941
1070    POKE53269,PEEK(53269)AND247:AC=1
1080    RETURN
```

> Print the scores; end the game and prompt for another.

```
2000    REMPLAYERTWO
2005    GOSUB1070
2010    L2=L2-1
2020    PRINT" ▨ ▨ ▨ ▨ ▨ ▨ ▨ ▨ ▨ ▨ ▨ ▨ ▨ ▨ ▨ ▨
        ▨ ▨ ▨ ▨ ▨ ▨ ▨ ▨ ▨ ▨ ▨ ▨ ▨ ▨ ▨ ▨
        ▨ ▨ ▨ ▨ ▨ ▨ ▨ ▨ ▨ ";L1
2030    PRINT" ▨ ▨ ▨ ▨ ▨ ▨ ▨ ▨ ▨ ▨ ▨ ▨ ▨ ▨ ▨ ▨
        ▨ ▨ ▨ ▨ ▨ ▨ ▨ ▨ ▨ ▨ ▨ ▨ ▨ ▨ ▨ ▨
        ▨ ";L2
2040    IFL2=0THENL2=4:L1=L1-1
2050    IFL1=0THEN3000
2055    ·SS=PEEK(53278):SB=PEEK(53279)
2060    GOTO70
2500    REMPLAYERONE
2505    GOSUB870
2510    H1=H1-1
2520    PRINT" ▨ ▨ ▨ ▨ ▨ ▨ ▨ ▨ ▨ ▨ ▨ ▨ ▨ ▨ ▨ ▨
        ▨ ▨ ▨ ▨ ▨ ▨ ▨ ▨ ▨ ▨ ▨ ▨ ▨ ▨ ▨ ▨
        ▨ ▨ ▨ ▨ ";P1
```

154

```
2530    PRINT" ▱ ▱ ▱ ▱ ▱ ▱ ▱ ▱ ▱ ▱ ▱ ▱ ▱ ▱ ▱ ▱
        ▱ ▱ ▱ ▱ ▱ ▱ ▱ ▱ ▱ ▱ ▱ ▱ ▱ ▱ ▱ ▱
        ▱ ";H1
2540    IFH1=0THENH1=4:P1=P1-1
2550    IFP1=0THEN3100
2555    SS=PEEK(53278):SB=PEEK(53279)
2560    GOTO70
3000    PRINT" ◰ ◰ ▱ ▱ ▱ ▱ ▱ ▱ PLAYER ▲ ONE ▲ ";
3010    GOTO3150
3100    PRINT" ◰ ◰ ▱ ▱ ▱ ▱ ▱ ▱ PLAYER ▲ TWO ▲ ";
3150    POKE53269,0
3200    PRINT" ◰ WON."
3250    PRINT
3300    PRINT"ANOTHER ▲ GAME. (Y/N)"
3310    IFPEEK(197)=25THENRUN
3315    IFPEEK(197)<>39THEN3310
3320    PRINT" ◰ ":STOP
```

> Data for the up, down, left and right versions of tank.

```
5000    REM UP TANC
5010    DATA0,0,0,0,0,0,0,60,0,0,24,0,7,24,224,7,24,224,7,24,224,7
        ,24,224
5020    DATA7,255,224,7,255,224,7,255,224,7,255,224,7,255,224,7,25
        5,224
5030    DATA7,0,224,7,0,224,7,0,224,7,0,224,0,0,0,0,0,0,0,0,0,0
5050    REM DOWN TANC
5060    DATA 0,0,0,0,0,0,0,0,0,7,0,224,7,0,224,7,0,224,7,0,224,7,2
        55,224,7,255,224
5070    DATA7,255,224,7,255,224,7,255,224,7,255,224,7,24,224,7,24,
        224,7,24,224
5080    DATA7,24,224,0,24,0,60,0,0,0,0,0,0,0,0
5100    REM RIGHT TANC
5110    DATA0,0,0,0,0,0,0,0,0,0,0,0,3,255,224,3,255,224,3,255,224,
        0,62,0,0,62,0
5120    DATA0,62,8,0,63,248,0,63,248,0,62,8,0,62,0,0,62,0,3,255,22
        4,3,255,224
5130    DATA3,255,224,0,0,0,0,0,0,0,0,0,0,0
5150    REMLEFT TANC
5160    DATA0,0,0,0,0,0,0,0,0,0,0,0,3,255,224,3,255,224,3,255,224,
        0,62,0,0,62,0
5170    DATA8,62,0,15,254,0,15,254,0,8,62,0,0,62,0,0,62,0,3,255,22
        4,3,255,224
5180    DATA3,255,224,0,0,0,0,0,0,0,0,0,0,0
9000    PRINTPEEK(197):GOTO9000
```

155

CHECKSUM

0=0	241=143	830=1002
10=0	242=3270	840=1006
20=2242	244=3321	850=1006
30=2529	245=527	860=1002
40=1864	246=3320	870=1897
50=4807	248=3264	890=143
60=4342	249=527	900=903
65=3313	300=567	905=1437
66=5922	310=1885	910=2248
67=3191	350=143	920=1004
68=6143	400=0	930=1008
69=251	402=2057	940=1008
70=294	405=364	941=1405
71=991	410=2444	942=534
72=1050	420=2447	943=1406
75=298	430=2441	944=535
76=1954	435=2447	945=1456
77=1294	440=1502	946=536
78=1296	441=143	947=1455
80=476	442=3268	948=541
90=2191	444=3313	950=1993
91=2148	445=531	960=1995
92=2024	446=3312	970=1994
93=2124	448=3262	980=1347
94=2136	449=531	990=2022
95=2028	600=578	1000=1727
96=2560	610=1502	1020=143
97=2508	650=143	1030=1000
98=2377	700=854	1040=1004
100=2367	705=1423	1050=1004
101=1965	710=2248	1060=1000
102=1965	720=998	1070=1901
103=2331	730=1002	1080=143
104=2331	740=1002	2000=0
108=2343	741=1346	2005=351
109=2319	742=530	2010=667
110=2343	743=1347	2020=2284
111=2659	744=531	2030=1824
180=1172	745=1405	2040=1808
181=2706	746=532	2050=896
190=143	747=1404	2055=1954
200=0	748=537	2060=476
203=2051	750=1985	2500=0
205=365	760=1987	2505=306
210=2428	770=1986	2510=662
220=2431	780=1347	2520=2013
230=2425	790=2010	2530=1820
235=2431	800=1673	2540=1835
240=1885	820=143	2550=901

```
2555=1954        3320=585         5120=3944
2560=476         5000=0           5130=1751
3000=1530        5010=3491        5150=0
3010=580         5020=3444        5160=4134
3100=1523        5030=2916        5170=3920
3150=532         5050=0           5180=1862
3200=539         5060=4383        9000=1283
3250=153         5070=4100
3300=1564        5080=2098        TOTAL=  284764
3310=1217        5100=0
3315=1494        5110=4134
```

Machine Language Sprite Management

This short program is a machine language routine that controls all sprite movements, in a manner that is totally independent of BASIC!

For the technically minded, the routine is interrupt-driven — that is, every 5Øth of a second the machine language program looks to see if anything needs to be done to each sprite.

The routine is so fast that it takes up virtually no time and thus has almost no effect on the speed of your BASIC program.

ABOUT SPRITES

Sprites are shapes that can be moved anywhere on the screen by specifying their position. The Commodore 64 has facility for up to 8 sprites to be displayed at any one time, and these are numbered Ø-7. Let us call this sprite number, SP. The following properties must be defined for each sprite, as a minimum.

Sprite enable
This determines whether a particular sprite is to be ON (i.e. displayed) or OFF (not displayed).

The information about this is held in a single byte (the variable called ENSP in this program). This byte is at location 53269, and the information is as follows:

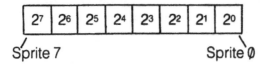

with each 'cell' holding a 1 or a 0.

To turn ON a sprite that is off:

POKE ENSP, PEEK(ENSP) + 2 ↑ SP

To turn OFF a sprite that is on:

POKE ENSP, PEEK(ENSP) − 2 ↑ SP

Sprite colour
Each sprite can be any of the Commodore's 16 colours, and this information is held in a table of 8 bytes starting at location 53287 (variable COLSP). To make the sprite white, say (colour 1) then:

POKE COLSP + SP, 1

Define its position
The screen position range for each sprite is from (24, 50) to (344, 250), where the X-position goes from 24 at left to 344 at right and the Y-position goes from 50 at the top to 250 at the bottom.

(There are values possible outside this range, but it means that the sprites are not visible — e.g. a sprite at (0, 0) is too high for you to see.)

The position of each sprite is held in a table starting at 53248 which is set out as follows:

X-position sprite 0
Y-position sprite 0
X-position sprite 1
Y-position sprite 1
. . . etc.

In order to set a sprite's position:

POKE XSP + 2 * SP, . . . : POKE YSP + 2 * SP, . . .

with the appropriate values inserted into the line.

You will probably be aware that the highest number that can be POKEd is 255, and so you cannot POKE X-values above this into this table.

The Commodore 64 has a special byte at 53264 (called HIGH in this program) which indicates if any sprite's X-position is greater than 255.

This byte is similar to the sprite enable byte:

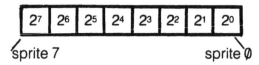

If any of the 'bits' in this byte are on, it indicates that 256 needs to be added to the X-value for that sprite in the X-position table.

For example, to set an X-position of 320 (256 + 64) then do:

POKE XP + 2 * SP, 64 : POKE HIGH, PEEK (HIGH) + 2 ↑ SP

Define its shape
Each sprite has to have a shape defined for it, and elsewhere in this book we give you a program that enables you to design sprite shapes easily (see SPRITE CREATE).

The Commodore 64 has a table at the end of the screen that tells it where to find the shape data. NOTE that each sprite requires 63 bytes to define it, and that for other reasons the Commodore 64 requires that the shape data be:

1. in the same 16K block as the screen.
2. start on a 64 byte boundary.

There are only 256 such 64K areas, and so we can specify where to find the shape data in a simple byte.

The Commodore 64 screen is usually in the first 16K of memory from 1024 to 2047 and the shape data pointers are from 2040 onwards.

To tell the Commodore 64 that the shape data for a particular sprite is in the 13th 64K block (memory locations 832 to 895):

POKE 2040 + SP, 13

In the standard Commodore 64, running a BASIC program, it is safe to place sprite shape data in the following 64K blocks:

13, 14, 15, 250, 251, 252, 253, 254, 255.

About this program
The power of Machine Language Sprite Management is that it enables you to control each sprite in a very simple manner once you have defined it, as shown above.

For each sprite, three variables are defined:

    XINC — its horizontal speed
    YINC — its vertical speed
    DIR   — the directions it is allowed to go in.

XINC and YINC are both in tables, and to set a sprite's movement at the slowest non-zero speed:

    POKE XINC + SP, 1 : POKE YINC + SP, 1

The DIR variable allows you to choose either no allowed movement, movement in only one direction (such as right) or movement in diagonal directions (by allowing both up and right movement, for example).

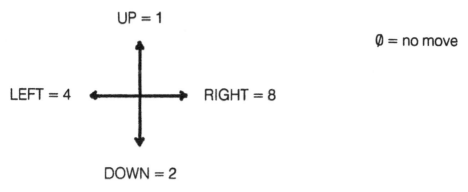

UP = 1

$\emptyset$ = no move

LEFT = 4

RIGHT = 8

DOWN = 2

To set movement to right and up (1 + 8 = 9):

    POKE DIR + SP, 9

Using this program
The program lines listed can be added to any of your own programs, and the Sprite Management Program is called by using GOSUB 8000.

NOTE that once this has been set up, and sprites enabled, the sprites will continue even when the program has finished running! It can be quite amusing to see sprites on the screen when editing a program.

To stop the sprites being shown, you can dis-enable all sprites by POKE 53269, $\emptyset$. (This will not stop the routine being called each interrupt.) To stop the routine, press RUN STOP/RESTORE.

```
8000    XINC=49309:YINC=49317:DIR=49301:ATAB=49293:OTAB=49285
8010    PRI=53275:SCLN=53278:MULT=53276:BAKCLN=53279:ENSP=53269:CO
        LSP=53287
8015    XSP=53248:YSP=53249:HIGH=53264
8020    FORI=0TO148:READA:POKE49152+I,A:NEXT
8030    FORI=0TO7:POKEDIR+I,0:POKEXINC+I,0:POKEYINC+I,0:NEXT
8040    POKE56333,127:POKE788,0:POKE789,192:POKE56333,129
8050    RETURN
9000    DATA162,7,138,10,168,24,189,149
9010    DATA192,133,251,70,251,144,14,185
9020    DATA1,208,201,51,144,7,56,253
9030    DATA165,192,153,1,208,70,251,144
9040    DATA14,185,1,208,201,226,176,7
9050    DATA24,125,165,192,153,1,208,70
9060    DATA251,144,36,173,16,208,61,133
9070    DATA192,208,7,185,0,208,201,25
9080    DATA144,21,185,0,208,56,253,157
9090    DATA192,153,0,208,176,9,173,16
9100    DATA208,61,141,192,141,16,208,70
9110    DATA251,144,36,185,0,208,201,64
9120    DATA144,11,173,16,208,61,133,192
9130    DATA208,21,185,0,208,24,125,157
9140    DATA192,153,0,208,144,9,173,16
9150    DATA208,29,133,192,141,16,208,202
9160    DATA16,128,76,49,234,1,2,4
9170    DATA8,16,32,64,128,254,253,251
9180    DATA247,239,223,191,127
```

CHECKSUM

```
Ø       REM EXAMPLE PROGRAM A
```

> Call Sprite Management routine.

```
100     GOSUB 8000
```

> Choose sprite #0, make it white.

```
110     SP=0 :POKE ENSP,2^SP
120     POKE COLSP+SP,1
```

> Define sprite's position.

```
130     POKE XSP+2*SP,170 :POKE YSP+2*SP,140
```

> Make the shape a square blob

```
140     FOR I=0 TO 63 :POKE 832+I,255 :NEXT I
```

> Tell the C64 where the shape data is.

```
150     POKE 2040+SP,13
```

> Wait until RUN STOP is pressed.

```
1000    GOTO 1000
```

CHECKSUM

```
   Ø=Ø
 100=355
 110=1414
 120=1006
 130=2538
 140=1866
 150=869
1000=579

TOTAL= 8627
```

163

```
Ø        REM EXAMPLE PROGRAM B.1
100      GOSUB 8000
110      SP=Ø :POKE ENSP,2^SP
120      POKE COLSP+SP,1
130      POKE XSP+2*SP,170 :POKE YSP+2*SP,140
140      FOR I=Ø TO 63 :POKE 832+I,255 :NEXT I
150      POKE 2040+SP,13
200      POKE XINC+SP,1:POKE YINC+SP,1
210      POKE DIR+SP,8
220      IF PEEK(HIGH)=Ø THEN 220
230      POKE DIR+SP,4
240      IF PEEK(XSP+2*SP)>30 THEN 240
250      GOTO 210
1000     GOTO 1000
```

```
Ø        REM EXAMPLE PROGRAM B.2
100      GOSUB 8000
110      SP=Ø :POKE ENSP,2^SP
120      POKE COLSP+SP,1
130      POKE XSP+2*SP,170 :POKE YSP+2*SP,140
140      FOR I=Ø TO 63 :POKE 832+I,255 :NEXT I
150      POKE 2040+SP,13
200      POKE XINC+SP,2:POKE YINC+SP,1
210      POKE DIR+SP,9
220      FOR I = 1 TO 2000: NEXT I
230      POKE DIR+SP,6
240      FOR I = 1 TO 2000: NEXT I
250      GOTO 210
1000     GOTO 1000
```

```
Ø        REM EXAMPLE PROGRAM B.3
100      GOSUB 8000
110      SP=Ø :POKE ENSP,2^SP
120      POKE COLSP+SP,1
130      POKE XSP+2*SP,170 :POKE YSP+2*SP,140
140      FOR I=Ø TO 63 :POKE 832+I,255 :NEXT I
150      POKE 2040+SP,13
200      POKE XINC+SP,1 :POKE YINC+SP,1
210      POKE DIR+SP,8 :FOR I=1 TO 1000:NEXT
220      POKE DIR+SP,2 :FOR I=1 TO 1000:NEXT
230      POKE DIR+SP,4 :FOR I=1 TO 1000:NEXT
240      POKE DIR+SP,1 :FOR I=1 TO  999:NEXT
250      GOTO 210
1000     GOTO 1000
```

Example of using the Sprite Management Program

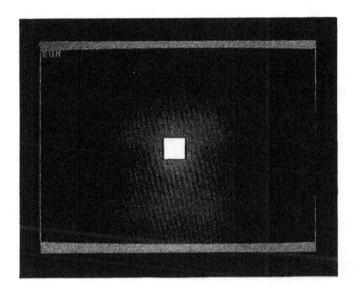

Following the Sprite Management Program, you will find Example Program A.

Type this in together with the Sprite Management Program, and RUN it. You will that find a large square sprite in the centre screen will be continuously displayed (because the program is in the infinite loop of line 1000).

NOTE that if you hit the RUN STOP key the execution of the program stops, but the sprite is still there.

Add afterwards any of the programs listed as Example Programs B. Each one will create a different movement pattern for the sprite, to give you familiarity with the capabilities of this program.

'Sprite Create'

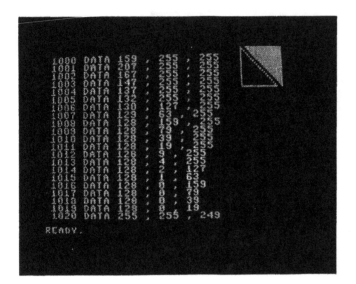

The following program allows you to use the cursor keys to draw a sprite by editing DATA statements. Type RUN 1, then use the cursor keys to move around the DATA statements. Use the shift Q character to signify a pixel-ON and a full-stop to signify a pixel-OFF. When you have finished drawing your sprite, move the cursor to the top of the screen, then keep hitting the RETURN key until you have entered all of the DATA statements. Now type RUN, and the program will generate the sprite and the DATA statements needed to generate that sprite. To store these DATA statements, use the same method as you used on the last set of DATA statements.

```
0 GOTO10 : REM *** SPRITE CREATE ***
1 POKE 650,128:PRINTCHR$( 147):POKE53269,0:LIST29-50
10 PRINTCHR$( 147):FORI=0TO63:POKE832+I,0:NEXT
15 POKE53280,6:POKE53281,6
20 GOTO 60
29 REM...012345678901234567890123
30 DATA "●..●●●●●●●●●●●●●●●●●●●"
31 DATA "●●..●●●●●●●●●●●●●●●●●●"
32 DATA "●.●..●●●●●●●●●●●●●●●●●"
33 DATA "●..●..●●●●●●●●●●●●●●●●"
34 DATA "●...●..●●●●●●●●●●●●●●●"
35 DATA "●....●..●●●●●●●●●●●●●●"
36 DATA "●.....●..●●●●●●●●●●●●●"
37 DATA "●......●..●●●●●●●●●●●●"
38 DATA "●.......●..●●●●●●●●●●●"
39 DATA "●........●..●●●●●●●●●●"
40 DATA "●........●..●●●●●●●●●"
41 DATA "●.........●..●●●●●●●●"
42 DATA "●.........●..●●●●●●●"
43 DATA "●..........●..●●●●●●"
44 DATA "●..........●..●●●●●"
45 DATA "●...........●..●●●●"
46 DATA "●...........●..●●●"
47 DATA "●.............●..●●●"
48 DATA "●.............●..●●"
49 DATA "●.................●..●●"
50 DATA "●●●●●●●●●●●●●●●●●●●●..●"
60 V=53248:POKEV+16,1:POKEV+1,50 :POKEV+21,1:POKEV+39,3:POKE2040,13
70 POKEV+23,1:POKEV+29,1
80 FORI=0TO20:PRINT1000+I;"DATA";:READA$:FORK=0TO2:T=0:FORJ=0TO7:B=0
90 IF MID$(A$,J+K*8+1,1)="●"THENB=1
100 T=T+B*2↑(7-J):NEXT:PRINT T;",";:POKE 832+I*3+K,T:NEXT:PRINT"█ ":NEXT
110 END

READY.
```

CHECKSUM

0=535	40=3516	110=129
1=2478	41=3372	
10=2408	42=3225	TOTAL= 102386
15=1182	43=3047	
20=476	44=2898	
29=0	45=2750	
30=5067	46=2599	
31=5065	47=2449	
32=4896	48=2296	
33=4728	49=2144	
34=4557	50=5091	
35=4387	60=4108	
36=4214	70=1332	
37=4042	80=4747	
38=3867	90=2497	
39=3693	100=4591	

167

Clucky Chook

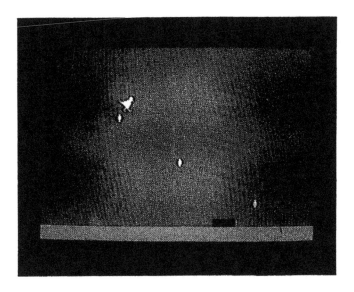

A clucky chook has escaped from the hen house and has gone on an egg laying spree. After plugging your joystick into port 2 you must control the pan at the bottom of the screen. Catch the eggs before they fall and break. The incorporation of 'Sprite Move' makes this game both fast and addictive.

VARIABLES

T	= Time between chook changing direction
AD	= Direction of chook
LAY	= Time between laying eggs
FR	= Number of eggs on screen
I	= Temporary variable
HX	= Temporary high × position of sprites
MT	= Temporary sprite collision register value
TALLY	= Number of eggs caught
	end

```
Ø       REM CLUCKY CHOOK
```

┌───┐
│ Initialisation routines.   │
└───┘

```
5       GOSUB7ØØØ
1Ø      GOSUB8ØØØ
25      GOSUB6ØØØ
```

┌───┐
│ Set player's direction from joystick.   │
└───┘

```
1ØØ     POKEDIR+1,15-(PEEK(5632Ø)AND15)
```

┌───┐
│ Move chook.   │
└───┘

```
2ØØ     T=T-1:IFT>ØTHEN24Ø
21Ø     AD=AD*-1:POKEDIR,PEEK(DIR)+AD
22Ø     T=3*(RND(Ø)+1)
```

┌───┐
│ Lay egg.   │
└───┘

```
24Ø     LAY=LAY-1:IFLAY>ØTHEN3Ø5
25Ø     LAY=2:IFFR=ØTHEN 3ØØ
26Ø     I=ETAB (FR):FR=FR-1
264     HX=PEEK(HIGH)
265     IF(HXAND1)=1THENPOKEHIGH,PEEK(OTAB+I)ORPEEK(HIGH):GOTO27Ø
266     POKEHIGH,(PEEK(ATAB+I))ANDPEEK(HIGH)
27Ø     POKEXSP+2*I,PEEK(XSP):POKEYSP+2*I,1Ø8:POKEDIR+I,2
```

┌───┐
│ Check if eggs caught or missed.   │
└───┘

```
3Ø5     HT=PEEK(SCLN)
31Ø     FORI=2TO7
314     POKEDIR+1,15-(PEEK(5632Ø)AND15)
315     HT=PEEK(SCLN)ORHT
32Ø     IF PEEK(YSP+2*I)<215THEN4ØØ
33Ø     IF (HT AND2)=ØTHEN42Ø
34Ø     POKEDIR+I,Ø:POKEYSP+2*I,Ø:FR=FR+1:ETAB (FR)=I:TALLY=TALLY+
        1
4ØØ     NEXT
41Ø     GOTO1ØØ
```

```
420    POKEDIR,0:POKEDIR+1,0
425    POKE54273,40:POKE54278,245:POKE54296,15:POKE54276,129
430    FORI=0TO7:POKE990+3*I,25*I:NEXT
435    POKE53271,252:POKE53277,252
440    POKE54276,128
450    PRINT" [S] YOU _ FRIED _ ";TALLY;" _ EGGS"
500    INPUT"DO _ YOU _ WANT _ ANOTHER _ TRY";A$
510    IFA$="Y"THENRUN
520    END
```

Set up screen and sprites.

```
6000   FORI=2 TO7:POKEYINC+I,1:POKECOLSP+I,7:POKEYSP+2*I,0
6001   NEXT
6020   FORI=2TO7:ETAB (I)=I:NEXT
6030   FR=7:POKEHIGH,0:POKEPRI,255:POKE53277,0:POKE53271,0
6034   PRINT" [.] "
6035   POKE53280,2:POKE53281,6:I=PEEK(SCLN)
6036   FORI=1024+23*40TO1024+25*40:POKEI,160:POKE55296-1024+I,5:
       NEXT
6042   LV=2:AD=4:T=10:LAY=5
6043   POKEXINC+1,3:POKECOLSP+1,0:POKEXSP+2,164:POKEYSP+2,218
6044   POKEXINC,LV:POKECOLSP,1:POKEXSP,164:POKEYSP,100:POKEDIR,8
6049   POKEENSP,255
6050   RETURN
```

Set up sprite shapes.

```
7000   POKE53269,0
7005   FORI=0TO191:POKE832+I,0:NEXT
7010   FORI=0 TO 45 STEP3:READ A:POKE832+I,A:READA:POKE833+I,A:
       NEXT
7020   FORI=0TO23:POKE920+I,255:NEXT
7030   FORI=0TO7:READ A:POKE990+3*I,A:NEXT
7031   POKE2040,13:POKE2041,14
7032   FORI=2042TO2047:POKEI,15:NEXT
7040   RETURN
7050   DATA0,0,0,12,0,30,0,26
7060   DATA0,126,135,249,127,248,63,248
7070   DATA15,248,7,240,1,224,1,224
7080   DATA3,64,4,32,4,20,2,8
7110   DATA24,24,60,60,60,60,24,24
```

Insert "Sprite Move" here.

170

CHECKSUM

```
       Ø=Ø              7Ø32=1688
       5=352            7Ø4Ø=143
      1Ø=355            7Ø5Ø=1Ø77
      25=351            7Ø6Ø=17Ø9
     1ØØ=1941           7Ø7Ø=146Ø
     2ØØ=1478           7Ø8Ø=11Ø7
     21Ø=2321           711Ø=14Ø6
     22Ø=114Ø
     24Ø=191Ø        TOTAL= 96391
     25Ø=1454
     26Ø=1625
     264=937
     265=4Ø44
     266=2359
     27Ø=3647
     3Ø5=937
     31Ø=657
     314=1941
     315=1293
     32Ø=1883
     33Ø=122Ø
     34Ø=5428
     4ØØ=131
     41Ø=525
     42Ø=129Ø
     425=2752
     43Ø=22Ø5
     435=1381
     44Ø=645
     45Ø=2112
     5ØØ=2257
     51Ø=914
     52Ø=129
    6ØØØ=3733
    6ØØ1=131
    6Ø2Ø=1693
    6Ø3Ø=297Ø
    6Ø34=372
    6Ø35=221Ø
    6Ø36=4281
    6Ø42=1873
    6Ø43=38Ø2
    6Ø44=3529
    6Ø49=696
    6Ø5Ø=143
    7ØØØ=532
    7ØØ5=1745
    7Ø1Ø=3376
    7Ø2Ø=1772
    7Ø3Ø=22Ø2
    7Ø31=1127
```

Soldier

The game begins with you as a Soldier within the safety of your tank. While you reside within the tank you are protected against the continuous barrage of enemy missiles. The objective is to leave the tank and weave your way through the mine field while dodging enemy missile explosions, and make your way to the ammunition dump behind the enemy missile launchers. Carry a single missile back through the mine field to your tank and attempt to destroy one of the enemy missile launchers. Continue this manoeuvre until all of the launchers have been destroyed. This game is joystick controlled.

VARIABLES

TRUE	= Logical TRUE compare
FALSE	= Logical FALSE compare
VID	= Start of video chip
SID	= Start of sound chip
JOY	= Joystick location
BDR	= Border colour
BCK	= Background colour
RB	= Sprite register number for first missile
RM	= Sprite register number for current missile
RP	= Sprite register number for player
RT	= Sprite register number for tank
RV	= Sprite register number for player's missile
NE	= Number of enemies
NL	= Number of land mines
SP	= Speed of player
SM	= Speed of missile
TS	= Speed of tank
SV	= Speed of player's missile
XP	= X position of player
YP	= Y position of player
XE( )	= X positions of missile launchers
YE( )	= Y positions of missile launchers

```
5       REM SOLDIER
10      GOSUB10000
```

```
                        Main loop
```

```
500     GOSUB1000
530     IF (PEEK(JOY)AND15)=15 THEN POKE DIR+RP,0:POKE DIR+RT,0
550     GOSUB7000
560     IF (PEEK(JOY)AND15)=15 THEN POKE DIR+RP,0:POKE DIR+RT,0
699     IF (FD=FALSE)AND(FC=FALSE) THEN 500
700     FOR K=0 TO 7:POKE DIR+K,0 :NEXT
720     IF FC THEN GOSUB6000
730     IF FD THEN GOSUB6200
790     RUN
999     STOP
```

```
                        Move missile
```

```
1000    POKE ENSP,PEEK(ENSP) AND R :R=255
1020    M=M+1:IF M>NE THEN M=0
1040    GOSUB 1500
1060    IF (YY>BM) AND (FX(M)=FALSE) THEN 3000
1070    IF FX(M) THEN GOSUB 2000
1080    M1=M:M=INT(RND(0)*NE)
1090    IF FX(M) THEN M=M1:GOTO 1499
1110    GOSUB 1500
1120    GOSUB 3000
1130    M=M1
1499    RETURN
```

```
                        Pre-calc reference variables
```

```
1500    RM=RB+M :RS=2^RM :RR=255-RS
1530    XX=PEEK(XSP+RM*2):YY=PEEK(YSP+RM*2)
1999    RETURN
```

```
                        Fire missile
```

```
2000    FX(M)=FALSE
2007    POKE VID+29,PEEK(VID+29) AND RR
2008    POKE VID+23,PEEK(VID+23) AND RR
2010    E=RND(0)*(NE+1)
2020    XE=XE(E):YE=YE(E)
2040    POKE DIR+RM,D(SGN(INT(PEEK(XSP+RP*2)/16-XE/16)*16)+1)
2050    POKE COLSP+RM,0
2060    POKE XSP+RM*2,XE:POKE YSP+RM*2,YE
```

174

```
2070    POKE HIGH,PEEK(HIGH) AND RR
2080    POKE ENSP,PEEK(ENSP) OR RS
2090    IF (PEEK(JOY)AND15)=15 THEN POKE DIR+RP,0:POKE DIR+RT,0
2999    RETURN
```

```
┌─────────────────────────────────────────┐
│  Explode                                 │
└─────────────────────────────────────────┘
```

```
3000    FX(M)=TRUE :R=RR
3010    POKE COLSP+RM,7
3025    POKE SID+4,0:POKE SID+4,WAVE+1
3030    POKE DIR+RM,0
3031    X=PEEK(XSP+RM*2)-12:IF X<0 THEN X=0
3032    Y=PEEK(YSP+RM*2)-10
3033    POKE XSP+RM*2,X
3034    POKE YSP+RM*2,Y
3040    POKE VID+29,PEEK(VID+29) OR RS
3041    POKE VID+23,PEEK(VID+23) OR RS
3045    IF FT THEN 3090
3050    IF ABS(X+12-PEEK(XSP+RP*2))>24 OR ABS(Y+10-PEEK(YSP+RP*2))
        >20 THEN 3090
3060    IF SGN(PEEK(HIGH)AND(2^RP))=SGN(PEEK(HIGH)AND(2^RM)) THEN
        FD=TRUE
3090    IF (PEEK(JOY)AND15)=15 THEN POKE DIR+RP,0:POKE DIR+RT,0
3999    RETURN
```

```
┌─────────────────────────────────────────┐
│  Move soldier                            │
└─────────────────────────────────────────┘
```

```
5000    POKEDIR+RP,15-(PEEK(JOY)AND15)
5030    IF (PEEK(BAKCLN)AND(2^RP))=FALSE THEN RETURN
5040    IF (PEEK(YSP+RP*2))<YM THEN POKE COLSP+RP,1:FG=TRUE:GOTO 5
        099
5050    FD=TRUE:POKE DIR+RP,0:S1=M:S2=FX(M):S3=R:M=RP-RB:GOSUB 150
        0
5060    GOSUB 3000:M=S1:FX(M)=S2:S1=R:R=S3
5099    RETURN
```

```
┌─────────────────────────────────────────┐
│  All enemys destroyed                    │
└─────────────────────────────────────────┘
```

```
6000    PRINT" ▧ SOLDIER ▲ DEAD"
6199    RETURN
```

```
┌─────────────────────────────────────────┐
│  Soldier dead                            │
└─────────────────────────────────────────┘
```

```
6200    REM SOLDIER DEAD
6299    RETURN
```

```
6300    IF F2=FALSE THEN 6310
6306    POKE ENSP,PEEK(ENSP)ANDS1
6307    POKE VID+23,PEEK(VID+23)ANDS1:POKE VID+29,PEEK(VID+29)ANDS
        1
6308    POKE COLSP+RV,Ø:F2=FALSE:FH=FALSE:FV=FALSE:IF ED>NE THEN F
        C=TRUE
6309    RETURN
6310    Y=PEEK(YSP+RV*2)
6320    IF FH THEN IF Y<YE(EH)+3Ø THEN 6330
6325    IF Y>BT+3Ø THEN RETURN
6330    POKE DIR+RV,Ø
6340    S1=M:S2=FX(M):S3=R:M=RV-RB:GOSUB 15ØØ
6350    GOSUB 3ØØØ:M=S1:FX(M)=S2:S1=R:R=S3
6355    IF EH=-1 THEN 6490
6360    POKE 214,(YE(EH)-5Ø)/8:PRINT:POKE 211,(XE(EH)-24)/8:PRINT
        EB$;
6365    FOR K=Ø TO NE:IF XE(K)=XE(P2)THEN XE(K)=XE(P1):YE(K)=YE(P1
        )
6366    NEXT K
6490    F2=TRUE
6499    RETURN
```

```
7ØØØ    IF FV THEN GOSUB 63ØØ
7Ø1Ø    J=PEEK(JOY)
7Ø2Ø    IF FT THEN 71ØØ :REM(IE. TANK)
7Ø25    IF PEEK(YSP+RP*2)<YT THEN 5ØØØ
7Ø3Ø    IFABS(PEEK(XSP+RP*2)-PEEK(XSP+RT*2))>1Ø THEN 5ØØØ
7Ø35    IF SGN(PEEK(HIGH)AND(2^RP))<>SGN(PEEK(HIGH)AND(2^RT))THEN
        5ØØØ
7Ø5Ø    FT=TRUE:POKE ENSP,PEEK(ENSP)AND(255-(2^RP)):POKE SID+11,12
        9
71ØØ    IF FL THEN 73ØØ :REM-FIRE
712Ø    POKEDIR+RT,12-(JAND12):POKE SID+8,15+(PEEK(DIR+RT)=Ø)*5
715Ø    IF ((JAND16)=Ø)AND(FG=TRUE)THEN FL=TRUE:GOTO7299
716Ø    IF (JAND1)=1 THEN 7299
717Ø    FT=FALSE:POKE DIR+RT,Ø:POKE DIR+RP,Ø:POKE SID+11,128:POKE
        COLSP+RP,Ø
7175    POKE XSP+RP*2,PEEK(XSP+RT*2):POKE YSP+RP*2,PEEK(YSP+RT*2)-
        22
7176    POKE HIGH,PEEK(HIGH)AND(255-2^RP)
7177    POKE HIGH,(PEEK(HIGH)OR((2^RP)*SGN(PEEK(HIGH)AND(2^RT))))
718Ø    POKE ENSP,PEEK(ENSP)OR2^RP
7181    PK=PEEK(VID+3Ø)
7299    RETURN
```

176

```
7300    FL=FALSE:FG=FALSE:FH=FALSE:FV=TRUE:EH=-1
7350    POKE DIR+RV,1
7360    X=PEEK(XSP+RT*2):Y=PEEK(YSP+RT*2)
7370    FOR K=0 TO NE
7380    IF ABS(X-XC(K))<10 THEN FH=TRUE:EH=K:XC(K)=-1
7390    NEXT K
7400    IF EH=-1 THEN 7500
7420    ED(EH)=-1:ED=ED+1
7430    FOR K=0TONE:IF ED(K)=0 THEN P1=K
7440    NEXT K
7450    P2=EH
7500    POKE XSP+RV*2,X:POKE YSP+RV*2,Y
7510    POKE HIGH,PEEK(HIGH)AND(255-2^RV)
7520    POKE HIGH,(PEEK(HIGH)OR((2^RV)*SGN(PEEK(HIGH)AND(2^RT))))
7530    POKE ENSP,PEEK(ENSP)OR(2^RV)
7599    RETURN
7600    FOR K=0 TO 3*64-1:READ D:POKE 13*64+K,D:NEXT
7620    DATA 0,0,0,224,0,14,224,0,14,224,0,14,48,0,24,24,0,48,12,5
        6,96
7630    DATA 6,124,192,3,255,128,0,254,0,1,255,0,1,255,0,0,254,0,1
        ,255,0
7640    DATA 3,125,128,6,56,192,12,0,96,24,0,48,240,0,30,224,0,14,
        224,0,14,0
7650    DATA 0,40,0,0,40,0,0,40,0,62,111,62,127,239,254,170,170,17
        1,175,239,235
7660    DATA 175,239,251,127,239,254,63,238,248,63,171,248,63,171,
        248,63,215,248
7670    DATA 63,255,248,63,255,248,127,255,254,175,255,251,167,255
        ,235
7675    DATA 170,170,171,127,255,254,62,127,62,0
7680    DATA 0,192,0,1,96,0,2,240,0,2,244,0,1,106,0,0,250,0,3,252,
        0
7690    DATA 55,252,0,47,252,0,47,252,0,31,232,0,31,224,0,11,240,0
        ,3,240
7695    DATA 0,7,240,0,7,240,0,7,248,0,7,232,0,11,232,0,9,176,0,6,
        0,0,0
7999    RETURN
8000    XINC=49309:YINC=49317:DIR=49301:ATAB=49293:OTAB=49285
8010    PRI=53275:SCLN=53278:MULT=53276:BAKCLN=53279:ENSP=53269:CO
        LSP=53287
8015    XSP=53248:YSP=53249:HIGH=53264
8020    FORI=0TO148:READA:POKE49152+I,A:NEXT
8030    FORI=0TO7:POKEDIR+I,0:POKEXINC+I,0:POKEYINC+I,0:NEXT
8040    POKE56333,127:POKE788,0:POKE789,192:POKE56333,129
8050    RETURN
9000    DATA162,7,138,10,168,24,189,149
9010    DATA192,133,251,70,251,144,14,185
9020    DATA1,208,201,51,144,7,56,253
9030    DATA165,192,153,1,208,70,251,144
9040    DATA14,185,1,208,201,226,176,7
```

```
9050    DATA24,125,165,192,153,1,208,70
9060    DATA251,144,36,173,16,208,61,133
9070    DATA192,208,7,185,0,208,201,25
9080    DATA144,21,185,0,208,56,253,157
9090    DATA192,153,0,208,176,9,173,16
9100    DATA208,61,141,192,141,16,208,70
9110    DATA251,144,36,185,0,208,201,64
9120    DATA144,11,173,16,208,61,133,192
9130    DATA208,21,185,0,208,24,125,157
9140    DATA192,153,0,208,144,9,173,16
9150    DATA208,29,133,192,141,16,208,202
9160    DATA16,128,76,49,234,1,2,4
9170    DATA8,16,32,64,128,254,253,251
9180    DATA247,239,223,191,127
```

┌──┐
│   │
│   Initialisation   │
│   │
└──┘

```
10000 GOSUB 7600
10003 GOSUB 8000
10005 TRUE=1:FALSE=0
10010 VID=53248 :SID=54272 :JOY=56320
10011 BDR=0:BCK=2
10015 RB=0:RM=RB:RP=5:RT=6:RV=7
10020 NE=5-1:NL=10:E$=" ▨ ▨ ▼ ─ ◣ ▨ ▮▮ ▮▮ ▮▮ ▮ ● ▮ ▨
      ▮▮ ▮▮ ▮▮ ▬ ◣ ▨ ─ ▬ ▼ ":MINE$=" ▬ ▁ "
10021 DUMP$=" ▨ ▨ ▼ ▼ ◢ ◣ ▨ ▮▮ ▮▮ ▮▮ ▮▮ ▼ ▲ ▬ ▬
      ▨ ◢ ◣ "
10022 EB$=" ▬ .. ▨ ▨ ▮▮ ▮▮ ● . ▨ ▮▮ ▮▮. ▨ "
10025 D(0)=6:D(1)=2:D(2)=10
10030 SP=1:SM=1:TS=1:SV=1
10035 POKE XI+RP,SP:POKE YI+RP,SP
10036 POKE XI+RT,TS:POKE YI+RT,TS
10037 POKE XI+RV,00:POKE YI+RV,SV
10038 FOR K=0 TO NE:POKE XI+RM+K,SM:POKE YI+RM+K,SM:NEXT
10050 BT=50:BB=230:BL=24:BR=255:BM=120
10060 XT=150:YT=BB-8:XP=XT:YP=YT
10120 FOR E=0 TO NE:READ XE(E),YE(E):NEXT
10130 DATA 0,11,7,7,14,3,21,7,28,11
10150 YM=YE(2):XG=XE(2):YG=YM-3
10200 SID=54272 :WAVE=128 :EX=1
10220 FOR K=0TO24:POKESID+K,0:NEXT
10230 FOR K=0TO24:READ D:POKE SID+K,D:NEXT
10240 DATA 1,0,0,128,10,0
10250 DATA 0,10,0,0,128,0,80
10260 DATA 0,0,0,0,0,0,0
10270 DATA 0,100,243,47
10500 GOSUB 11000
10510 FOR E=0 TO NE:XE(E)=24+XE(E)*8:YE(E)=50+YE(E)*8
10515 XC(E)=XE(E):YC(E)=YE(E):NEXT:YM=50+YM*8
10520 PK=PEEK(VID+30)+PEEK(VID+31)
10600 FOR K=0 TO NE:FX(K)=TRUE:NEXT K:R=255
10999 RETURN
```

```
11000 PRINT" 💀 ";
11012 POKE 53280,BDR:POKE 53281,BCK
11015 FORK=1TONL:POKE214,6+RND(0)*10:PRINT:POKE211,RND(0)*40:
      PRINT MINE$;:NEXT
11017 POKE 214,YG:PRINT:POKE211,XG:PRINT DUMP$;
11018 FOR E=0 TO NE:POKE214,YE(E):PRINT:POKE211,XE(E):PRINT E$;:
      NEXT
11050 POKE 2040+RT,14:POKE 2040+RP,15:POKE 2040+RV,13
11055 FOR K=0 TO NE:POKE 2040+RM+K,13:NEXT
11100 POKE ENSP,0
11130 POKE XSP+RP*2,XP:POKE YSP+RP*2,YP
11135 POKE XSP+RT*2,XT:POKE YSP+RT*2,YT
11140 POKE COLSP+RP,0:POKE COLSP+RT,0:POKE COLSP+RV,0
11150 FOR K=0 TO NE:POKE COLSP+RM+K,1:NEXT
11190 POKE ENSP,2^RP+2^RT:POKE HIGH,0
11195 POKE VID+23,0:POKEVID+29,0
11197 POKE VID+29,2^RP
11999 RETURN
```

CHEXSUM

5=0	2007=1921	5030=2637
10=402	2008=1907	5040=4616
500=348	2010=1228	5050=4841
530=3466	2020=1438	5060=2521
550=352	2040=4149	5099=143
560=3466	2050=993	6000=1165
699=2347	2060=2524	6199=143
700=1687	2070=1433	6200=0
720=806	2080=1509	6299=143
730=810	2090=3466	6300=1255
790=139	2999=143	6306=1460
999=145	3000=1390	6307=4022
1000=1887	3010=997	6308=5624
1020=1690	3025=2057	6309=143
1040=352	3030=823	6310=1410
1060=2389	3031=2745	6320=1961
1070=1012	3032=1681	6325=1166
1080=1669	3033=1116	6330=831
1090=1711	3034=1117	6340=2911
1110=352	3040=1909	6350=2521
1120=348	3041=1895	6355=1105
1130=387	3045=691	6360=3744
1499=143	3050=5511	6365=4311
1500=2524	3060=4672	6366=206
1530=3135	3090=3466	6490=629
1999=143	3999=143	6499=143
2000=899	5000=2044	7000=826

179

```
7010=786          9040=1574         11130=2534
7020=743          9050=1642         11135=2538
7025=2044         9060=1726         11140=3321
7030=3644         9070=1571         11150=2338
7035=4203         9080=1630         11190=2213
7050=4266         9090=1586         11195=1626
7100=735          9100=1703         11197=1132
7120=4258         9110=1651         11999=143
7150=3465         9120=1688
7160=1190         9130=1630         TOTAL= 394269
7170=4986         9140=1584
7175=4997         9150=1769
7176=2123         9160=1346
7177=3895         9170=1590
7180=1749         9180=1165
7181=1153         10000=356
7299=143          10003=355
7300=3941         10005=1274
7350=831          10010=2298
7360=2952         10011=983
7370=749          10015=2403
7380=3569         10020=6385
7390=206          10021=3074
7400=1105         10022=1771
7420=1583         10025=1571
7430=2106         10030=1833
7440=206          10035=1853
7450=456          10036=1863
7500=2371         10037=1796
7510=2123         10038=3513
7520=3897         10050=2710
7530=1849         10060=2534
7599=143          10120=1923
7600=2729         10130=1432
7620=3286         10150=2250
7630=3441         10200=1922
7640=3726         10220=1722
7650=4048         10230=2098
7660=4222         10240=986
7670=3333         10250=1040
7675=2079         10260=799
7680=3099         10270=783
7690=3420         10500=402
7695=3339         10510=3832
7999=143          10515=3227
8000=4370         10520=2200
8010=6035         10600=2506
8015=2443         10999=143
8020=2186         11000=435
8030=3646         11012=1551
8040=2508         11015=4394
8050=143          11017=2034
9000=1646         11018=3299
9010=1773         11050=2853
9020=1527         11055=2228
9030=1701         11100=574
```

180

Birthday Party

This program makes use of the Sprite Management Program, described earlier in the book.

BIRTHDAY PARTY is an animated birthday greeting for your favourite mother.

You will see a birthday cake appear, a greeting, then Mum comes on, and blows out the candles!

This is achieved by using Sprite Movement as well as switching sprites (to get animation).

You can use this idea and the Sprite Management Program to create your own individualised greeting cards, or cartoon animation sequences, or amusing title page animations for your own programs.

```
Ø        REM BIRTHDAY CARD
```

```
100      GOSUB 8000
110      XXPND=53277:YXPND=53271
120      POKE XXPND,255:POKE YXPND,255
130      PRINT" 🔲 🔳 ":POKE 53280,6
```

```
200      FOR SP=Ø TO 3
210      POKE COLSP+SP,1
220      READ X,Y:POKE XSP+2*SP,X:POKE YSP+2*SP,Y
230      POKE 2040+SP,240+SP:SHAPE=64*(240+SP)
240      FOR I=Ø TO 62:READ A:POKE SHAPE+I,A:NEXT I
250      NEXT SP
260      POKE ENSP,15
```

```
300      FOR SP=Ø TO 1
310      SHAPE = 64*(244 + SP)
320      FOR I=Ø TO 62:READ A:POKE SHAPE+I,A:NEXT I
330      NEXT SP
```

```
400      FOR I=1 TO 1Ø
410      PRINT "HAPPY ▃ BIRTHDAY,MUM"
420      NEXT I
```

```
500      FOR SP=4 TO 7
510      READ X,Y:POKE XSP+2*SP,X:POKE YSP+2*SP,Y
520      POKE 2040+SP,242+SP:SHAPE= 64 * (242+SP)  ·
530      FOR I=Ø TO 62:READ A:POKE SHAPE+I,A:NEXT I
540      NEXT SP
550      POKE COLSP+4,12:POKE COLSP+5,15:POKE COLSP+6,3:POKE COLSP+
         7,3
560      POKE ENSP,255
```

> Get alternate shape for mum blowing candles.

```
600    SHAPE=64 * 250
610    FOR I=0 TO 62:READ A:POKE SHAPE+I,A:NEXT I
```

> Set movement speed, get mum moving left until she reaches cake, then stop moving.

```
700    FOR SP=0 TO 7
710    POKE XINC+SP,1:POKE YINC+SP,1
720    NEXT SP
730    FOR SP=4 TO 7:POKE DIR+SP,4:NEXT SP
740    IF PEEK(XSP+8) > 140 THEN 740
750    FOR SP=4 TO 7:POKE DIR+SP,0:NEXT SP
```

> Get correct position for mum in front of cake.

```
800    FOR SP=4 TO 7
810    READ X,Y:POKE XSP+2*SP,X:POKE YSP+2*SP,Y
820    NEXT SP
```

> Mum is blowing candles:
> Change candle and face sprites in delay loop

```
830    FOR I=1 TO 4
840    FOR W=1 TO 200:NEXT W
850    POKE 2042,244:POKE 2043,245:POKE 2045,250
860    FOR W=1 TO 200:NEXT W
870    POKE 2042,242:POKE 2043,243:POKE 2045,247
880    NEXT I
```

> Big blow : move cake off the screen

```
900    POKE 2042,244:POKE 2043,245:POKE 2045,250
910    FOR PSS=20 TO 0 STEP-1
920    FOR SP=0 TO 2 STEP 2
930    POKE XSP+2*SP,PSS:POKE XSP+2+2*SP,PSS+48
940    NEXT SP
950    NEXT PSS
960    POKE ENSP,250
970    FOR PSS= 47 TO 0 STEP-1:POKE XSP+2,PSS:POKE XSP+6,PSS:NEXT
       PSS
980    POKE ENSP,240
```

```
990    POKE 2045,247
1000   GOTO 1000
8000   XINC=49309:YINC=49317:DIR=49301:ATAB=49293:OTAB=49285
8010   PRI=53275:SCLN=53278:MULT=53276:BAKCLN=53279:ENSP=53269:CO
       LSP=53287
8015   XSP=53248:YSP=53249:HIGH=53264
8020   FORI=0TO148:READA:POKE49152+I,A:NEXT
8030   FORI=0TO7:POKEDIR+I,0:POKEXINC+I,0:POKEYINC+I,0:NEXT
8040   POKE56333,127:POKE788,0:POKE789,192:POKE56333,129
8050   RETURN
9000   DATA162,7,138,10,168,24,189,149
9010   DATA192,133,251,70,251,144,14,185
9020   DATA1,208,201,51,144,7,56,253
9030   DATA165,192,153,1,208,70,251,144
9040   DATA14,185,1,208,201,226,176,7
9050   DATA24,125,165,192,153,1,208,70
9060   DATA251,144,36,173,16,208,61,133
9070   DATA192,208,7,185,0,208,201,25
9080   DATA144,21,185,0,208,56,253,157
9090   DATA192,153,0,208,176,9,173,16
9100   DATA208,61,141,192,141,16,208,70
9110   DATA251,144,36,185,0,208,201,64
9120   DATA144,11,173,16,208,61,133,192
9130   DATA208,21,185,0,208,24,125,157
9140   DATA192,153,0,208,144,9,173,16
9150   DATA208,29,133,192,141,16,208,202
9160   DATA16,128,76,49,234,1,2,4
9170   DATA8,16,32,64,128,254,253,251
9180   DATA247,239,223,191,127
10000  DATA20,200
10010  DATA3,144,16,5,254,16,5
10020  DATA111,240,5,111,255,5,111
10030  DATA255,5,111,255,5,111,255
10040  DATA5,111,255,5,111,255,5
10050  DATA111,255,5,111,255,13,111
10060  DATA255,23,111,255,35,111,255
10070  DATA33,239,255,16,127,255,16
10080  DATA31,255,12,0,31,3,128
10090  DATA0,0,120,0,0,7,255
10100  DATA68,200
10110  DATA8,9,224,8,127,160,15
10120  DATA221,160,255,221,160,255,221
10130  DATA160,255,221,160,255,221,160
10140  DATA255,221,160,255,221,160,255
10150  DATA221,160,255,221,160,255,221
10160  DATA176,255,221,232,255,221,196
10170  DATA255,223,132,255,222,8,255
10180  DATA248,8,248,0,48,0,1
10190  DATA192,0,254,0,255,0,0
10200  DATA20,158
```

184

```
10210 DATA0,0,0,0,0,0,0
10220 DATA0,0,0,0,0,2,0,0
10230 DATA2,0,1,0,0,65,0
10240 DATA0,64,2,0,0,2,2
10250 DATA1,2,2,65,2,0,65
10260 DATA18,0,65,18,2,81,2
10270 DATA2,81,15,2,67,240,2
10280 DATA126,0,3,128,16,2,16
10290 DATA16,4,16,16,4,16,16
10300 DATA68,158
10310 DATA0,0,0,0,0,0,0
10320 DATA0,0,64,0,0,64,128
10330 DATA0,0,128,0,0,2,0
10340 DATA64,2,64,64,128,64,64
10350 DATA128,0,64,130,0,72,130
10360 DATA64,72,130,64,64,138,64
10370 DATA240,138,64,15,194,64,0
10380 DATA62,64,8,1,192,8,8
10390 DATA32,8,8,32,8,8,32
10500 REM ALTERNATE SHAPE LEFT CANDLES
10510 DATA0,0,0,0,0,0,0
10520 DATA0,0,0,0,0,0,0
10530 DATA0,0,0,29,0,0,0
10540 DATA0,7,2,1,192,2,0
10550 DATA1,50,14,65,2,0,65
10560 DATA2,2,65,114,2,65,2
10570 DATA2,241,15,2,67,240,2
10580 DATA126,0,3,128,16,2,16
10590 DATA16,4,16,16,4,16,16
10600 REM ALTERNATE SHAPE RIGHT CANDLE
10610 DATA0,0,0,0,0,0,0
10620 DATA0,0,0,0,0,0,0
10630 DATA0,192,0,0,3,128,0
10640 DATA64,0,0,64,142,0,64
10650 DATA129,192,64,130,0,64,130
10660 DATA64,64,130,64,56,130,64
10670 DATA240,186,64,15,194,64,0
10680 DATA62,64,8,1,192,8,8
10690 DATA32,8,8,32,8,8,32
11000 DATA233,140
11010 DATA1,255,0,15,255,192,63
11020 DATA255,224,127,255,248,255,255
11030 DATA252,255,255,252,255,255,254
11040 DATA7,255,254,1,255,255,0
11050 DATA255,255,0,63,255,0,15
11060 DATA255,0,15,255,0,31,255
11070 DATA0,31,255,1,191,254,1
11080 DATA255,254,1,255,254,1,255
11090 DATA252,0,255,248,0,127,192
11100 DATA227,146
11110 DATA0,0,0,0,0,0,0
11120 DATA0,0,0,0,0,30,127
11130 DATA128,31,255,128,15,127,128
11140 DATA47,127,128,127,255,128,95
11150 DATA255,128,63,255,128,125,255
```

```
11160 DATA128,0,255,128,47,127,128
11170 DATA16,127,128,16,127,128,24
11180 DATA255,128,31,255,128,15,248
11190 DATA0,7,128,0,0,0,0
11200 DATA255,170
11210 DATA0,0,0,0,0,0,0
11220 DATA0,0,0,120,0,5,86
11230 DATA0,21,85,0,85,85,0
11240 DATA85,85,192,85,85,64,85
11250 DATA85,64,85,85,64,85,85
11260 DATA64,85,85,64,85,85,64
11270 DATA85,85,64,85,85,64,85
11280 DATA85,64,85,85,64,85,85
11290 DATA64,85,85,64,85,85,64
11300 DATA207,170
11310 DATA0,0,0,0,0,0,0
11320 DATA0,0,0,0,0,0,0
11330 DATA0,0,0,0,0,248,0
11340 DATA3,84,1,3,84,5,5
11350 DATA85,85,5,85,85,13,85
11360 DATA85,13,85,85,21,85,85
11370 DATA21,85,85,21,85,85,53
11380 DATA85,85,53,85,85,85,85
11390 DATA85,85,85,85,85,85,85
11400 REM ALTERNATE DATA FOR FACE
11410 DATA0,0,0,0,0,0,0
11420 DATA0,0,0,0,0,30,127
11430 DATA128,31,255,128,63,255,128
11440 DATA14,127,128,111,255,128,95
11450 DATA255,128,191,255,128,123,255
11460 DATA128,135,255,128,255,255,128
11470 DATA255,255,128,95,255,128,127
11480 DATA255,128,63,255,128,63,248
11490 DATA0,15,224,0,0,0,0
11500 DATA140,140
11510 DATA134,146
11520 DATA162,170
11530 DATA114,170
```

CHEXSUM

0=0	320=2344	700=751
100=355	330=297	710=1936
110=1866	400=711	720=297
120=1692	410=1684	730=2070
130=1013	420=206	740=1619
200=751	500=751	750=2066
210=1006	510=2822	800=751
220=2822	520=2946	810=2822
230=2942	530=2344	820=297
240=2344	540=297	830=655
250=297	550=4167	840=1070
260=635	560=696	850=1952
300=751	600=1028	860=1070
310=1475	610=2344	870=1947

186

```
880=206          10170=1534       11120=970
900=1952         10180=1126       11130=1534
910=1305         10190=1178       11140=1525
920=979          10200=447        11150=1584
930=3302         10210=799        11160=1462
940=297          10220=799        11170=1445
950=383          10230=865        11180=1522
960=692          10240=858        11190=906
970=4070         10250=924        11200=500
980=691          10260=1039       11210=799
990=581          10270=1101       11220=973
1000=579         10280=1164       11230=1049
8000=4370        10290=1099       11240=1299
8010=6035        10300=459        11250=1245
8015=2443        10310=799        11260=1245
8020=2186        10320=1014       11270=1255
8030=3646        10330=903        11280=1245
8040=2508        10340=1239       11290=1245
8050=143         10350=1290       11300=498
9000=1646        10360=1338       11310=799
9010=1773        10370=1331       11320=799
9020=1527        10380=1049       11330=912
9030=1701        10390=971        11340=919
9040=1574        10500=0          11350=1167
9050=1642        10510=799        11360=1244
9060=1726        10520=799        11370=1235
9070=1571        10530=860        11380=1255
9080=1630        10540=913        11390=1252
9090=1586        10550=1052       11400=0
9100=1703        10560=1039       11410=799
9110=1651        10570=1147       11420=970
9120=1688        10580=1164       11430=1535
9130=1630        10590=1099       11440=1523
9140=1584        10600=0          11450=1643
9150=1769        10610=799        11460=1652
9160=1346        10620=799        11470=1587
9170=1590        10630=1050       11480=1527
9180=1165        10640=1103       11490=982
10000=440        10650=1421       11500=500
10010=1177       10660=1332       11510=502
10020=1385       10670=1345       11520=502
10030=1389       10680=1049       11530=496
10040=1286       10690=971
10050=1448       11000=498        TOTAL= 251347
10060=1530       11010=1283
10070=1456       11020=1652
10080=1218       11030=1644
10090=1014       11040=1288
10100=452        11050=1275
10110=1218       11060=1276
10120=1631       11070=1229
10130=1635       11080=1391
10140=1635       11090=1400
10150=1631       11100=504
10160=1636       11110=799
```

Mastering the Commodore 64

Mark Greenshields